MICHELANGELO THE PAINTER

VALERIO MARIANI

MICHELANGELO
THE PAINTER

HARRY N. ABRAMS, INC., PUBLISHERS, NEW YORK

THIS VOLUME HAS BEEN PUBLISHED UNDER THE AUSPICES OF THE
ITALIAN NATIONAL COMMITTEE HONORING MICHELANGELO IN
COMMEMORATION OF THE FOURTH CENTENNIAL OF HIS DEATH

Standard Book Number: 8109-0307-5
Library of Congress Catalogue Card Number: 73-178969
Copyright 1964 in Italy by Arti Grafiche Ricordi S.p.A., Milan
All rights reserved. No part of the contents of this book may be
reproduced without the written permission of the publishers
Harry N. Abrams, Incorporated, New York
Printed and bound in Japan

Photography: Del Priore, Rome

COAT OF ARMS OF THE DELLA ROVERE FAMILY

to which Popes Sixtus IV and Julius II belonged. Placed on the vault, painted by Michelangelo below the figure of the Prophet Zachariah in correspondence with the principal entrance.

Rome, Vatican-The Sistine Chapel

CONTENTS

TEXT

PLATES

CHAPTER ONE

BEGINNINGS – EARLY STUDIES – JUVENILE WORKS
THE *DONI MADONNA*

MICHELANGELO BUONARROTI was born on March 6, 1475. On April 1, 1488, his father Ludovico apprenticed the thirteen-year-old Buonarroti to Domenico and David Ghirlandaio, stipulating that he remain with them for three years.

This event was documented by Giorgio Vasari, who claimed to have transcribed it from one of Domenico Ghirlandaio's books. The version which he copied reads as follows: "1488. I, Ludovico of Lionardo of Buonarota, herewith set forth that, on this day, the first of April, I yield my son Michelangelo to Domenico and David of Tommaso of Currado for the next three years in accordance with the following terms: that the said Michelangelo must remain with the aforesaid for the agreed upon time in order to learn to paint and to execute the agreed upon exercises and all that which the aforesaid will order him to do; and the said Domenico and David must give him twenty-four sealed florins: six florins the first year, eight florins the second, and ten florins the third; in all, the sum of ninety-six lire."

Before his apprenticeship to those overworked painters, Michelangelo's literary studies had been under the guidance of Francesco d'Urbino, who enjoyed a certain fame in those days for his knowledge of Greek and Latin. Michelangelo's contemporaries recalled that his artistic tendencies were so pronounced as to cause him to ignore his books for drawing and to seek his friends among artistic apprentices rather than fellow Humanities students.

Because of this, and possibly heeding the advice of Francesco Granacci, a nineteen-year-old student of Ghirlandaio who was among the first to appreciate Michelangelo's precocious genius, his father decided to direct him toward art instead of literature.

Domenico Ghirlandaio, together with his brother David, was then working on the choir of Santa Maria Novella, and the two artists used the large group of boys in their studio for the preparation of the cartoons for the project. At their side, Michelangelo conceived his first notions about technique and had his first practical experience in painting and drawing. He was always of independent temperament and preferred to choose by himself the subjects which really interested him. He chose subjects which manifested the natural sculptural tendencies to which he was drawn and which remained the basis of his future style.

One gathers from Ascanio Condivi's biography of the artist, a work which was enriched by direct information from Michelangelo himself (at certain points, one would say dictated by Michelangelo), that Francesco Granacci had a more notable influence on Buonarroti's artistic formation than did Domenico Ghirlandaio, with whom teacher-pupil relations never really developed as they should have. According to the biographer, it was Granacci who furnished his young friend with drawings and prints, and who took him to see works from which he could derive enrichment.[1]

It must be accepted as a matter of course that the adolescence of Michelangelo is a period which we know mainly through anecdotes, even more so because we have no certain examples of his artistic output.

Art historians have proposed various hypotheses in their attempts to reconstruct those formative years; according to some, the start which Domenico Ghirlandaio gave him in technique and in an initial style of drawing was of notable significance, especially since he was apprenticed to Ghirlandaio's shop with precise working terms; according to others, his friend Francesco Granacci, from whom Michelangelo may have derived his interest in linear drawing and colors which were used in a sculptural sense, was more influential; still others think that Michelangelo developed by himself, following the dictates of his own genius, independent from anything that Ghirlandaio and Granacci would have been able to teach him.

Actually, each of these hypotheses may be partially true, especially when we think about the youth of the artist, who, notwithstanding his independence and autonomy (his need to differ from the conventional taste of the times), was still searching for a personal way of expressing himself, and therefore absorbed and learned from the others' styles.

It is important to bear in mind that the first certain drawings are studies from the paintings of Giotto, Masaccio, and a few other Tuscan masters, almost all of which are executed with pen and demonstrate an obvious relief effect. In their insistent search for the direction of the planes, underlined by the direction of the strokes, the drawings give a more intense and sculptured rendering which can be verified by comparison with the originals. This clearly demonstrates, in addition to his precocious genius, Michelangelo's power of selection which led him outside the sphere which Ghirlandaio and Granacci represented and into a synthesis of mass and an incisiveness in chiaroscuro which were unknown to his contemporaries and were actually more typical of the great Florentines of the fourteenth and fifteenth centuries.

The boy Michelangelo, having already absorbed his artistic "grammar" from Ghirlandaio's shop, was already striking out on his own, identifying with complete freedom in the tradition of Tuscan painting that which represented a starting point for him in the development of his own personal style.

We must not forget, too, that his vivid curiosity attracted him to the study of ancient sculpture. This served him not only as experience in the plastic arts but also in drawing and painting. Leon Battista Alberti already had said in his treatise that "he who wishes to acquire a knowledge of form should draw from sculpture rather than paintings."[2] The statement has particular significance for Michelangelo whose genius, which was stimulated by forms in relief, discovered in ancient sculpture an exemplary representation of the human form translated into a clear volume relationship. He discovered a compositional method, especially in the sarcophagus reliefs, in which space is fully realized by the linked mass of the figures with a strong emphasis on filled rather than empty space.

From childhood, Michelangelo demonstrated a very retentive visual memory. Both of his contemporary biographers agree about this and justifiably emphasize this characteristic which is so germane to one's understanding of the artist, a characteristic which they discovered by experience and direct conversation with Michelangelo.

Condivi says that Michelangelo "had a very retentive memory, so much so that although he painted many thousands of figures, he never made one which resembled another or which was placed in the same attitude. On the contrary, I heard him say that he never drew a line which he didn't remember and that he would erase one in public which he hadn't drawn."[3]

Critics have discovered the repetition of some figures, very often done at widely varying times, in the different works of the artist; these, however, represent recurring motifs which were dear to the imagination and taste of the artist and which were always repeated for a precise reason. This suggests the development of a nucleus of ideas which reappear in successive works, each time with a different function.

Vasari has a more interesting anecdote to offer, which seems to have been recounted by Buonarroti himself, and which leads us to several considerations about Michelangelo's artistic ideals.[4]

Perhaps reflecting Condivi, he also says: ". . . Michelangelo was of a retentive and profound memory"; but he underlines this quality in relation to other works, and continues: ". . . when he saw others' works only once, he retained them completely, and used them so that nobody ever became aware. He never did anything of his own which was exactly like what he had done before because he remembered everything that he had done." It is clear that the biographer is referring here to Michelangelo's interest in the pictorial works of Luca Signorelli, as well as those of a few others. He underlines the fact that Michelangelo's "copying" was original and interpretative and that his motive was not to "steal." The anecdote itself refers to an episode in the artist's youth: among a group of friends, Michelangelo wagered a free dinner to the one who could best draw a figure "which had no proportion, which was awkward like the puppets made by inept craftsmen and which soil the walls." Michelangelo, who already had an exceptionally secure drawing technique, won the wager because he remembered having seen one of "these awkward figures" scrawled on a wall and was able to mentally reproduce it as if it were before his eyes.

Here Vasari concludes, ". . . a difficult thing for a man who was so full of drawing, so accustomed to chosen things." This is an important notation about Buonarroti who must have considered drawing to be an almost absolutely expressive language. Among the very earliest of Michelangelo's boyhood exercises, the biographers refer to a copy of Martin Schongauer's *Temptation of Saint Anthony* which dates back to the days of the friendship with Granacci, who introduced Michelangelo to this work for copying purposes. Michelangelo's feeling for drawing is documented by his copying of "Martin the German's" graphic work, Schongauer having enjoyed a certain success in the early days of Florentine curiosity about Nordic graphic art. It had seemed that all hope to ever recover this early Michelangelo exercise was lost, until a *tempera on wood* painting which reproduces that Schongauer was placed on auction in London recently which manifests certain Ghirlandesque qualities, leading one to believe that it may be in Michelangelo's adolescent style. There is also another one of importance to be found in a private collection in Bologna.

We know, from further information furnished by Condivi, that this was a painted exercise and not merely a copied drawing. He called it "a little painting," and tells how Michelangelo was very assiduous in his gathering of details for the experiment, even going to the fish market to observe the different types of fish, the colors of the fins and scales, because "he [Michelangelo] did not use a single color that he had not personally confirmed from nature." We may also ask ourselves just what attracted Michelangelo in this Schongauer print. When one considers the work from compositional and graphic points of view, it is not difficult to find the answer. The print reveals a certain dynamism, even though it is the fruit of a late Gothic impulse, in the monstrous demons who torment the Saint, who is raised off the earth and surrounded by a strange saraband of devils who mistreat him and pull him by his cassock. A composition which has so much movement but which is at the same time circumscribed in space had clear appeal for the young artist. From a drawing standpoint, he was probably interested in the manner in which Schongauer rendered the folds and defined the chiaroscuro.[5]

Michelangelo probably derived his first style of pen drawing, in which each stroke is clearly separated from the others, from these German prints. They offered a patient and clear graphic language which Michelangelo swiftly turned to a synthetic rather than an analytic purpose. They could, indeed, offer little else because of their expressionist characteristics which were quite far from the sculptural definition of bodies which Michelangelo, even in his copies, immediately realized. If we wish to discuss his assiduous attention to the detailed effects in the painting, we should recall certain subtleties which one can still note in the *Manchester Madonna*, which is his first known painting extant.

To orient ourselves a little to this delicate but significant period in the youth of Michelangelo the painter, we may refer to an authenticated drawing in the Louvre which reproduces two figures by Giotto from the *Resurrection of Saint John* fresco in Santa Croce. It is a pen drawing in which the two figures to the left of Giotto's composition have been isolated. One is standing up and the other is bent over; both are intently watching the empty sepulchre. It would be difficult to discover in the juvenile works of any great artist a more decisive testimony and prediction of what was to be his future development (figs. 1 and 2).

Michelangelo is interested in the two figures as if they formed an isolated group. It is possibly the contrast between the standing figure, immobile and statue-like, and the other figure, bearded, bent double by a brusque movement of his body, which instinctively led Michelangelo to choose these two personages among so many others. In the drawing, however, which is already so energetic, a sense of sculptured relief emerges from the pictorial values of Giotto. If we ignore the real source of the exercise, we could easily imagine that it was copied from a bas-relief rather than a painting. That it was a sculptured feeling which drew Michelangelo to the study of this Giotto is confirmed by the technique which Buonarroti uses, and the particular way in which he employs that technique. We are speaking of a pen drawing which has long been an expressive means of doing a study which does not fade with the passing of time. Pen drawing is, however, a method which requires extreme sureness in notions about form, because it is impossible to make corrections and still present a clearly defined image.

This drawing by Michelangelo is different from all other Renaissance drawings. It is completely opposed to those of Leonardo in the same technique, and can only be compared to the technique of marble sculpture.

It may very well be, as we have already said, that the young artist might have sensed from his studies of fifteenth-century prints the value of the delineation of form which one can obtain in sketching when following the planes indicated by the relief of the images. Here, certainly, Michelangelo is already an autonomous artist, in possession of a precise personal vision of things and their robust individualization in space. We are fortunate to be able to follow Michelangelo's method in the Louvre drawing because while the standing figure is complete, the other is barely sketched, giving evidence of his working procedure. It seems that from a lightly sketched pencil outline (if he needed one), he delineated the edges of the figures and then systematically finished the relief effect in chiaroscuro. His conception is not the pictorial, atmospheric, and suggestive conception of Leonardo in which the image is evoked by subtle shadings in a nervous hailstorm of one-directional strokes. Michelangelo, instead, models his form with clear distinct strokes which are sometimes crossed (but never confused in the manner of a painter) as he attempts to determine the volume masses of the body.

This is Michelangelo's adolescent drawing method and returns very often, even in his later and more tempestuously imaginative periods. It is as if he wished to return to a certainty in form when he was about to lose faith in the consistency of reality. Even taking into account his successive maturation, his later drawings still display the same characteristics as in, for example, the youthful rendering of the *Madonna and Saint Anne* in the Louvre, the nude for the *Battle of Cascina* in the British Museum, and the Christ study for the Roman church of Santa Maria sopra Minerva in the Louvre. These confirm the fact that the artist liked this method of delineating form decisively in relief without concessions to shading. All this leads us to conclude that of the young Michelangelo's interests (at that point painting and sculpture were of equal importance), drawing assumed a dominant position as a means of expressing an idea in plastic form.

Such a priority had evolved in Florence until it became the essential characteristic of this school of painting. During the Renaissance, the same concept of drawing assumed an even deeper significance. One can gather this from the *Treatise* of Cennino Cennini (near the end of the fourteenth century) who, speaking with an ideal pupil, discusses pen drawing

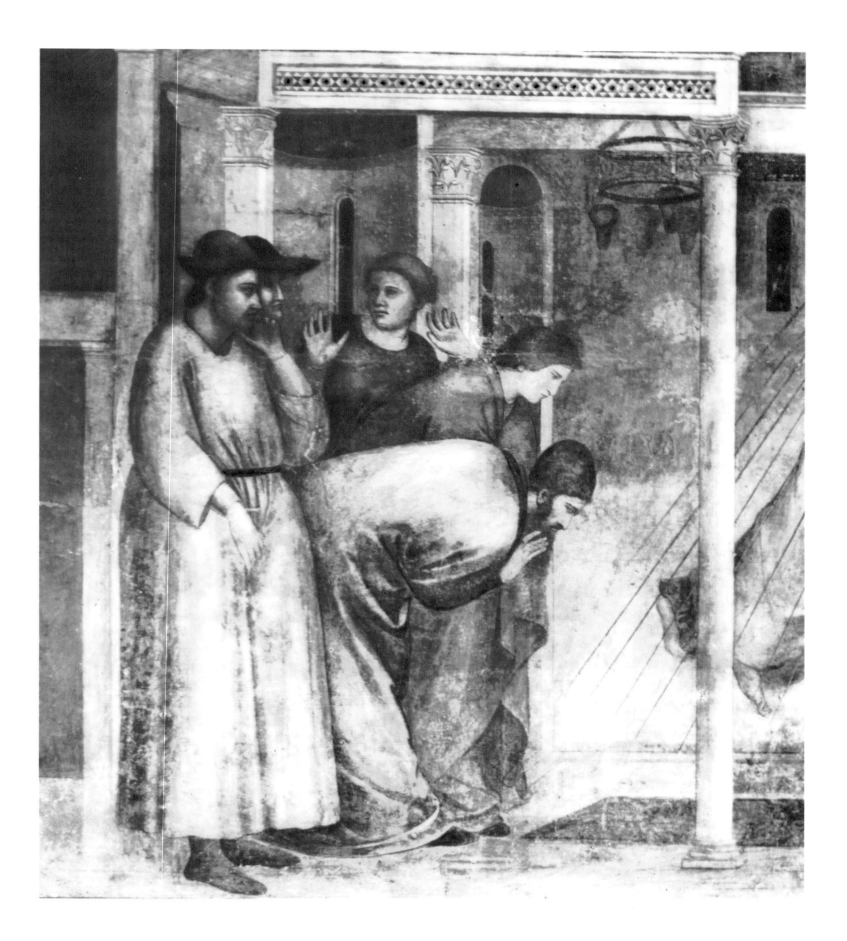

Fig. 1—GIOTTO. *"The Ascension of the Evangelist"*—*Florence, Santa Croce (Michelangelo's copy of this work is done in pen, and is in the Louvre)*

as follows: "Do you know what will happen to you as you exercise with pen drawing? You will become expert, practiced, and capable of much drawing in your head."[6] We should not forget what the exercise of drawing meant to Leonardo, who utilized it as a language capable of expressing everything which is expressible from rigorous scientific demonstration to the most liberal pictorial invention.

We can therefore say that in the young Michelangelo, the simultaneous tendency towards painting and sculpture was fused with drawing, a method of articulating the typical Michelangelesque values of both.

Until 1492, the year of the death of Michelangelo's friend and protector Lorenzo the Magnificent, the young artist's experiences were varied and intense as he discovered the secrets of his art. The good luck of his becoming a "member" of the Medici family, after Lorenzo had noticed him working in the garden of San Marco, led to Michelangelo's further study of the humanities. This came about through his frequent contacts with Poliziano, with the Neoplatonic ideas of Marsilio Ficino, and his reading of the *Divine Comedy* (which he came to love so much that he could recite the entire work by heart).

We have at least two authenticated sculptures of those youthful years, the *Madonna of the Stairs* and the *Battle of the Centaurs* (both now in Casa Buonarroti, and the latter done on Poliziano's recommendation). It is more difficult, however, to distinguish among the various paintings dated at this period (and which manifest characteristics of the art of Francesco Granacci or, indirectly, Ghirlandaio) those which should be attributed to Michelangelo.

Recent Michelangelo criticism concerns a group of paintings which are considered by some to be among his early exercises. Others attribute this group to the master of the *Manchester Madonna* (the temporary title of the *Madonna and Child* in London). We feel that they are works which certainly come from the hand of Michelangelo. We must, however, confess that there is still at the present time much uncertainty about the youthful paintings of Michelangelo.[7]

Granacci's influence on Buonarroti has become emphasized in the various critical hypotheses after Fiocco's changing of what was formerly considered Granacci's birth date of 1477 to the correct date of 1469. Fiocco, who thoroughly explored the youthful painting activities of Michelangelo, attributed the *Madonna and Child with the Infant Saint John* in the Dublin Gallery to Buonarroti. It is certainly a notable work, but according to Bertini and our own opinion, it is, rather, a product of Granacci, whose artistic nature was easily influenced and who might have drawn from the vigorous personality of Michelangelo. Another *Madonna and Child* in the Contini Collection was also attributed to Michelangelo but it lacks his expressive force and seems closer to Granacci, as does a *Madonna* in a private collection in Baden near Zurich. These and other similar works, linked by a certain affinity, simply do not come near the singular autonomy of the *Manchester Madonna*. They demonstrate the characteristics of a fifteenth-century Mannerism rather than the power of a new idea. Even if we keep in mind that the young artist must have revealed some stylistic uncertainty, these paintings demonstrate none of that irrepressible "élan" so characteristic of Michelangelo. The argument over works which were done during Michelangelo's youth, even if not by his hand, must depend on point of view rather than details in the works themselves. Certain works do not seem to be Michelangelo's because they do not contain that newness of idea, that independence of conception which are fundamental elements of his art.

Stating in advance that Buonarroti was thirsty for conquest in his youthful period, and paying attention to his maturation as he came into contact with the great art of the past (and his curiosity about developments in the Florentine artistic circles of the time), we must immediately add that a total examination of these experiences reveals that his youthful impetus produced apparently contrasting results—results which manifest themselves in the creative activity of any

Fig. 2—MICHELANGELO *original pen drawing: copy from a detail to the left of Giòtto's fresco "The Ascension of the Evangelist" in Santa Croce (Paris, Cabinet des Dessins, Louvre)*

genius in search of himself, who already possesses extremely original ideas which anticipate the characteristics of his more mature style.

If this is true in his sculpture (think of the dates of the *Madonna of the Stairs* and the *Battle of the Centaurs*) it is even more symptomatic of his painting. Here we have the artist who already manifests a decidedly sculptural concept translated by drafting and coloristic means which are still immature. His search for an incisive and almost metallic linear vigor is evident, along with a tormented inquiry into modelled form which is not free of those accents which already assumed manneristic characteristics in the hands of his less gifted contemporaries.

To this we must add, in repetition, the exercise which he gained from the Nordic prints in which he perceived (if only dimly) the possibility of giving form to that inner anger which always characterized his exceptional temperament and which he so vigorously expressed in the *Battle of the Centaurs*. Michelangelo undoubtedly produced some paintings at this time and also did some fresco work. A study of the Florentine paintings datable to the close of the fifteenth century which present characteristics akin to the *Manchester Madonna* in composition, design, and color reveals a possible precocious influence, if not the direct hand, of the young Michelangelo on his contemporaries, the interpreters of what we may call the crisis of the "fin de siècle."

Plate I In our opinion, however, of all the various works that are continually being accepted and refused as products of the twenty-year-old Michelangelo, the *Manchester Madonna* seems to display the most singular Buonarrotian characteristics. We can consider it to be in his first group of works, mainly because the undeniable elements of his art do not appear as reflections or copies but as predictions of what the artist developed in future works, not only as a painter but also as a sculptor.

The incomplete painting (this, too, is a factor although not conclusive, which is rather typical of the artist's restlessness) depicts the Madonna and Child with the infant Saint John at the center of the composition and four angels standing in pairs to the sides in the act of reading and alluding to a song. The two angels to the left are delineated in preparation for painting, while the two to the right are completely finished and reveal, as does the Madonna, a very careful, almost tormented search for the modelled form in the faceted planes of the material and in the curved vitality of outline. The outlines are accentuated by the characteristic chromatic effect of acute and almost piercingly metallic harmonies. These harmonies already contain the dominant tones which are so decisively expressed in the *Doni Madonna* and the early Sistine Chapel figures.

The London painting has very great interest from a coloristic point of view. The recurrence of orange pinks in the angels' tunics and in the border of the Madonna's dress seems to be used as a pretext to eliminate the young flesh of the adolescents and is in contrast with the brownish green of the Virgin's mantle which has a light slate-colored highlight. The preparation of the painting's surface is in olive green, that "earth green" tone which was used in monochromes and which recurs in Michelangelo's work when he wishes, as he does here, to create a plastically modelled form for the sweet face of the Virgin, and to resolve in clear relief the sharp folds of the mantle. In these folds and shadows, we discover those subtle and incisive brush strokes which correspond to the pen-drawing technique used by the young artist.

Finally, the play of the knotted cloth or that held up by the bands that delineate the sculptured substance of the bodies is underlined by the different color which they assume in relation to the highlights and shadings of the nearby tones (as will occur again in the *Doni Madonna*).

The idea for the couples of angels might have come to Michelangelo from the figures in the choir by Luca della Robbia. It seems much more probable, however, that the influence comes from the bas-relief *Jesus and Little Saint John* by Desiderio da Settignano in the Mellon Collection of the National Gallery in Washington.[8] This is an important element because it brings into focus the characteristics of subtle search by the artist who instinctively incorporated the bas-relief effect into the painting, although he does not yet produce a complete "tondo" like the *Doni Madonna* in the Uffizi.

The placement of the Madonna and Child group at the center of the painting is exceptional. The Virgin rising from a base of splintered rock is a characteristic which returns in other works and already anticipates the monumental base of the *Pietà* in St. Peter's. The greatness of the base is softened, however, by the attitude of the Virgin who, almost wanting to prevent the Child from reading the Holy Book, holds it away from him while he tries to climb on her knees to seize it. The clothes appear wrapped up, torn, open here and there (as in the very beautiful piece which reveals the virginal breast of the Madonna). This is a very personal idea which has no point of comparison in other works and would seem to be the fruit of an adolescent longing centered on the ancient motif of the Madonna of the Milk. It may seem excessive to accentuate this detail, but it is in such unpredicted inventions that the independence of Michelangelo's genius is revealed. Bearing in mind the character of the planned disorder of the clothes, and the primitive qualities which Michelangelo reveals in the plain garments around the youths, we must recognize that Michelangelo's taste is maturing. We are drawn, rather, to seek out the stimuli which brought about this development, and must return to the capricious and refined solutions of the aristocratic Sandro Botticelli to rediscover the thread.

Tuscan painting was not lacking in ideas of this type even in the fourteenth century. We can find an example in the frail image of Poverty, wearing elegantly torn clothes, who offers her hand in a gesture of ineffable sweetness to Saint Francis in the cloister vault of the tomb at Assisi. Let us leave to refined literary analysis any further discussion of the consequence of a "pre-Romantic" or "decadent" taste in these eventful years of Florentine painting.

The sweet and serious expression of the young Madonna with the smooth and pure brow is already the expression of the *Bruges Madonna,* just as the attitude of the Child is repeated with variations in the sculptured group (especially the characteristic fold of the Madonna's clothes, on which the Child rests his little foot).

One could not find any artist in those years who could conceive of so beautiful and original a composition, so close to Michelangelo's other works, unless it were Michelangelo himself. Because this painting not only contains points in common with established Michelangelo works, but also expresses the profound essence of his most intimate soul and imagination, it is not possible to consider it a copied work.

Another interesting factor is the "unfinished" painting technique used by the artist, which is also repeated in a painting which we believe to be an authentic Michelangelo, the *Deposition* in the London National Gallery. In the *Manchester Madonna* the completely finished section of the painting stops with a portion barely sketched and ready to be painted. (Contrast Leonardo's *Saint Girolamo* in the Vatican, for instance, the unfinished portions of which are already done in terms of chiaroscuro effects, or are impressionistically sketched even in the barely begun sections in order to prepare for the "painted" effect as opposed to the "sculptured" effect. This is very puzzling, indeed, in the Uffizi *Adoration of the Magi* in which it is very difficult to distinguish what is finished, what is not yet finished, and what he might never have intended to finish.) Michelangelo's procedure is the fresco method, which is also the sculptural method, in which the form is defined little by little over the sketch as in the process of working sculpturally.

Between the *Manchester Madonna* and the London *Deposition*, several years passed until 1494 during which Michelangelo (after the death of Lorenzo the Magnificent) stayed at his paternal home working by himself and meditating

Plate II

21

on religious problems. He was already under the influence of Savonarola's preachings and felt the influence of Savonarola's words until old age, as he confessed to Condivi. Much of the *Deposition*, however, demonstrates a more mature and developed art, both in conception and technique. We do not believe (as many have proposed) that the piece should be ascribed to the Sistine period because here again the analogies with the initial fresco compositions do not seem a consequence but rather an anticipation of the solutions which the artist develops more broadly in the Vatican Chapel. These are further reasons to encourage the hypothesis that this was executed between the *Manchester Madonna* and the *Doni Madonna*. These proofs arise from comparisons with works of sculpture which he executed at the time, in addition to chronological considerations.

The composition of the London painting is still in the line of development of a frontal concept, as in the *Manchester Madonna* (notwithstanding the search for a depth effect in the most original structure of the painting, which has Saint John and Mary Magdalene symmetrically placed at the center in the act of supporting the marmoreal body of Christ, and Saint Joseph of Arimathea, who supports Him under the armpits). It is almost in high relief which is emphasized by the figure of Mary of Cleophas and the other two female figures who are shown in close-up, Mary Salome to the left (she would have propped up the crown of thorns and the nails) and the unfinished Madonna.

The landscape is squalid and desertlike with rocky crags of Leonardesque taste which are, however, clearly sculptural in nature. A drawing of a kneeling Mary Salome in pen technique is known in which special attention is given to the nude who must then be clothed. According to some, this is a copy of an original and lost Michelangelo, but it loses no significance because of this. The clothes, as in the *Manchester Madonna*, swathe the body and emphasize in a particularly functional manner the gestures which are rich in energy. The forms become more plastic and the line less broken and metallic. The rendering of the figures, however, is equally nervous and clearly intended to bring out contrasting gestures and attitudes. The body of Christ is proof of an immensely significant factor which had been already included in the experience of the artist. This factor was the study of anatomy which gave him a freer command over the language implicit in the secret vitality of the muscles and tendons in action. It gave him an enriched poetry in the rendering of the nude in its heroic beauty. He poured infinite love into his molding of the colors and light in this perfect human image of Christ. We may also think back to his slightly smaller-than-life wood sculptured Crucifix which he created in gratitude to the Prior of Santo Spirito in Florence, who had allowed him to study anatomy directly from corpses, "a greater service than which," says Condivi, "he could not have provided."

The Santo Spirito Crucifix, which was considered lost, has been found by Margrit Lisner in the Santo Spirito convent. Notwithstanding the contrary opinion of several critics, it displays all the characteristics of the eighteen-year-old artist. For its close affinity to the ideal but young man on the Cross, it can be placed next to the London painting as an immediate antecedent. Its extraordinary and new naturalness, the contrasting motion, and the penetrating, delicate construction of Jesus' body seem offered to the adoration of the faithful also for the sake of sheer physical beauty.[9]

In a much later drawing, Michelangelo took up the walk of the carriers of Christ's body, as if in a funeral march for the death of a hero, but with a completely different sense of discomfort and pensive religiousness. The London composition represents the beginning of this conception which was to become typical and certainly made a strong impression in Florentine artistic circles of that period. We believe, in fact, that Raphael himself might have utilized more than one motif to invigorate his own style (besides the Holy Family of the *Doni Madonna*) for his *Deposition* in the Borghese Gallery in Rome (which was executed in 1507 for Atalanta Baglioni of Perugia).

In the London *Deposition*, in which space is defined by simple rocky crags and a terrain which is broadly and simply molded, there is a clear indication of a rough drawn stairway on that terrain to sustain the figures and justify their movements. To the right foreground near the rocks, the impressionistically treated, unfinished sepulchre is visible, displaying two small figures in the act of removing the stone. The rapid manner in which this detail is splattered on is also to be found in the more distant portions of the *Flood* in the Sistine vault. This is not really extraneous to Michelangelo's taste which, in the episode in the foreground, arrives at Greco-Roman effects because of the spontaneity of its inventiveness and the constant sculptural sense.

The existence of the molded steps on which the foreground figures are placed in the mass of terrain is of notable significance. We are led to think of Christ's bearers in the act of withdrawal rather than advancement, this being a more logical movement in view of the ascent to the sepulchre. One can thus explain the tension in the gestures, the movement of Saint John's feet and the brusque turning of the slim, singular figure of Mary Magdalene, who reacts "in opposition" to the heroic image of the Apostle. As far as the characteristic disposition of the two bearers goes, they assume poses which are widely spread due to their strained action. We may refer to a drawing in the British Museum in which the motif is taken up again, perhaps for the *Battle of Cascina* or possibly for the *Brazen Serpent* in the Sistine Chapel.

We should not be surprised by the artist's anticipation and reuse of certain dominant motifs. Bertini says, "It is characteristic of Michelangelo's art that several preferred motifs were precociously conceived which persisted and obstinately renewed themselves until his old age." This is an attitude which we consider fundamental to Buonarroti, and indicates his development in a continual search for solutions to the exigencies of his insatiable creative spirit.

We know that Michelangelo left Florence in 1494, perhaps because of anxiety over the consequences implicit in the fall of the Medici. He went to Venice and Bologna. In the latter city he was a guest of Gianfrancesco Aldobrandi, who loved to hear the artist read from Dante and Petrarch. Michelangelo deepened his knowledge of the Humanities while simultaneously working on sculpture and by taking an interest in the Ferrarese school of painting which he could study at first hand. Many have offered this new experience as an explanation of that nervous and linear zest which one finds in his youthful paintings and sculpture up to the time of the *David*. Although the artist was interested in the singular style of Cosimo Tura and Ercole de Roberti, we do not think the neo-Gothic expressionism of the Ferrarese school was necessarily an element in the formation of Michelangelo, who came from the country of Pollaiuolo and Verrocchio.

His first period in Rome, which extends from 1496 to 1501, is characterized by a renewal of enthusiasm for ancient sculpture, notwithstanding the fact that his masterpiece of that period, the *Pietà* in Saint Peter's, is without classical elements. It expresses, on the contrary, a deepening of Tuscan taste, invigorated by a knowledge of Jacopo della Quercia's works, in a very intense climate of spiritual concentration.

The *Pietà* in Saint Peter's has its own particular value in relation to the artist's tastes in painting and drawing. This work is determined in space as a high-relief in which the essential element is enhanced by light. It is realized by an exceptional control over sculptural methods which, starting from a frontal vision, fully develop the motif of Christ laid out on the Mother's knees (a theme very dear to painters).

Michelangelo has developed, to the utmost point of luministic sensibility, the sharply modelled forms in the marble. He accentuates the folds in the beautiful mantle of the Virgin, from the knee to the base in an analogous fashion to certain drawings of folds by Leonardo highlighted in white lead.

He has emphasized the purposely clean break between the nude figure of Christ, invested with light raining from above which causes Him to grow mortally pale, and the complex movement of the Mother's clothes. The result is almost a "tonal painting" effect.

Relationships to painting are indicated by the almost sad incisiveness of the drapery folds, the linear strokes of the details of Christ's body, and the Madonna's face. Here too, the supposed stimuli which the artist received from the fifteenth-century Ferrarese style during his stay in Bologna are cited as significant. Such stimuli, we believe, might have been better incorporated into a more generic affinity of expressive means, which one already notes in the London *Pietà* or, even more so, in the *Manchester Madonna*. Since we know that Michelangelo tended to transplant his struggle with drawing technique into sculpture in such an individual fashion, the comparison between the rendering of the drapes in the *Manchester Madonna* and the marble drapes of the *Pietà* is almost obvious.

In the Vatican group, which expresses such an intense religious concentration at the moment of the classical trend in Michelangelo's art, there is also a vivid trace of the effect of Savonarola's preaching on his spirit. If, however, the austere vision of the sacred drama has some affinity with the words of the friar who cried out for severity in art, it also responds to a particular moment in the Florentine Renaissance; a moment in which the better artists renounced decoration on the one hand and documentary realism on the other. This was an effort to get away from the crisis of the fifteenth century. Leonardo, Michelangelo, and Raphael were to determine, each in his own individual but analogous fashion, new human ideals by means of a more profound inquiry into reality conceived as life reborn. It is really the works of Michelangelo in this period, the *Pietà* in Saint Peter's, the *Bruges Madonna*, the "tondos" in Florence and London, and the *Doni Madonna*, which spontaneously reflect the admonitions of Savonarola to the artists of his time. These admonitions were so definite and allusive as to almost make Ghirlandaio, for example, their target (and we know how Michelangelo valued Ghirlandaio).

Savonarola said in 1496, "The images which you paint in the Churches are images of yourselves. The young people go around saying to this woman and that, 'she is the Magdalene, he is Saint John, there is the Virgin . . . .' Do you believe that the Virgin went around dressed as you depict her? I tell you that she was dressed simply as a poor woman and was covered so that you could barely see her face." [10]

We must keep in mind the presence of Savonarola's personality during Michelangelo's youth in Florence. His influence on the artist, although it matured with the years, was favored by an artistic and intellectual condition in art which determined a common climate of rethinking on problems of form and content. This affected Michelangelo as it affected, in a different way, Leonardo.

Plate III At the close of 1503, for the wedding of Agnolo Doni and Maddalena Strozzi, Michelangelo painted the *Doni Madonna*, which is now in the Uffizi. This is considered by several scholars to be the only certain autograph painting on wood by Michelangelo—a judgment which, in our opinion, seems excessively strong.

This famous painting, so much admired by Michelangelo's contemporaries, must be put into relation with the two marble "tondos," the *Madonna and Child with the Infant Saint John* for Bartolomeo Pitti, in the National Museum in Florence, and the other for Taddeo Taddei in the Royal Academy in London. Even if we can construct a compositional rapport between these sculptured works and the *Doni Madonna*, Michelangelo reaches a richer complexity in the painting. He realized the full three-dimensional relief effect in the space which surrounds the principal group and makes them appear to stand in statuary isolation. This echoes his new spatial vision in the background with the figures of the young bathing nudes, which are perspectively removed from the imposing compositional knot of the Holy Family.

The vision which Michelangelo realized in the *Doni Madonna*, allowing the group to create the illusion of space surrounding it, seems to be fundamental to a more measured interpretation of the "single image" so happily discovered by Aru in 1937, and which has been rapidly accepted by the majority of the critics.

According to the "single image" concept, Michelangelo conceived his figures as if drawn from the block. This was necessarily related to painting, through plastic values, but was not to give the impression that sculptors call the "full round." This is a rather common phenomenon among the majority of sculptors of any period.

If this phenomenon is to be mentioned in sculpture, where even isolated figures like the *David* often presuppose a base from which they can draw their eloquent relief, the bridge from sculpture to painting is slightly more difficult to deduce. This is particularly true, however, if we maintain that the artist, as much as he considered himself mainly a sculptor, was more at ease as a painter where he was free to impose his "single image" on his figures.

In the *Doni Madonna*, for example, what the Mannerists call the "serpentine line" (meaning spiral) is done with complete naturalness. It uninterruptedly facilitates the complete freedom of the figures in space, even though it begins from a central point of view which is so clearly indicated by the Madonna's gesture. (If we wish to consider the work as an exception in Michelangelo's art, it leads us to the necessity of calling countless other examples exceptions, since his creative scope was so diversified). We can logically deduce that Michelangelo paid more attention to Leonardo's works after returning to Florence. Evidence of this is to be found in several autograph drawings, especially the one in the Louvre, in which it is possible to trace the artist's attitude with respect to Leonardo's new compositional style, a style founded on the centralization of the figures and the reciprocal relationships obtained in a complex play of interlaced positions. In the Louvre sketch, treated in pen with his typical sculptural energy as he dashes off the planes, one reads in the artist's handwriting, "Who would ever say that this was by my hand?" These words express his implicit surprise in studying groupings of this type.

To get the *Doni Madonna* away from the Leonardesque ideas and the artist's own marble reliefs, it is useful to take note of its singular energy, the very original linked composition, and the re-echoing of perspectives in the curve of the architectural exedra where the youths seem to be preparing to bathe (this, in the opinion of many critics, alludes to the pagan world which is superseded by the advent of Christ). All this provokes, in Michelangelo's creative intuition, a sense of absolute plastic clarity which has by now been transferred without any reticence to his paintings, after his sculptural experiences.

If we wished to find a work from which Michelangelo may have derived the stimulus for this "launch into space," we might refer to the *Holy Family* of Luca Signorelli in the Uffizi. Not only are several elements of content reproduced (such as the nudes in the background), but also the same type of painter's vision is employed. This is a sign of the value which Michelangelo already gave to that painter's style and which is later employed in the composition of the frescoes in the San Brizio Chapel in Orvieto, from which he drew motifs for the *Last Judgment*. (Here, we must mention the error of several critics who reverse the chronological and stylistic relationship by claiming that Signorelli's *Holy Family* comes after the *Doni Madonna*.)

The hypothesis which might favorably explain the staggering originality of ideas in Michelangelo's work and place the strong sculptural solutions of Signorelli in a generic dependence on the world of Michelangelo is unacceptable for stylistic reasons since the date of the *Doni Madonna* cannot be set before the Doni-Strozzi wedding. One would have to place the Signorelli after 1503 when Signorelli's powers were considerably flagging and no longer demonstrated those characteristics which we find in the *Holy Family* or the frescoes in Orvieto which are clearly anterior in date. These characteristics are: the heroic construction of the bodies, the mastery over broad pictorial effects, the typology of the Virgin (so close to those sculptured feminine images which we find in the more serene portions of the frescoes), and the importance given to perspective and foreshortening effects (almost symbolic as, for example, in the large half open book which re-echoes typical Pierfrancescani and Florentine problems of the fifteenth century). These make us think of the rigorous elements in the chapel paintings (especially the famous portrait of Dante). Signorelli's work seems quite certainly to anticipate Michelangelo's *Doni Madonna* and represents from many points of view the nearest influence on the formation of Michelangelo's heroic style.

Although he evidently feels close to Signorelli's vigorous and sculptural taste, in the *Doni Madonna* Michelangelo goes beyond the mere advancing of tradition and announces innovations which are more monumental and "classical." These innovations are concerned with complex and articulated composition and reach beyond lifelike study to an idealization of form.

The idea of including groups in a circle was already present in the Renaissance mentality which sought the circular form as a sign of perfect equilibrium and supreme harmony. If painters like Sandro Botticelli (think of the *Madonna of the Magnificat* or the *Madonna of the Pomegranate*) were interested in its musical qualities and in the echo of the curve within the pictorial space, Michelangelo meets the difficult compositional problems by cancelling the surface of the paintings from our vision. He transmutes the surface into a transparent crystal sphere in which the images assume their attitudes in complete freedom of movement, in a space which has become three-dimensional.

To suggest this new conquest which replaces the perspective vision of the fifteenth century and totally involves the human figure in its movements, Michelangelo's compositions gradually unwind in successive planes until they induce a singular expansion of the atmosphere. The figures then move with complete dominance in the composition.

The group of the Holy Family is so closely knit (and so harmoniously linked in its movements) that our eyes cannot help following its helicoidal motion. It continues uninterruptedly until finishing with the proud face of the Child, a small classical deity, illuminated with Christian spirituality. From the compositional point of view, the work reveals a high degree of harmony achieved through contrasts. Saint Joseph, kneeling behind the Virgin who reads the Holy Book, is so well inserted into the group that he represents the ideal background against which the figure of the Virgin is perfectly drawn.

It does not seem very important to understand the precise reasons for the gestures of the harmonious figures (the harmony of a perfect unity being what Michelangelo was striving to attain). It seems unnatural, however, to have to explain the gestures of the protagonists, as if the Virgin were entrusting Saint Joseph with the small, proud Child. It is, instead, a normal gesture on the Mother's part, who is about to gather the Child to her bosom, the Child who wishes to climb on her shoulders and tenderly pull her hair while she watches him with infinite tenderness.

Without complicating the symbolic value of the composition, which for us is non-existent here, it seems like a spontaneous inspiration on the part of Michelangelo (who did the work for the Doni marriage) to conceive of a Holy Family in the act of uniting itself. It is the moment in which the Child is about to be clasped to the Mother's bosom to form the traditional Madonna with Child on her knees; this is emphasized because the book, bound in red and abandoned on the lovely azure drape of the Madonna, seems to indicate a preceding moment in which the Virgin was reading.

As always, Michelangelo paid extraordinary attention to real-life studies. He made accurate drawings, especially of details, in preparation for the *Doni Madonna*, as he did for the Sistine Chapel. (The complete set of studies is not known, however.)

For the Virgin's face, the artist made a very careful study in a sanguine drawing which is now in the Casa Buonarroti. It is very well known, being one of the few extant studies of heads by the artist. The reference to the *Doni Madonna* was supported by Berenson, who was seconded by others in the opinion. Some, however, think of it as a sketch for the head of the prophet Jonah, although drawn in reverse.

In the characteristic tension of the head which is turned upward and the insistent isolation of the gradually molded chiaroscuro, the drawing is referable to the *Doni Madonna*. It is also natural that any eventual idealized splendor will not be present in a study which seeks to document real life.

This painting is of essential importance. We know that in a few years, Michelangelo developed this same volumetrical vision in the great Sistine poem, and we recognize that here the artist is concluding an intense period of search of which the exemplary results found in the *Doni Madonna* are a clear manifestation. The marble-like, limpid construction recalls the London *Deposition* and particularly the figure of the nude Christ. We are also reminded of the typology of Saint Joseph of Arimathea, the quality of the sharp folds in the clothes, the original pose of the seated female figure in the foreground, and above all, the terrain with its rocky crags (which, in the *Doni Madonna*, is molded in azure to determine the final circular horizons of a perfectly finished world).

We also feel very near to the *Pietà* in Saint Peter's for the marvelous draperies of the Virgin which are translated in such an expressive manner in the painting of the Madonna's clothes.

Here, Michelangelo's painting style has reached its full autonomous significance in the rapport between form and color. Invested with an almost zenith-like light, the modelled form is reworked with tints that exalt its significance to the fullest. In the precise separation between one zone and another, the various sculptured masses of the composition were formed out of precious blocks of polychrome marble. The blue of the Virgin's clothes serves as a base for the antique rose garment out of which her beautiful arm, which is ready to receive the Child, can be seen. The limpid turning of that face, so rich with intense expression, towards the Son who is modelled with bronze skin (as if he were the child Hercules) is extraordinary. The sharp tone of Saint Joseph's clothes seems to be the illuminating element of a painting which is almost gleaming with ancient and precious reflections.

The color scheme of the *Doni Madonna* is directly derived from the sharp, contrasting tints which we saw in the *Manchester Madonna* and the *Deposition* in London. The artist considers color as a necessary and integral element of the form. He thus links himself with Florentine painting back to the time of Giotto, since the iridescent effect in the drapes (an effect which the Mannerists developed to a high degree) is still tied to a sculptural sense which is, in turn, produced by violent contrasts in tone.

Buonarroti is not, however, insensitive to the interplay of reflections and reverberations of color. One need only observe the border of the Virgin's azure drape on the left knee, which becomes almost green as it approaches the orange-yellow of Saint Joseph's mantle. One may also observe how the Child is inserted between the pink of Mary's dress and a strip of Saint Joseph's yellow mantle.

The group inhabits its own abstract climate precisely because of the attention which Michelangelo has given to the luminosity of the colors which maintain their initial purity within the limits of the design. What can we say about the solar beauty of those nudes which seem to live in a gilt sunset against the receding hills? Here we already have Michelangelo's full palette. The palette acquires new modulations and singularly truthful accents in the Sistine vault. In this Holy Family, the artist demonstrates the fullness of his heroic style in matters of form and color, where he reaches his autonomous solution.

Raphael, among others, studied the *Doni Madonna*. His work on the portraits of Agnolo and Maddalena Doni gave him the opportunity to come in contact with Michelangelo's painting. After passing through a series of variations, he arrived at a Virgin of sculptural values in the group of Marys to the right in the Borghese *Deposition*. Raphael used, above all, the new spiral line which was necessary to unify the figures who hover around the fainting Virgin. This is one of the first exercises of his interest in Michelangelo, whose compositional and monumental solutions he meditated on and utilized until his final works. This painting was also studied by artists like Pontormo and Rosso Fiorentino, whose interests were primarily coloristic. Their studies were almost a "surrealistic rendering of the transposition of the plastic sentiment into a chromatic play of modern suggestion." This prodigiously firm work stands at the center of Florentine art as the most discussed antithesis to the "shaded" conception introduced into painting by Leonardo. It is an affirmation of that sculptural energy which constituted the backbone of Florentine painting, and a courageous testimony to an artistic innovation—the monumental grandeur of images transferred from the daily plane of realism to a heroic evocation.

Such a conception was definitely affirmed by Michelangelo with his colossal *David*, which he executed from 1501 to 1504. This image of civic pride became gigantic and assumed a high value both as a symbol of a sculptural vision and as a symbol of a world which is Man's creation. It was impossible that repercussions would not be felt in painting as well.

(1) *Michelangelo*, his life as gathered from the writings of his disciple Ascanio Condivi, revision, introduction and notes by Paolo d'Ancona. Milan 1928.

(2) Here is the L. B. Alberti quotation from the treatise *Della Pittura* (1435): ". . . and if you would like to reproduce some work because you have more feeling towards that than towards live things, I would prefer to copy a mediocre sculpture than a fine painting. From a painting, nothing is acquired other than a knowledge of copying; but from a sculptured piece, one learns to copy and also acquaints himself with the copying and knowledge of light." L. B. Alberti: *Il trattato della pittura*. Lanciano 1934 (page 92).

(3) A. Condivi: op. cit., page 196.

(4) G. Vasari: *La vita di Michelangelo*, with comments by Paola Barocchi, Milan—Naples 1962. Page 124 and note 727 which records the developments of the Vasari anecdote.

(5) C. Champion-Schongauer: Paris 1925, plate XV and page 88. The print was considered by the author "si dissemblable des oeuvres habituelles du Beau Martin . . . que Michel-Ange en fit . . . une copie peinte."

(6) *Il libro dell'arte or Trattato della pittura* of Cennino Cennini. Florence 1859, chapter XIII, page 9.

(7) One may refer to the ample treatise in the first volume of those devoted to Michelangelo by Charles De Tolnay. Princeton University Press (1943–1960).

(8) G. Galassi: *La scultura fiorentina del Quattrocento*, Milan 1949, page 202.

(9) M. Lisner in "Kunstchronik," vol. XVI, page 1–2 (1963); and for the critical developments: V. Mariani: *Il Crocifisso di Michelangelo* in "Il Giornale d'Italia," May 9th-10th, 1963.

(10) G. Savonarola: *Prediche sopra Amos e Zaccaria* (1496).

CHAPTER TWO

THE CARTOON FOR THE *BATTLE OF CASCINA* IN THE PALAZZO VECCHIO

IN THE AUTUMN OF 1503, the "Signoria" of Florence decided to commemorate the war exploits of the Republic on the walls of the council chamber of the Palazzo Vecchio. In May of 1504, Leonardo was summoned to paint the *Battle of Anghiari* which he began in 1505, after having drawn the famous cartoon with a technique derived from readings of classical authors; this technique was chosen due to his hostility towards the fresco method in which corrections are not possible after a mistake has been made.

In the autumn of 1504, the Gonfaloniere Pier Soderini had, however, invited Michelangelo to paint the *Battle of Cascina* next to Leonardo's version, and the cartoon seems to have been finished in 1505. Thus a competition between the two artists began. It may not have been the original intention of the order but the competition accorded well with the vivid sentiments of Florentine civic pride during those years.

Leonardo, after having completed the cartoon depicting the Florentine victory of 1440 against the Visconti leader Niccolò Piccinino, started experiments on the wall but had to stop because the paint had been melted by the heat he had used for glazing the painting on the wall in accordance with an ancient encaustic formula.

After having done many studies, Michelangelo drew his cartoon which represented the Florentine victory over Pisa in 1364. The episode which he used is mentioned in Philip Villani's chronicle and refers to a dramatic moment in the Pisan war. The Florentines are bathing in the Arno near Cascina when they are surprised by the enemy. Into the midst of the crowd of combatants, Mario Donati breathlessly arrives and cries, "We are lost!" The soldiers then hurry ashore, dress rapidly and arm themselves to join in the battle.

The famous, definitive drawings which both artists prepared for the walls reasserted the fundamental principles of these two Florentine geniuses. Exhibited in the "Hall of the Pope" and successively transported to the Medici palace, they created an enormous impression and were, in Benvenuto Cellini's words, "the school of the world."

Condivi said of Michelangelo's work that "all those who later put their hands to a brush received light from it." When Condivi wrote his biography (published in 1553), the Michelangelo cartoon had already been dismembered since he adds that "I have not learned the cause of that misfortune which happened, Michelangelo having left it in the Hall of the Pope, the place which is so named in Florence (at S. Maria Novella). One can see, in various places, some of the pieces which are preserved with great care as being holy things."

Vasari, who it seems did not see the cartoon when it was still an integral whole, said that its study offered a chance to an entire generation of painters who lived or worked in Florence to deepen their knowledge of the drawing of the nude. As he concludes his description of the work, he solemnly affirms, "Because they were filled with wonder and admiration at seeing the summit of art in such a picture as that shown them by Michelangelo . . . ."[1]

Fragmentary notes on payment which Michelangelo received as the work proceeded are known. They were published by Gaye, and refer to October and December of 1504 and February and August of 1505. In the latter year, the work should have been finished if the expenses covered the actual painting process, but that was not possible since Michelangelo had to leave for Bologna to meet Pope Julius II.

From Vasari's biography, we can also deduce the artist's drawing technique. It would appear that it was not the same for the entire work. While the greater part of the fighting semi-nude figures was completely in chiaroscuro, other parts of the cartoon were sketched. This is not because, as his biographer imagines, Michelangelo wished to "demonstrate how much he knew about this craft" but because he went about the whole work in single groups.

Each group contained several figures "in various sketched styles, outlined in charcoal, drawn with strokes or shaded with illuminated white lead." We are actually talking about a cartoon which, as such, had to be finished and illuminated with white lead like the *School of Athens* by Raphael in the Ambrosiana in Milan. Its moving from one place to another and the flocking of young artists to copy it caused the cartoon's dismemberment. Vasari says that when it was placed in the Medici palace while Giulio de Medici was sick, "nobody paid attention to it, so that it was torn and divided." Some of the pieces ended up at the Strozzi house in Mantua where they were offered in sale to the Grand Duke of Tuscany in 1575. We must acknowledge, however, that nothing of Leonardo's or Michelangelo's cartoons remains, and we must reconstruct the two compositions with the aid of partial copies, contemporary descriptions and the rare autograph sketches of the artists.

We know that Leonardo developed his theme by giving the main emphasis to the battle of the Knights, the most famous part of the episode (which Rubens copied) being the *Conquest of the Standard*. After having originally toyed with an idea analogous to Leonardo's, Michelangelo concentrated on the moment in which the combatants are surprised at their bath in the Arno, depicting the knightly incident in the background.

The sudden alarm permitted the artist to develop the young combatants' bodies in a diverse, sculptural manner, and many were drawn nude in the water or in the act of arming themselves. Vasari illustrates with great vivacity the drawing pretext which Michelangelo so fully developed: ". . . while they came out of the water to dress, one saw from Michelangelo's divine hands, those who hurried to aid their companions, others who buckled on their armor, and those who were fully armed . . . ."

In the various combat situations, Michelangelo found a reason for sculptural solutions of great originality and vigorous relief. He gave full play to those effects of movement and modelling which his anatomical studies and real-life drawing had developed to an exceptional degree. In certain realistic episodes, he undoubtedly took the opportunity in order to express the intimate physical life of the bodies, the play of the muscles and the participation of each figure in the dynamic action.

In this connection, it is interesting to quote the section in Vasari's description in which he expresses his curiosity about a detail. It is a very characteristic detail which one sees in the foreground of the great composition (and also in the copies and etchings) and which was done with special care: "There was among the other figures, an old man who had an ivy garland to shade himself. Having sat down to put on his stockings, he could not finish the act because his legs were wet and, hearing the tumult of the soldiers and the shouts and noise of the drummers, forced on a stocking. Besides all the muscles and tendons of the figures which one saw, he made a facial grimace which showed how much he was suffering, to the very tips of his toes."

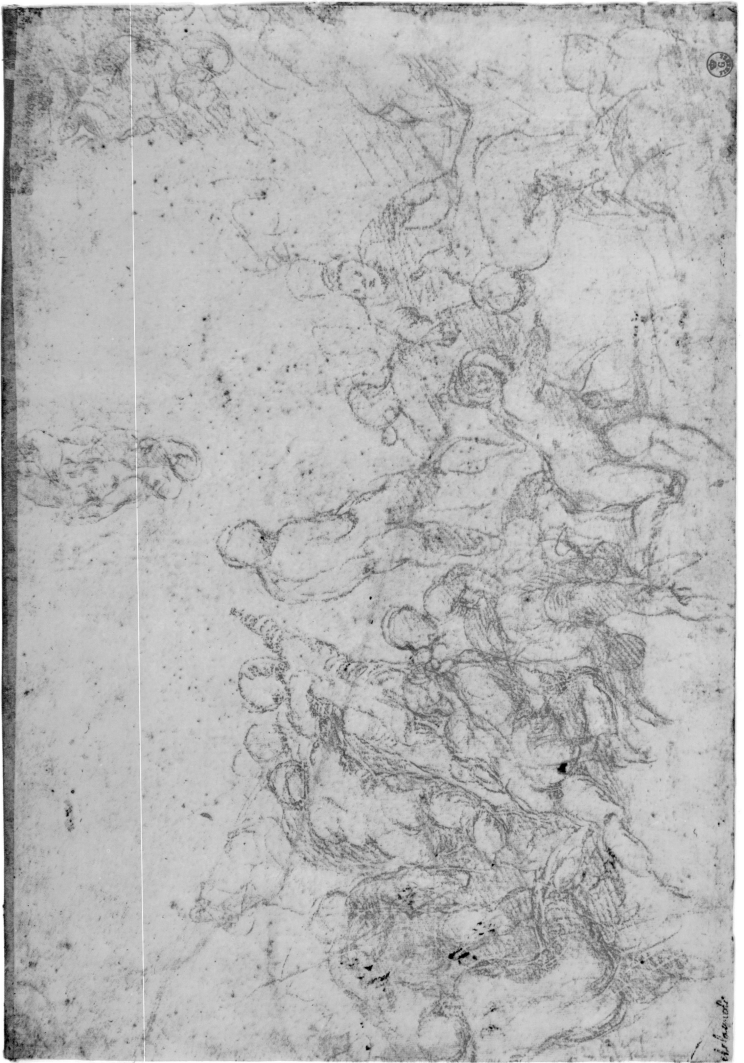

Fig. 3—MICHELANGELO *autograph drawing for the composition of the "Battle of Cascina" cartoon. An important sketch in black pencil and silver point, very much discussed by the critics but to be considered an original. It is one of the rare pieces of evidence which we have of the composition of the famous lost cartoon (Florence, Uffizi, 613 F. See Exhibition of drawings by Michelangelo. Catalogue edited by P. Barocchi, Florence, Holschki, 1962, page 6 and illustration II, III)*

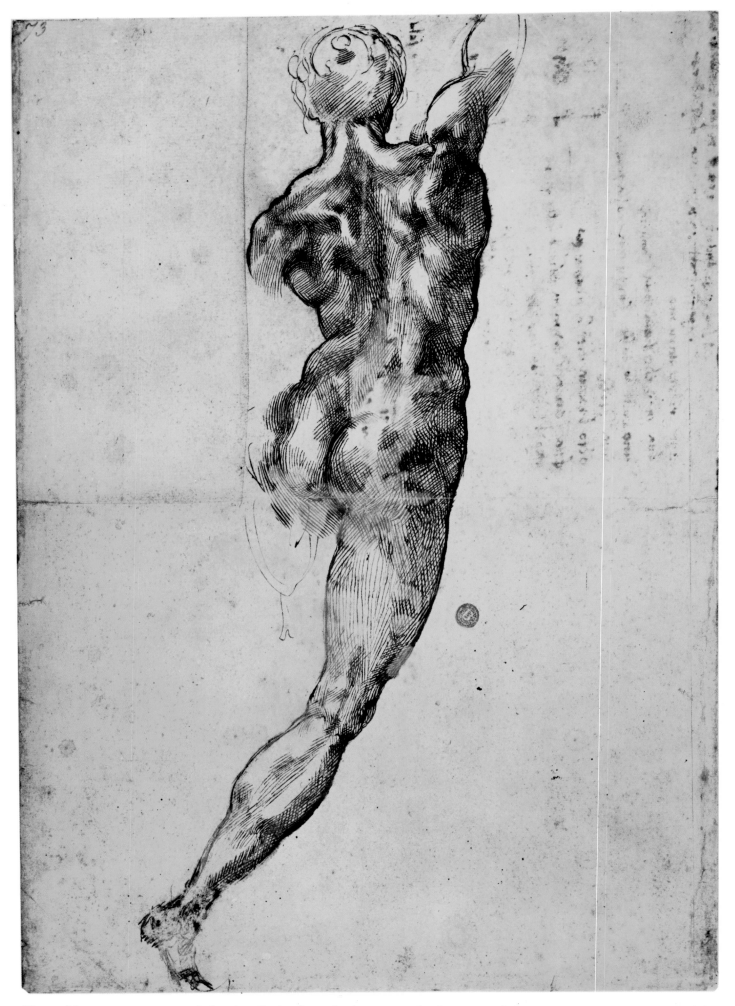

Fig. 4—MICHELANGELO *autograph drawing. Study of a nude, done in pen for the cartoon of the "Battle of Cascina," but derived from motifs of Greco-Roman sculpture, probably from a sarcophagus with the "Labors of Hercules" of the Lateran type (Florence, Casa Buonarroti, 73 F. See Exhibition of drawings by Michelangelo. Catalogue edited by P. Barocchi, Florence, Holschki, 1962, page 7, illustration I)*

*Fig. 5—*MICHELANGELO *autograph drawing. Study of a nude, done with pen, for one of the figures of the cartoon of the "Battle of Cascina" (London, British Museum)*

Here is evidence of the way in which Michelangelo re-links himself with the pure Florentine painting tradition, from Giotto to Masolino and Masaccio, in the study of details which those masters so often used (for instance, in the scene from the *Baptism of Christ*). This revealed his growing interest in the nude, for its vitality and the flexible expression of the psychology of the characters.

Of the various partial copies and engravings derived from Michelangelo's lost cartoon, only the monochrome in the Leicester Collection has conserved a broader perspective. This permits us to imagine the whole, conceived as a series of groups of figures which are linked by their gestures to those personages engaged in combat in the background.

It is not, therefore, a battle like the *Battle of the Centaurs* in the Casa Buonarroti which the artist sculpted as a youth on the advice of Poliziano. It represents instead the progressive development of the battle provoked by the call to arms and realized in various gestures all of which refer to the background, in order to excite a succession of responses to the far-off appeal in a brisk contrast of poses.

We are far from Pollaiuolo's nude battles in which we are present during the action in single contrasts, as if they were Greco-Roman bas-reliefs. We have, instead, arrived at the conception of a series of movements held together by a central motif which determines various episodes but does not bring us into the actual combat, as does Leonardo's *Battle of Anghiari*.

It seems that Leonardo gave prime importance to the battle for the conquest of the standard and knotted the knights and horses violently together in a dramatic grouping which was to assume the symbolic value of the pitiless fatality of the war. Michelangelo seems to have concentrated his compositional ability on the episode of the combatants, who, having climbed onto the bank of the river, help one another to arm themselves for battle. The largest part of the drawing which was taken from the cartoon isolates this scene to which the artist returns in the *Flood* in the Sistine Chapel, and even in the central part of the *Last Judgment*.

The sixteenth-century engravers usually completed the single motifs with elements of landscape.[2] Marcantonio Raimondi, copying three of the nudes on the river bank, added houses and trees in the German taste. Agostino Veneziano engraved five figures, including the soldier who is putting on his armor, and set them in an alpine landscape. Michelangelo's autograph sketches, even though they are limited to a few feverish strokes or particular studies, are more effective and, at least, permit us to reconstruct the artist's strength in the composition of this cartoon (figs. 3–7).

There is a drawing in the Uffizi which is a first idea with variations of the central episode. Another at Oxford is a rapid sketch of a knight and combatant on foot, both nude, and marked out in a happy synthesis. The well-known pen drawing in the British Museum is a sculptural study, very accurately done from the point of view of anatomic relief. The drawing is of a young man sitting on the bank and brusquely turned toward the background in a body torsion which is typical of the artist and is used by him elsewhere.

Another very well known drawing in the Casa Buonarroti refers to one of the two nudes in the foreground. It is executed with great attention and incisiveness of pen technique and also bears black pencil traces, perhaps belonging to an initial sketch. It displays the majestic plastic force of the artist who seems to model on paper the sculptural reliefs of a young body, which is seen from the back and is sensed to be ready to rush ahead like an athlete. This drawing is also of interest because it does not appear to have been completely executed from a living model but rather, as Wilde initially suggested, is inspired from a figure on a late Roman sarcophagus decorated with a *Labors of Hercules* of the Lateran type.

Other similar solutions to a theme which was very much in favor in imperial Roman sculpture are in existence. They are probably replicas of a more famous Hellenistic work which is now lost. Notwithstanding its affinity with

*Fig. 6—*MICHELANGELO *autograph drawing. In pen and pencil. The nude figure in the center is from the studies for the cartoon of the "Battle of Cascina" which was to have been painted for the Palazzo Vecchio in Florence. The smaller pen sketches seem to be early ideas for the "Bruges Madonna" (Florence, Gabinetto dei Disegni e delle Stampe, Uffizi)*

ancient sculpture, it is certain that the artist used this drawing for his *Battle of Cascina* cartoon. While the plastic qualities of the study seem to preserve traces of the sculptured model, it is the motif of the youth's tension which interested Michelangelo. Once inserted into the group of combatants, it was destined to construct a center of propulsion amid the general dynamism. From this we are able to confirm the constant attention which Michelangelo paid to ancient sculpture, even during the elaboration of original and challenging works like this cartoon. The reference to classical art was not a cultural attitude for the artist, but rather a living use of it. He placed it on the same level with the real-life model, as an exemplary stimulant for the sculptural solutions to be found in the moving bodies.

One of the most important drawings is the sketch of the whole in black pencil and silver point in the Uffizi, which is, unfortunately, in very bad condition and is considered by some scholars to be a copy (fig. 3). The central idea of a large portion of the composition is indicated here with a few essential strokes. The argument in favor of the composition's originality, as Barocchi has correctly observed, is supported by singular analogies to Michelangelo's later drawings, in addition to the quality of the pencil strokes and the notable variations which it demonstrates (when compared with Holkham's copy, and others). A good example of the analogies in later sketches might be shown in the drawing in the Casa Buonarroti which illustrates the first idea for the *Last Judgment*.

Michelangelo improvises the group of combatants gathered on the bank as if they were on a reef. We recognize (although very rapidly sketched) the young man in the foreground who turns toward the background and the beautiful figure of the warrior who is arming himself and is seen from the back in so monumental a pose as to constitute the fulcrum of the composition. The groups of other young nudes seem to gather around this energetically virile image and are almost united in a bunch as they climb ashore and quickly throw themselves behind a companion who gestures toward the background with a tense arm.

To the right, we indistinctly see other figures who do not appear in the better known copies. Among these figures, which are very important, even if only hinted at, we see a warrior breathlessly arriving from the field of combat who is turned toward the climbing nudes and seems to call his companions. The young men on the river bank and another to the right turn towards that figure. This is the group for which the beautiful pen drawing in the British Museum served as a study.

From this, as from the other drawings related to the lost cartoon, we can confirm our impression of what was the nucleus of Michelangelo's composition. That nucleus is the group of soldiers who gather together on the river bank. We should not exclude the possibility that he deliberately chose this aspect of the event in order to contrast with Leonardo, who had centered his attention on the *Conquest of the Standard* episode.

Both Leonardo's and Michelangelo's cartoons affirmed a new artistic conception which indicated horizons very different from those explored in the fifteenth century. Leonardo opposed the sensitive, musical and sometimes sad line of Botticelli and the realist conception of Verrocchio with a furious confusion of humanity caught up by the demon of war in a battle which had even vaster implications: an almost cosmic drama which he molds through a palpitating investigation of reality. It is a penetration of the secret movements of the body and a synthesis of contrasts into a never ending vibration of shading.

Michelangelo departed broadly from the impassiveness of Piero della Francesca, from the stoic monumentality of Masaccio, from the movement of Pollaiuolo and from the linear functional quality of Botticelli. By articulating the language of the sculptured forms of the nude as a vigorous celebration of the priority of man, he linked the sentiments provoked by the vital impulse of the action.

Thus the two artists who were so dissimilar in their confrontation of the new century revealed the same idealistic

*Fig. 7—*Michelangelo *autograph drawing. Study in red pencil for one of the combatants in the cartoon of the "Battle of Cascina" (Florence, Gabinetto dei Disegni e delle Stampe, Uffizi)*

exigence. Having passed through the study of reality, Michelangelo succeeded in overcoming its infinite variety of manifestations, and it was this which drew the flocks of young artists to study the intimate secrets of the two battle cartoons.

Many foreigners were among the artists who considered the study of Michelangelo's cartoon to be a necessary experience in their perfection of the art of drawing. These included Alonso Berruguete, for whom Michelangelo had a particular affection. Michelangelo wrote a letter from Rome to his brother which, when consigned to the young painter, would serve him as authorization for the keys to the Hall of the Pope in Santa Maria Novella: "The bearer of this is a young Spaniard who comes to learn painting and has asked me to see the cartoon which I began in the Hall. Do what you can to let him have the keys and if you can do anything to help him, do it for love of me, because he is a good lad."

We know that Berruguete was unable to see the drawing at that time even with Michelangelo's recommendation. If Vasari remembers correctly, he saw and copied it later with the other young artists who went to study this work which was considered the "light of the century" along with Leonardo's cartoon.

The influence of Michelangelo's cartoon, like Leonardo's, was not only limited to the study which it received before its dismemberment. The various partial copies, the drawings and engravings no matter how unfaithful, perpetuated certain compositional solutions and certain motifs into the seventeenth and eighteenth centuries and even into Romantic painting, in which style one of Michelangelo's greatest admirers, Théodore Géricault, worked.

We do not know what stimulated the dramatic French painter to study the principal episode in the *Battle of Cascina* cartoon. It seems certain, however, that the first compositional idea for the famous *Raft of the Medusa* came from Michelangelo's cartoon. The group of nudes whom Michelangelo depicted in the variously articulated attitude of heeding the battle cry from the background seem to antedate the reciprocal movements of the desperate figures in the Géricault. They have a different significance, but still conserve something of Michelangelo's flavor filtered through Romantic sensibility.

NOTES FOR CHAPTER TWO

(1) One may also see the vivacious description of Vasari in the accurate and informed comments of P. BAROCCHI in: G. Vasari, op. cit., page 24, with related notes.

(2) M. PITTALUGA: *L'incisione italiana del Cinquecento*, Milan 1928, page 139. Here are the comments about these prints which come from the Michelangelo cartoon and particularly about that of Marcantonio Raimondi: ". . . if, with those of Agostino Veneziano, Schiavonetti and the other *Arrampicatore* of Raimondi, such work has importance because it gives an idea of a great thing which was never realized, in the field of art it has no claim to fame."

CHAPTER THREE

THE VAULT OF THE SISTINE CHAPEL

MICHELANGELO'S pictorial work for the hall of the Palazzo Vecchio was interrupted by Julius II's invitation to Rome. He turned his attention to the great task of creating the mausoleum for the Pope which was never completed, although it constituted a forty-year nightmare for the artist and caused a dramatic alternation of extremes of hope and bitter disillusion. We find Michelangelo returning abruptly to Florence in August, 1506, when he had only just begun work with great enthusiasm, because he had not been received by the Pope.

A reconciliation was effected with the Pope in Bologna the same year and Michelangelo executed the bronze figure of Julius which was destroyed by a mob in 1511. He finally returned to Rome in 1508 on another Papal invitation, not to take up his work on the tomb again as he had hoped, but to face the task of painting on the vault of the Sistine Chapel. This was a project which the Pontiff had evidently been considering for two years.[1]

The relationship between the two tasks, one to be completed at an undetermined time, and the other an immediate reality, invested Michelangelo's art with a new, more profound and constructive factor. He remained, however, the same artist with his sculpturing and painting ideals and succeeded in passing from one theme to the other while always maintaining his vital and powerful personality.

It is known that the idea for Julius' tomb, due to external reasons and personal troubles, underwent at least six changes. It passed from the conception of a colossal mausoleum inspired by classical monumentality, through successive simplifications. At the time of the painting of the Sistine Chapel, however, Michelangelo still believed that he would be involved in a gigantic undertaking, populated by statues of Sibyls and Prophets, of captives symbolizing the virtues of the Pope linked together by his death, and of reliefs and allegorical images. The architectural structure of the work would be animated and made eloquent by the sculptures and would unite with them into an organic whole.[2]

To understand the whole, born from the relationship between the constructed parts and the sculpted figures, we need only think of how Buonarroti also conceived an architectural and figurative whole, rich with vitality, in his painting. The Prophet and Sibyl figures are in agreement with the architecture and united with it to produce a dynamic and sculptural "expression" in the unity of the painting medium.

The condition of the Sistine Chapel, at the moment in which Michelangelo began his great task, was as follows: the vast and harmonious structure, executed with singular skill under Sixtus IV, had the precious marble decorations of the transept and the choir, and a beautiful floor divided in the traditional Roman marble technique. It also contained a group of rapidly executed frescoes on the walls which were done in 1481–1482 by a group of Florentine painters whom the Pope had selected. Among these painters, Botticelli had played the principal role since three of the paintings were his. One must attribute to him the idea for the decoration of the upper walls with the false niches containing the figures of the Popes.

The fifteenth-century frescoes were also continued on the wall of the high altar where Michelangelo would eventually paint his *Last Judgment*. The Chapel vault, which bent over small pedestals with a singular elegant monuméntality, was covered by a spacious starred ceiling, the modest work of Pier Matteo d'Amelia. The Sistine Chapel, thus, had a stylistic unity in itself. It lacked nothing because of the fact that its harmonious structure, emphasized by the decorations of Botticelli, Perugino, Luca Signorelli, Pinturicchio, Piero di Cosimo, Cosimo Rosselli, and Domenico Ghirlandaio, was in harmony with late fifteenth-century taste.

We do not know the real reason for which Julius II wished to erase the blue ceiling with gold stars and substitute the prodigious work of Michelangelo. He certainly did not want to make up for any lack of decoration.

It was customary in those days that when the walls of a religious edifice were covered with "religious histories," the vault should contain a starry sky, perhaps with some isolated figuration. From what we know of Julius' bellicose nature, his declaration that he "knew not of letters" and his volatile and authoritarian nature, we may conclude that the decision to replace this purely decorative work with another of larger significance sprang from his same restlessness of spirit. This restlessness possibly caused him to commission Raphael to create grandiose paintings for his Vatican suite, thus removing Pinturicchio's work which had been done for Alexander VI (and was, therefore, odious to the new Pontiff), and replacing it with work of a new philosophic-religious thought which had matured in his times and not without his authoritarian influence.

When Michelangelo accepted the task, he did not have an immediate intuition as to how he might fill the immense space. Initially, thinking of the twelve cloisters of the vault, he planned to depict the twelve Apostles and complete the rest of the space with decorated compartments. This is made evident by the pen drawing in the British Museum, which sketches a figure seated on a small throne in a shell-shaped niche flanked by two small winged figures. The figures are connected to the central part of the vault with round and rectangular partitions and dominated from above by a diamond-shaped section which designates the central axis of the ceiling (fig. 9).

Other drawings in Detroit and in the British Museum simplify the composition which, although more autonomous, appears linked to a conception bound to the wall decoration. Michelangelo spoke of this first idea, of which he did not seem overly convinced, in a letter to Fattucci, written several years later in 1524. He reconstructed the circumstances surrounding the composition as follows: "The first drawing of the said work was of the twelve apostles in lunettes and the rest a certain filling up with ornamentation, as customary. Thence, having begun the said work, it seemed to come out poorly and I told the Pope that making only the Apostles seemed to produce a poor work. He asked me why and I told him, because the Apostles were also poor. He then commissioned me to do what I wished and said that I should paint down to the frescoes below."[3]

This letter, which the artist wrote after a period long enough to grant him some objectivity in viewing the original circumstances, makes his dissatisfaction with the initial concept quite clear. His phrase "a certain filling up with ornamentation, as customary," implies criticism of the decorative tastes of the time. He confirms, however, the great liberty which the Pope granted him, both in theme and space, by allowing him to choose his subject and execute it "down to the frescoes below." This extended the scope of the work to include the space around the windows as well as the architectural portion of the vault.

There is the allusion to the work's "poor appearance" in its original version which refers to the excessive simplicity of the originally imagined elements. Presented in typical Michelangelo fashion, there is a criticism of custom, which he repeated at the moment of the painting's unveiling when the Pope wished the whole to be retouched with gold. We must, therefore, conclude that the theme of the Sistine Vault sprang largely from the thoughts and imagination of Michelangelo who, having received the new commission from the Pope, turned with renewed impetus to the gigantic work.

The beginnings of the work are documented by the artist, who left us a note on the financial arrangements, written with great simplicity in the form of a receipt. "This day, the tenth of May, 1508, I, Michelangelo the sculptor, received from his Holiness Pope Julius II 500 ducats for the painting of the vault of the Chapel of Pope Sixtus for which I am beginning work today."

He wrote, almost simultaneously, to the priest Jacopo Gesuato in Florence, asking for a stock of colors. The letter is purposely vague pertaining to the work at its outset. He insists, instead, upon the quality of the colors and the method of payment. "Brother Jacopo, having to have certain things painted here, or rather, to paint, it falls to me to advise you that I need a certain quantity of good blues and if you can serve me in the present exigence, it would be of great help. See that you send here to your priests that quantity which you have if they be of good quality and I promise to return the just price . . . and before I take those blues, you will have your money paid, here or where you like."

Michelangelo obviously had to turn to Florence for a blue of good quality and did not indicate the desired quantity but issued a blanket request for as much as the priest could send, making the offer attractive by the prospect of immediate payment.

The interesting detail, however, is that Michelangelo, perhaps not wanting to specifically name the painting in which the colors would be used, or because he did not yet know if he would be working alone or in collaboration, employed purposely vague phrases: ". . . having to have certain things painted here, or rather, to paint." It would seem almost impossible that "certain things" could refer to anything but the painting of the Sistine Chapel vault.[4]

There are a few letters to relatives and others in Florence which indicate that the great work proceeded well. The opus covered more than 500 square meters of fresco and was executed between 1508 and 1512. The artist accepted some help on the decorative elements and a minimal figurative collaboration at the beginning of the work. He soon became dissatisfied with the collaboration and continued the gigantic task by himself.

In September of 1510, half of the work was finished. The Pope wanted the unveiling to take place August 14, 1511, but the final unveiling occurred on October 31, 1512, the eve of All Saints' Day, being celebrated with a solemn "Te Deum."

There is a wealth of documentation (also by Michelangelo's contemporaries) attesting to the fact that, after having expressed his discontent over the first idea to the Pope, Michelangelo was left free to develop the new theme as he wished. We cannot, however, believe that the vast and complex thematic structure emerged full blown and completely autonomously from Michelangelo's head.

Raphael had consulted with the learned priests and Humanists of the Vatican when he was working on the frescoes for the Pope's rooms (above all, regarding the "Stanza della Segnatura" which demonstrates such dense philosophic and religious content). Michelangelo must have also relied on similar sources for the Sistine Vault in order to arrive at a connective tissue for the various concepts to be presented, although he interpreted the ideas with his usual freedom.

Starting from this supposition, critics have long been deeply interested in determining what the central inspiration for the work was in order to better interpret the already clear forms. As often happens in investigations which are based on a knowledge of Humanistic culture and the tendency to develop figuratively allegorical and conceptual motifs, the focus of the problem has been shifted. This shift from intellectual origins to a study of the religious-philosophical conceptions of the time, while producing notable results in the cultural history of the Renaissance, has diminished interest in the essential and determining fact: the manner in which Michelangelo surpassed the allegorical motifs through his exceptional vigor and sculptural independence.

It is not very useful, therefore, to discuss the various hypotheses as to the cultural content of the Sistine Vault. We might mention De Tolnay's theory which perceives a reflection of Neoplatonic doctrine, and the progressive liberation of Man from his bodily prison in successive stages until he arrives at liberty in God. Hartt's examination of the writings of Marco Vigerio, whose book is dedicated to Julius II, is based on the devotion to the "Lignum Vitae," the Tree of Life, according to Franciscan religious thought. The critic proposes that the Biblical scenes can be interpreted as a prophetic figuration of Christ incarnate, the fruit of the Tree of Life. This idea would also reflect an allusion to the heraldic emblem of the Rovere family, of which Julius II was a member. This emblem depicted an oak tree which, in fact, appears in the vault's decorative motifs, and in the heavy garlands which the nudes entwine around the shields above the thrones of the Prophets and Sibyls.[5]

The suggestions and stimuli which were incorporated into the painting of the chapel may have come from these or even more complicated sources. The interest, however, lies in the fierce urgency which drove Michelangelo to use these sources as a bare schematic outline onto which he immediately grafts a vaster poem of Creation, Original Sin and the waiting for Redemption, articulated in forms and colors which are so eloquent in themselves.

The artist always leaned toward an expression of universal values, even when the germ of the opus was born of a complex cultural theme. We have noted this phenomenon from the earliest period of his works, in particular, the *Battle of the Centaurs* which was based on a mythological theme suggested by Poliziano. The young Michelangelo, who might have followed the advice of his more learned elders, emphasizes, in his depiction of the battle, the violent contrast between beastly force and the heroic onslaught of the young men; an interpretation which is projected to include the entire field of the battle within this dominant motif, understood in the dynamics of the nude bodies.

This must be kept in mind as we study the Sistine Vault, in order not to lose contact with that formal expression which in Michelangelo's art conditions the thematic development, even if the great complexity of the narrative and textual motifs is in high relief in the central portion of the four large vaults and lunettes. This is true especially in the *Battle of Cascina*, which was his first great encounter with such problems in painting. He was at the time occupied in the preparation of studies and cartoons. According to the custom of the times, the artist had to conceive the general scheme of the work in proportion to the spaces to be decorated, and in an organic and complex distribution of the various elements. The establishment of a coherent theme and compositional structure of great clarity was therefore necessary; otherwise, it would not be possible to explain the relationship between the various parts of the immense composition. It would also have been impossible for the artist to attain the extraordinary unity which he reached in the whole of his painting cycle notwithstanding the presence of so many diverse elements.

A perennial source of wonder is the way in which Michelangelo surpassed such a concise, architectural conception in a free execution, powerful and thick with spontaneous solutions. This remains as a sign of the creative maturity which the artist had achieved in this glorious period.

Michelangelo, by substituting the second idea for the first, did not wish to ignore the concept of the painters of Sixtus IV's days. Some critics tend to consider the decoration of the vault as a conception which was fulfilled in complete independence of the vision of the fifteenth-century painters. They had used the stories of Moses and Christ to celebrate one theme. The salvation of Man through the Redemptive mission, considered within the "syncretism" of the Old and New Testaments, was also an often used scheme in the older cycles of painting.

SISTINE CHAPEL. *View from the principal entrance. Built at the wish of Sixtus IV (1471–1484) and consecrated to the Assumption of the Virgin Mary. It was constructed by the architect Giovannino de' Dolci with the help of Baccio Pontelli. Of a single nave (which measures 40.25 by 13.41 meters and 20.73 meters in height), it is one of the most solemn and grandiose examples of Renaissance architecture in Rome. While the exterior has the austere aspect of a fortified edifice, the interior contains masterpieces of fifteenth-century and early sixteenth-century art. The floor is in "opus alexandrinum" of the style traditional to the Roman marble-cutters and the elegant transenna which divides the ambience in two parts, according to medieval liturgical usage, is the work of Mino da Fiesole and collaborators, as is the choir which faces the interior, from the right wall.*

The pictorial decoration from Sixtus IV's times includes the frescoes on the lower sections of the walls, with the stories of Moses and Christ, and the painted architecture above the cornice, in the alternating spaces of the windows, with figures of the Popes. Julius II (1503–1513) ordered Michelangelo to paint the vault with the scenes of the Creation and the Prophets and Sibyls.

Much later, Paul III (1534–1550) took up Clement VII's (1523–1534) project again of having Michelangelo paint the great wall at the end with the "Last Judgment." The artist, in order to have the entire surface at his disposition for his unified composition, had the existing fifteenth-century windows walled up, and destroyed the fifteenth-century paintings (including the two lunettes which he had painted himself during the period of the frescoes on the vault).

Michelangelo, instead, imagining the episodes of the Creation, the Fall, the Flood and the new life of humanity on earth with Noah and his family, composed the "Preface" to the stories of Moses and Christ which are narrated on the walls. The seven Prophets and five Sibyls announce the coming of the Messiah to the Jews and the pagans.

The new power which Michelangelo so impetuously introduced into the Chapel might have inserted an unexpected monumentality into the harmony of the fifteenth-century decorations. It cannot, however, be concluded that the artist wished to negate the constructional and decorative values of the ambience. He imagined an ideal architecture which would be substituted in the vault, parting from the outline of the construction and linking its structure to a large rectangular frame along its entire length. This would be held firmly by the sculptured composition of the thrones on which the Prophets and Sibyls sit. In the central spaces, alternately open or framed and flanked by muscular athletes who hold large bronze shields entwined with ribbons and garlands, the successive scenes of the Creation would unfold as if in solemn and heroic hymns.

This monumental architectural composition acquires its expressive life from its colors. What had been thought of for the tomb of Julius II is miraculously realized in an evocative vision of the Old Testament and the presence of the Protagonist: the Lord is realized with immense force as he hovers in the heavens, presenting His visage to mankind in all its sacred and mysterious beauty. He is no longer an immobile hieratic image but the active Creator in the fullness of His form. This is a conception which turns Renaissance ideals upside down. It develops these ideals to the extremes of their possibilities and combines an ancient expressive and dramatic vitality with the complexity of Michelangelo's experiences as he spiritually lived them.

The structure of the vault evidently came from the initial idea for the mausoleum of Julius II. This is evident in the composition of the *Prophets* and *Sibyls.* They immediately recall the placement of the *Moses* and the other figures which Michelangelo had thought of employing around the base of the tomb in addition to slaves and commemorative reliefs. The ideal world of sculpture solicited a freer painting conception in the artist's imagination which is far from the original "sfondato" idea of perspective (like Mantegna's work in the *Camera degli Sposi* at Mantua). This conception is far from what Raphael executed in those same years on the vault of the "Stanza della Segnatura," which was traditionally planned in compartments linked by decorative motifs with complete respect for the surface over which the painting extends.

In the Sistine Chapel, Michelangelo exalts the value of the architectural composition. He creates a partition of spaces linked together by the organic vitality of the whole. This partition gives maximum effect to the gigantic figures of the Prophets and Sibyls. It enhances the nervous energy of the nudes and open spaces in which the Biblical episodes assume their expressive significance within the very limits of their confinement. This is an entirely personal conception and the logical consequence of Michelangelo's sculptural vision which sees painting as an exaltation of the values of both movement and relief.

At the heart of the formal aspect of this grandiose composition, a profound and new vitality of thought is expressed. The result is that the whole becomes an exteriorization of the interior energy from which the forms acquire singular force and inner life.

When the artist distributed his themes over the surface of the vault, he imagined that they would be seen from the principal entrance to the chapel in a logical sequence in accordance with the narration of the facts which proceeds from the first episodes of the *Creation* until reaching the *Flood* and the *Drunkenness of Noah* which are found directly above those who enter the vast hall. We know that he began work on the final Biblical scenes above the entrance.

This was due to various reasons (one being the idea of keeping the final section of the chapel with the main altar free for worship until the last possible moment) and confirms the necessity which bound the artist to rigorously prepare the development of the various scenes in cartoons to be then translated into painting. This was an immense task that Michelangelo faced for the first time. His preceding experiences were limited to paintings on wood (at least, as far as we know). The great cartoon of the *Battle of Cascina* had been interrupted in a preparatory state and never executed in fresco. We may deduce that from his apprenticeship to Ghirlandaio, he had already worked in fresco. He had, however, never before faced such a vast and complex task in which the technical problems were interlaced with deeper problems of style and thought. We should not overlook the serious difficulties implicit in painting the surface of a vault (an immense space which curves over us). This requires standing on scaffolding in contact with the wall, and continually turning one's glance upwards in the effort to imagine the effect of the painting as seen from below.

Michelangelo, in one of his early sonnets, succeeds in expressing with great courage the suffering produced by such an effort. This is done in an almost joking tone with the characteristic ironic taste of his Tuscan soul.[6]

The poem is dedicated to "Giovanni, the one from Pistoia" (Giovanni di Benedetto da Pistoia), who later became Chancellor of the Florence Academy and wrote bizarre sonnets addressed to Michelangelo. This explains the burlesque character of Buonarroti's poem. Besides the poetic value of the sonnet, which is Dantesque in flavor, in its images and improvised tone (already significant for Michelangelo's future poetical development), it is an excellent psychological document of the artist's state of mind during the period of this vast work. It is singular proof of his ability to see himself as if through a trick mirror, in such an unusual manner of painting which forces him to add a pen sketch of his difficult position beside the verses. With a few simple strokes (of the type which Leonardo used for quick sketches) he improvises a little nude figure painting and looking upwards in a graphic clarification of what the sonnet says.

For these reasons, the sonnet assumes a particular importance. In the verses that begin "I've grown a goiter by dwelling in this den," he describes the swelling of his neck from assuming unnatural positions as if he had a goiter. He complains that turning his head, he can feel the nape of his neck almost placed on his shoulders and his thorax swelling like those of the Harpies. His brush, soaked with paint, covers him with drops as if he were the floor. In such a contorted position his skin expands and contracts. All this is described in images which seem drawn from the *Divine Comedy*:

> In front my skin grows loose and long; behind,
> By bending it becomes more taut and strait;
> Crosswise I strain me like a Syrian bow:

More important, however, is the sonnet's bitter conclusion immediately following, in which the artist's discontent is indicated:

> Whence false and quaint, I know,
> Must be the fruit of squinting brain and eye;
> For ill can aim the gun that bends awry.
> Come then, Giovanni, try
> To succour my dead pictures and my fame;
> Since foul I fare and painting is my shame.

He complains that his "judgment" (or rather the possibility of judging the work) might be falsified by the unusual position, as when one blows through a dart-tube which is curved rather than straight. He finally recommends that his friend defend the "dead painting" (gloomy and without coloristic effects) and his artistic reputation since he is working in an unsuitable place and because painting is not his art.

In fact, Michelangelo wrote to his father on January 27, 1509, "My work does not proceed as it should and this is due to the difficulty of the task and to the fact that it is also not my profession . . . ."

It may seem out of place to discuss these "human" documents relative to the work on the chapel. They contain, however, many elements in addition to a vivid reflection of the artist's state of trepidation which are necessary to get to the bottom of the work's significance. In the sonnet, for example, which must have been written between 1508 and 1510, Michelangelo passes from a grotesquely ironic self-portrait to a statement about the "dead painting."

He re-echoes this in 1512 when the work is unveiled and when it was observed that the work seemed to lack gold and blue. He also invokes his friend's defense for the fact that he has been forced to work as a painter when he feels himself a sculptor. He affirms this attitude in this period on several other occasions; for instance, the reluctance which he demonstrated when the Pope set the task, in the receipt of the advance money on his initiating work, where he defines himself as "I, Michelangelo, sculptor" and in the letters to his relatives in which he insists that any correspondence should be mailed to "Michelangelo, sculptor in Rome" because he is known as a sculptor.

Notwithstanding his tendency to consider himself a stranger to painting of the type which was customary in those days, it was his conceptual independence which provoked the vigorous insertion of plastic vision into color and determined the Sistine masterpiece, and confirmed his conviction that painting became better as it approached sculpture.

In order to realize the full relief effect in his opus without using the deception of a general perspective which imposes certain points of view on the observer, Michelangelo established a progressive division along the longitudinal axis of the vault. Such a procedure was very well recalled by Vasari. As always, when he calls upon his artistic knowledge, Vasari knows how to find the correct terms to define even the most difficult attitudes in sixteenth-century taste.

In this case his words are really germane to the character of this composition: "In the divisions, he used neither an order of perspective which foreshortened nor the 'veduta ferma.' He accommodated the divisions to the figures rather than the figures to the divisions."

Michelangelo, in other words, did not seek out perspectives which created "sotto in sù" effects with the idea of fooling the eye, nor did he choose a determined point of view. He imagined the division (the architectural composition) in relation to the figures rather than vice-versa.

In the rhythmic development, the large arcs have the *Prophets* and *Sibyls* at their base. The careful choice of colors by the artist creates a chromatic effect which also contributes to the unity of the work in a new sense which is related to the various sections of the composition. These are the painted architecture, the Biblical scenes, the *Prophets* and *Sibyls*, the lunettes with the *Ancestors of Christ*, each zone with its own particular characteristics, harmonized into the whole.

The accurate studies which Biagetti did on the colors which Michelangelo employed on the Sistine Vault (published in 1936) are important in themselves. They are also important in relation to the investigations which the same writer did much later on the frescoes of the Pauline Chapel, where the colors are numerically less, but more subtly employed.

It seems that Michelangelo used no more than seven colors on the Sistine Vault. He gave precedence among these to the tones which most clearly adhered to the diverse material to be depicted. The fundamental colors are lime white, yellow ochre, red, siena red, earth green, ultramarine blues, and vine black. These are colors of the Tuscan tradition, to which the artist thought of adding some details in gold (of which traces remained in the balusters of the marmoreal thrones of the Prophets and Sibyls). This latter plan he did not carry through, however, because he probably felt that

AUTOGRAPH MANUSCRIPT OF MICHELANGELO's *famous sonnet "Io ho già fatto un gozzo in questo stento . . ."* addressed to Giovanni da Pistoia, *an amateur in comic poetry and later, in 1540, Chancellor of the Florentine Academy. In the poem, the artist describes the difficulties which he met when he painted the Sistine Chapel and he asks his friend to defend him from criticisms. The writing, typical of Michelangelo's youthful period, displays the characteristic abbreviations in use at the time.*
On the margin to the right, the artist has drawn with pen a small standing figure that shows the complicated and difficult position which he was obliged to assume in the execution of the Sistine Vault, standing on a wooden scaffolding, always looking upwards.
(from Michelangelo Buonarroti, Poems edited by Enzo Noè Girardi, p. 158, figure A.B. XIII son. F.6.A. Laterza, Bari, 1960)

the apparently "dead painting" was more appropriate to his severe spirit than the gilded sparkle which was still fashionable, and which we see in Raphael's first frescoes for the "Stanza della Segnatura." Here even gilt plaster reliefs are employed to obtain an even more vivid illumination in the context of the painting.

The execution of the fresco was carried out in four sections. As De Tolnay has pointed out, the first section included all the Noah stories and the second was from the story of the Original Sin to the creation of Adam. The third included almost all the final stories, excluding the lunettes around the windows and the *Ancestors of Christ*. The three sections were unveiled in 1511. The fourth section included all the rest and was finished just before the unveiling.

These divisions are obviously not intended in any absolute sense. The variations in Michelangelo's painting style during the course of the execution, however, were reflected in the various sections of the monumental painting, as he slowly progressed from the entrance of the Chapel to the walls at the end. We may not presume from the fervor and almost superhuman intensity with which Michelangelo worked on the scaffolding (profoundly immersed in the tempestuous world being created out of his imagination) that there were no interruptions in those four years, other than those due to the moving of the scaffolding and the unveiling of the first half of the pictorial cycle. The latter event, at any rate, was of the greatest importance to the artist. He could only then (for the first time in a complete fashion) comprehend the effect of his painting as seen from below and not examined from the wooden scaffolding in which he was almost barricaded in his closed and sometimes enraged creative solitude. The stylistic difference is evident in the passage from the rather analytic technique (although plastic and new) to a greater volumetric synthesis responding to the increased proportions of the figures which proceed from the Noah scenes to the first episodes in the Creation. They are stripped of detail and become more gigantic in their mass. The result is the broader, more vigorous, and freer style of painting. This is the style of an artist who has progressively conquered a new monumental vision of form with complete freedom of technique.

The increase in the proportions of the figures of the final *Prophets* and *Sibyls*, like the mysterious power of the image of the Lord (the solitary all-embracing presence in the Cosmos), has been placed in relation to the artist's desire to correct the diminution of perspective in his painting. This helps the observer who views the work from the entrance of the chapel. If this idea is possible, it is certainly the result of the considerations which the artist was able to take into account after seeing the wall which had been done in the first half of the vault.

If we follow the artist's correspondence during the final months of work on the painting, we discover that it was a dramatic period indeed. His relatives send letter after letter from Florence in which they speak about personal affairs and things which Michelangelo was not able to know, being so far away. It seems that they did not appreciate the seriousness of his task. On July 28, 1512, the artist writes to his brother: "I don't have time to answer your letter . . . if I had the time, I couldn't answer until I could see the end of my things here . . . . I am in more difficulty than ever before, with bad health and great fatigue but I still have the patience to reach the desired end . . . ." In a letter of August: "as for my return there [Florence], I cannot return if I do not finish my opus which I hope to complete in September; it is truly such a great task that I don't know whether I can set [my departure] at fifteen days . . . ." In the work itself, however, as often occurs in the mystery of artistic creation, we discover no trace of the anxieties and disillusionments which tormented the artist. We are, instead, in communication with a serious and virile artistic language.

Michelangelo separates the four large cloister vaults at the far corners of the ceiling from the complex architectural structure and plunges the triangles of the lunettes with the *Ancestors of Christ* into deep shadow. He thus indicates the sense in which we should interpret the sculptural and compositional values which animate the entire work with such vigor. The portion reserved for the architecture is inseparable from that which is filled with images. The former would appear empty and deprived of significance if we were to exclude the grandiose *Prophets* and *Sibyls* or the Biblical scenes. This is true because the architecture is intended as an expression of the sculptural vitality, whose energy is put to use in the groups of "children's figures" in false relief, to the sides of the *Prophets* and *Sibyls*. They soften the striking firmness of the frame with the intervention of a figurative element which, therefore, stands between the painted images and those conceived as marble effects.

As far as the continual interruptions which characterized his artistic activity on this work go, we must bear in mind the importance of the project for Julius II's tomb in relation to this passage from the original conception of the Apostles and simple "divisions" to the vaster and organic composition with the Creation stories and the painted architecture. We should also point out that the motif of a centralizing, isolated, architectural structure is later exchanged for the definitive structure extending along the walls which we find in the Medici Chapel. After the first sculptural plan, placed outside the centrally designed chapel, the composition of the sepulchres and statues follows in a complete inversion of the first idea. One has the sensation of being surrounded and almost swathed by the architecture into which one is introduced. Something similar occurs in the painting structure of the Sistine Vault which opens the architectural elements into a composition and which transforms the painted surface into an "open" construction over our heads. This construction is, at the same time, closed in by the vigorous architectural divisions. The latter serve as support for the living images which they accompany. They are animated by a fierce vitality in which all the richly moving elements participate and are realized as if they were closely linked to a comprehensive vision. The movement invests every part, determining the total expression of a force which is equally related to the full color figures and the simulated architectural structure.

Thus, the artist who did not want to be considered a painter succeeded with his own personal conception in translating his sculptural aspirations. This profoundly modified the traditional essence of painting into a more intense significance impressed upon painted forms.

When Michelangelo began his work with the scenes from the life of Noah and especially when he composed the *Flood* (the most crowded episode in the entire vault) his style was still that of the *Battle of Cascina.* This is true even if some sections in the material execution can be attributed to the artists whom Michelangelo had called to Rome from Florence. At any rate, they scrupulously executed Michelangelo's cartoon which had certainly been drawn with great care. Even if some of the linear outlines are slightly crude, the images conserve their great expressivity.

We can also find the marks of those artists whom Michelangelo had known ever since his apprenticeship to Ghirlandaio and his studies in the Medici garden of San Marco. They are to be found in the slightly cold colored portions and the minute execution of the brush strokes, which contrast vigorously with Michelangelo's new, strong sculptural conception. We are speaking of a very slight matter, however, since the artist, who could not stand any interference from others, sent them back to Florence and assumed full responsibility for the work. In a letter written to his father, he discussed his discontent with Indaco's collaboration and said: "A few days ago, Jacopo the painter whom I made come here departed. He complained about my affairs here, so I think that he will still complain there. Listen and pretend not to hear; that is enough, because he is a thousand times wrong, I feel sorry for him . . . ."

Notwithstanding the minimal amount of work done by others on the *Flood,* it is composed with a breadth and Plate VI innovating spirit which make Michelangelo's presence felt. The artist, remembering his cartoon for the Palazzo Vecchio, makes use of a similar episode to employ the nude motifs, which, caught up in the immediacy of the drama, make hastening gestures to one another similar to those in the cartoon. Paolo Uccello's *Flood* in the green cloister of Santa Maria Novella was also helpful to the entire composition in the artist's memory. From it, he drew the idea of the Ark which is almost besieged by castaway persons and by the trees which are violently twisted by the storm. From Botticelli's fresco of scenes from the *Life of Moses,* also in the Sistine Chapel, he re-evoked the procession of men, women, and children who reach safety by moving behind a rocky foreground. Michelangelo transforms this in a dramatic fashion with episodes of great vividness. The mother, for instance, is a gigantic primitive figure, who presses her son to her bosom in a whirlpool of clothes swollen by the wind. The other child, meanwhile, grasps her by her muscular leg. Here we have Michelangelo in the glory of his style which has been matured through the sculptural influence of Jacopo della Quercia, an interpreter of a profound and mysterious archaic sentiment.

In the tiring climb of this mass of humanity seeking the last avenue of escape, there are groups which carry rudimentary domestic articles. This is, to be sure, a pretext for articulating the language of the human body in more diverse attitudes. It is also an example of the impartial realism which he had already demonstrated in his youthful drawings. In one of these, it seems that the artist depicted the scaffolding which had been erected for Ghirlandaio's fresco in Santa Maria Novella, on which the students at work were seen.

The composition of the *Flood* is ingeniously imagined as if from the top of a bank. This constitutes the foreground against which the people, who are arduously climbing, can be seen trying to place themselves out of danger. Michelangelo wished to give the maximum relief to this piece of greenish earth which, by hiding a part of the crowd, gives the impression of a more numerous and larger one. On the top of the hill to the left, the slow ascent is concluded with the more sculptured and prominent groups. One sees mothers with children, embracing lovers, and another mother, who symbolizes absolute distress, leaning against a tree trunk indifferently watching the waters rise.

Behind her, the gilt yellow tone of an almost oriental robe indicates a group trying to save an old man and a child by mounting them on an ass. We notice, above all, the young man who seizes a tree bent by the wind. This is a stupendously painted effect, because of its inventive originality and robust colors. The rest of the scenes seem to be a memory of a flood of the Arno or the Tiber. To the right, the fugitives have hoisted a violaceous cloth between two trunks in vain. They are gathered there, making desperate gestures of invocation, or extending their arms to help other castaways. The white rocky structure on which the figures lean is almost cut into marble with sculptured intent. This may be a memory of the stone quarries.

The artist paints a grief-stricken father carrying the body of his son in his arms. He is in the act of climbing this final hill and is by this time surrounded by the waters. This is an episode worthy of Homer or Virgil. It is an isolated heroic testimony against the grey background in which men's egotism is unchained and revealed in the battle on a ship which is in danger of capsizing because of the desperate, Dantesque fury of their unconscious gestures. Unfortunately, a wide plaster section which fell in 1797 because of the powder-magazine explosion in Castel Sant'Angelo is badly restored in a neutral dye. It has robbed the colorful group to the right of its painted conclusion above, where the space was filled with the leaves of a tree through which several branches are seen. This robs the composition of very little, however, and it remains a vast organic work with tremendous new movement in its dramatic fascination.

Fifteenth-century painting is by now very far removed from Michelangelo's style. In its analytic and narrative aspects, his painting technique reveals, even more than that of his collaborators, scrupulous attention and some residue of the sharp execution of Botticelli and Signorelli. The images are decidedly sculptured and the bodies studied from real life have a spontaneous vigor and beauty in the limbs. An inspiring human influence which tends to successive developments hovers above all this.

Plates IV and V The composition of the *Drunkenness of Noah* seems ultimately to derive from some ancient sarcophagus. This is especially evident in the image of the Patriarch which is similar to the reclining figures of the rivers in Hellenistic and Roman sculptures. The section to the left, however, with Noah digging to plant the vines, reveals a singular readiness to outline in dense colors which are experimentally applied. This makes us reflect on the artist's constant search and the unforeseen results which he obtained as he realized the great work in a continual trial-and-error manner. He thus arrived at an ever broader new style in opposition to the detailed trifling of the fifteenth-century painters. The same can be said Plates VII and VIII (in its relation to classic art) of the somewhat sibylline representation of the *Sacrifice of Noah*. The figures are ably assembled around the altar and closely connected in their gestures.

Plate IX In the scenes depicting the Original Sin and the Expulsion from Earthly Paradise, however, the artist has already invented a scheme which unites the two episodes. He keeps them separate by the central element of the tree of Good and Evil from which guilt and punishment seem to break loose. By the effect of the long spiral of the serpent (which, in medieval fashion, terminates with the image of the deceitful woman), the leafy protagonist which Adam has seized seems to be an architectural element. It is almost a spiral-like column dividing the rectangular space of the fresco into a diptych.

The Adam and Eve group to the left recalls the studies for the *Doni Madonna* made more sculptural in relation to the theme. Perhaps no other female image was painted by Michelangelo with more intensity and warmth than this woman on the vault, a Roman type with eyes full of desire. It is also evident, in the group of the progenitors cast out by the Angel, that there is a reference to Masaccio's fresco in the Brancacci Chapel. Michelangelo has, however, interpreted and complicated it in a new expressive movement linked to the fatality of the path toward the unknown.

A testimony to the careful thought which the artist gave to this motif is to be found in a drawing in the Casa Buonarroti. In the drawing, Adam's defensive movement against the harsh, peremptory gesture of the Angel, as he

THE VAULT OF THE SISTINE CHAPEL

Completely covered with frescoes by Michelangelo, the vault bends with proportioned fullness arising from twelve crests which spring from the walls and form a natural spatial variety of which the artist has availed himself in conceiving his gigantic composition. He conceived a pseudomarmoreal architecture composed of twelve thrones on which the vigorous figures of the Prophets and Sibyls are seated. Above these, he painted pairs of young nudes who place bronze shields and garlands on the terminal cornice.

In the spaces drawn along the principal axis of the vault, open within imaginary arcades, he developed the central theme of the *Creation*, alternating minor scenes with scenes which are more ample and which occupy the space completely.

In the four large resulting cloister vaults at the angles of the vault, the artist painted Biblical episodes in close relation to the content of the *Creation*. The artist developed the theme according to a succession which, starting from the first episodes of the *Creation* which hang over the main altar (to the left), arrives at the *Drunkenness of Noah* (to the right) at the principal entrance of the Chapel. In the execution, however, he proceeded in the opposite direction, from right to left. The entire work was done between 1508 and 1512 with brief interruptions.

The two scenes in the right corner represent the *Crucifixion of Amman* (above) and the *Brazen Serpent* (below) and the two corresponding scenes to the right depict *David and Goliath* (above) and *Judith and Holofernes* (below).

Moving along the central axis of the vault from left to right, we find the various episodes of the *Creation* in the following order: the *Lord gives Order to Chaos*; the *Creation* (repeated twice in the same scene) *of the Sun, the Moon and the plants*; the *Separation of the Land from the Waters*; the *Creation of Adam*; the *Creation of Eve*; the *Original Sin and the Expulsion from Earthly Paradise*, the *Sacrifice of Noah*, the *Flood* and the *Drunkenness of Noah*.

The Prophets and Sibyls which surround the central zone at the base are in the following order: to the left above the wall of the altar is the figure of the *Prophet Jonah* and below from left to right we have—the *Libyan Sibyl*, the *Prophet Daniel*, the *Cumean Sibyl*, the *Prophet Isaiah*, the *Delphic Sibyl*; at the right, on the entrance wall we have—the *Prophet Zachariah*, and above, from left to right in symmetry with the preceding—the *Prophet Jeremiah*, the *Persian Sibyl*, the *Prophet Ezekiel*, the *Eritrean Sibyl* and the *Prophet Joel*. In the other remaining spaces of the Vault and in the lunettes above the windows, Michelangelo painted the *Ancestors of Christ* awaiting the Messiah.

Rome, Vatican-The Sistine Chapel

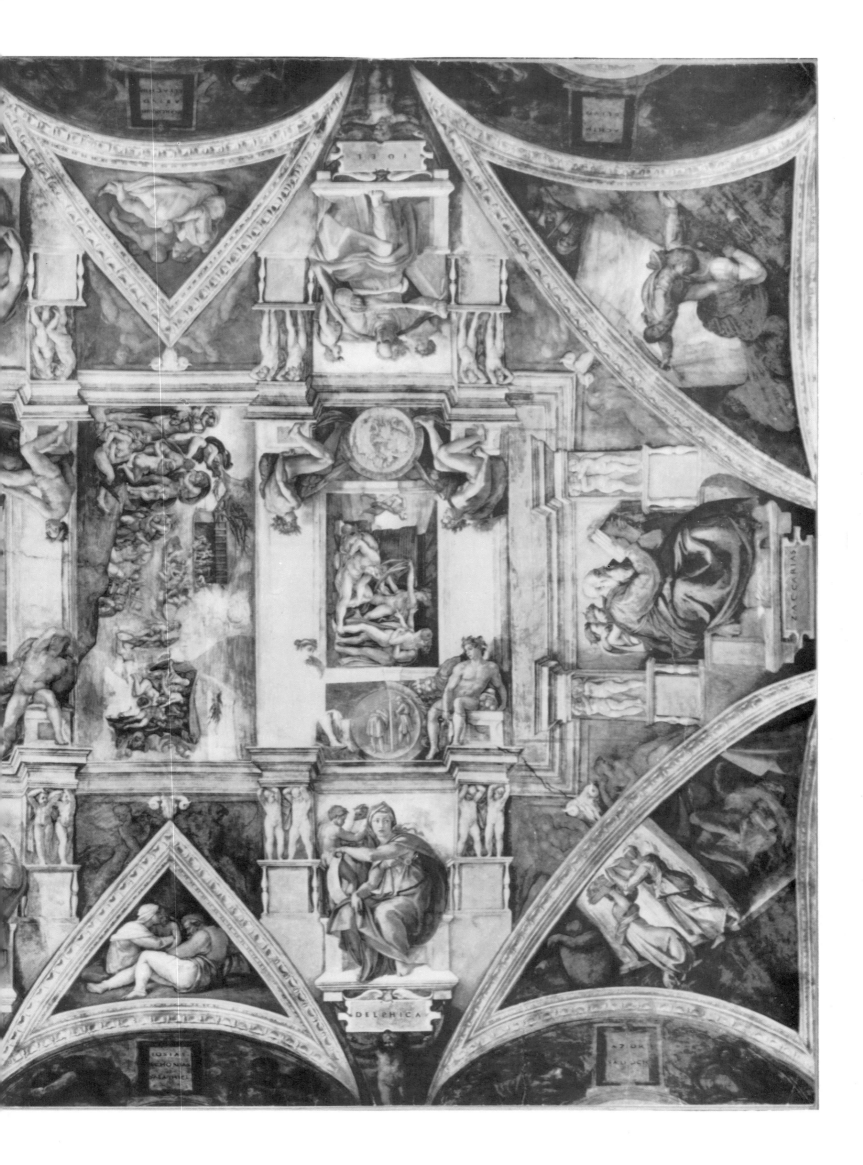

tries to fend off the fatal punishment, is interpreted with heightened energy in a few black pencil strokes. This drawing, certainly taken from a posed model, is very significant and leads us to speculate on what must have been the vast quantity of similar studies which the artist made in preparation for the definitive cartoons for the fresco (fig. 10). Here, the artist is interested in snatching from the play of the muscles the secret of the particular expression which he is seeking (aesthetic satisfaction is not of any importance to him in the drawing). This expression is born from a wide range of sentiments which are to be collected into a fundamental feeling of guilt. As always occurs in the studies which propose a specific problem of gesture, the muscular masses are outlined and fixed on the paper rather like sources of energy than harmonic elements of the human body. The rapid but incisive treatment of the torso results. The opposition of the arms is evident. One arm is barely alluded to and is almost absorbed into the mass of the full thorax while the other is projected outwards and analytically studied in the movement of the shoulder in a strong setting which determines the vividness of the gesture.

When the artist then passed to a painted realization of the complex movement of the nude, he modelled the forms in color with a greater sweetness, perhaps with the intention of making Adam's body more harmonious. He somewhat decreased the energy of the sketched figure in order to accentuate the grief at his own condemnation in Adam's face. He shifted his emphasis from the intense expression contained in a mere gesture to a more psychological rendering of the drama of the expulsion from Paradise. The sentiments implied in Eve's movements, however, are heightened. She dares to continue watching the punishing Angel in a combination of angry desperation and terror. The smaller square with the *Creation of Eve* is almost a parenthesis of rest. It shows Earthly Paradise as a typically Michelangelesque landscape, a barren stretch of land, barely interrupted by a truncated tree, which supports the sleeping Adam. The serious and austere image of the Lord is worth noting. He is like an ancient philosopher in the act of evoking the figure of Eve, the bridge of life between God and the first man, who is completely immersed in a primeval lethargic unconsciousness. Plates X and XI

Michelangelo's genius takes a sublime leap in the famous *Creation of Adam* scene in the newness of the idea and the exceptional expressive power. The artist's evident intention is to confront the physical beauty of the nude Adam with the beauty of the Lord, seen as a mysterious cosmic force suspended in the void of a timeless, seasonless heaven. Plate XII

On creating the indolent, perfect image of Adam, Michelangelo concentrated all his adoration for the young, firm body into this sublime living architecture of tendons and muscles. This is an harmonic synthesis of his formal language and his aspiration to compare himself with the ancient creators of nude bodies, Phidias and Praxiteles. In the pose of the nude, capturing a slow downward motion (which is echoed in the marbles of the Medici tombs), in the face which reveals an unforgettable, sweet melancholy (in which there is also a touch of blissfulness) as well as in the gesture of the left arm (weighed down by the primordial fatigue which overwhelms the limbs moved by instinct and not consciousness), Michelangelo succeeds in creating a new image. This image is rich with significant answers. It is perhaps the first which concentrates in itself, without exteriorization, an enormous intensity of inner life ready to be expressed. Plate XIII

The figure of the Lord, covered by a large mantle which snaps in the air like a sail swollen by the wind, is dense with tempestuous, heroically inspired strength. He is seen approaching His creature, who still lacks the life of the spirit, with the gesture of the great Creator whose fiat accomplishes the miracle.

The Lord is not depicted alone. The interpreting genii of his multiple powers carry Him along in space, and accompany him on His flight. Eve (still "in mente Dei") may also be protected by his vigorous arm, modelled in the shadow of his large mantle.

We might find the origin of the idea of suspending a group of figures swiftly wandering through space through the consideration of a composition which is, however, so different from Michelangelo's that the hypothesis must be broached with great discretion. We are referring to the two figures of Aeolus and Zephyrus, whom Botticelli depicted in the *Birth of Venus* in the Uffizi. This is a typical example of his frequent excursions into an imaginative vein which has been, perhaps too often, cited as a masterpiece of musical and poetic lyricism. This excursion is, however, completely unalterable in the firmness and impetus of its design. It is certain, however, that comparisons have little value when we face the maturity of style which Michelangelo had reached in this fresco, which is among the most singular and best realized of the entire Sistine cycle. The creative impetus is expressed with such decision in this work that we are hardly able to examine the opus unemotionally. We are confronted with the creation of an artist who, in contrast to all tradition, does not depict the Lord on His feet, erect in the supreme dignity of the moment. He molds the form soaring in space, which is so much more powerful. We may imagine the extent of the mass which gravitates in the vacuum like a tempestuous rain cloud, charged with unknown energy.

The scrupulous attention to reality through which Michelangelo arrived at such a high affirmation of the ideal is documented by the drawings done from models. The extant drawings are, however, very few in number, in comparison with the large number which (done for the Sistine Vault, as well as those for other works) have been certainly lost due to the artist's habit of systematic destruction. He did this to avoid the analytical reconstruction of the path he had trod from the embryonic idea to its ultimate definition, which he possibly wished to have considered as a quick inspiration.

There would be no other way of explaining the fears which he so often manifested in his letters. He feared that others might see his drawings and the extreme difficulty which he had in order to give his friends some small example of his prodigious power in draftsmanship.

There are several studies on the page in the British Museum which has the sketch of the first idea for the decoration of the Sistine Vault. This served for the right arm of Adam which rests upon the ground, and also for his left hand. These are essential to the expressive significance of the painting. Another sketch, also in London, reveals the study for Adam's face. This is in a different pose in right profile, however, tormented by the various corrections which often occurred when the artist was dissatisfied with his solution. Certainly the studies for this scene must have been numerous. It is easy to make such a supposition, especially when we take into account the two hands of God and Adam which so exceptionally synthesize the act of the Creation.

Notwithstanding the great insistence on the peremptory gesture of the Lord, who infuses life into Adam's indolent body, as always happens to a work of genius, the two figures are filled with an inexhaustible spiritual value.

The form here arrives at a maximum significance from the expressive point of view. Seeing it even from a distance, we are able to discern Michelangelo's intention to contrast the Creative Spirit and His Creature who is waiting to acquire life and consciousness. This has all been accomplished by the artist's full control over form, so intensely expressed that the two worlds become symbolized in the two hands which are on the brink of touching. The Lord's hand is charged with energy in the movement of the tense forefinger about to touch Adam's hand. Adam's hand, abandoned and inert, seems to be lifeless because the muscular arm which rests on his knee sustains it with effort. Such a detail indicates the extraordinary possibilities which Michelangelo's drawings afforded. They emphasized his continual nourishment on real life experience and above all indicate his faculty of impressing an absolute value on the pure sculptured significance of the form.

It remains to be seen how Michelangelo resolved one of his most difficult problems, given the fact that he regarded himself as a sculptor. In this episode, he attempts to realize the figure of the Lord who is cleaving through space (i.e.,

Plate XIV

how to make a mass articulated in the human form appear suspended in space and pushed along by an extremely fast motion, a figure which is determined with clear vigor from the relief of a strictly sculptural modelled form). His solution also gives us a clue as to his successive treatment of the Lord as the only protagonist of the following scenes for the *Last Judgment* and eventually the Pauline Chapel.

The Lord, Creator, who passes through the air is like a swimmer who freely moves in water. The simile is anything but paradoxical if we pay attention to the swift motion of the body which seems to be in its natural element. Note also the vigorous push that the other figures, at the same time, exercise against the invisible but real existence of the ambience in which they move. We should not be surprised at the analogy with the image that Dante (of whom Michelangelo was constantly aware) uses in the sixteenth canto of the *Inferno*; the image of the swimmer who returns to the surface after having liberated the anchor and of which Momigliano says "it is traced with vibrant clarity and sculptural corpulence upon reality." By now Michelangelo's God, brought to light after a profound gestation which has its origins in the sculptured images of ancient Zeus and passes through the most vital experiences of the fifteenth-century Renaissance, animates the final spaces with his authoritarian presence. The artist also employs this figure to simplify the composition to the maximum. (It was impossible for there to have been witnesses to the first acts of the Creation, if not the genii who sometimes accompany Him, marveling at His works, and becoming intermediaries of His divine truth at the sides of the *Prophets* and *Sibyls*.)

The existence, however, of a unique, grand image, which unites in itself the two essential characteristics of the Divinity, the "tremendum" and the "maiestas," inspired Michelangelo to actuate the striking foreshortenings. He seems to capture his joy in the solutions of the graphic difficulties involved in the work.

Perhaps this point of view is realized in its most absolute sense in the section which contains the *Separation of the Land from the Waters* and the *Creation of the Fish*. Here the Lord, whose garments are religiously supported by the genii who accompany Him, occupies with His power nearly all of the sky in which He advances with a prodigious perspective effect. The Lord annihilates the painted surface with a grand gesture of His arms which are open wide to bless and create. The imposing image advances, bringing into focus a face surrounded by the long, soft down of a beard. His eyes are veiled with an ineffable paternal sweetness. He seems to concentrate all of His expressiveness into the act of opening His arms before us as He flies over the immobile expanse of the waters. Plates XV and XVI

The figure comes out of the mantle in which it is draped as if coming out of a mysterious cave. The great mass profiled against the sky seems to extend itself in depth until it reaches the last horizon, indicated by a blinding metallic light.

In the more ample section, as in preceding compositions of the same size, the artist develops and uncouples the various elements. In the *Creation of the Sun, the Moon and the Plants* Michelangelo, perhaps recalling the efficacy of repetition of the protagonist in Botticelli's fresco with the Moses stories, imagines the Lord who completes His rapid action in two movements. In the first movement, to the right, to which Michelangelo gives the prime importance, He creates the sun and the moon with a new imperious gesture (long the subject of successive imitation). He throws open His arms and indicates their places to each of the celestial bodies. The creative power of God is thus manifested in one of the most peremptory and vigorous gestures which can be found in the vast range of poses in the Sistine Chapel. The value of the "sotto in sù" technique which is employed with such decision in the preceding section is united with the expressive force of the gesture. It is also reflected in the proud face with its wrinkled forehead, windswept beard accentuated by exceptionally vigorous brush strokes, drawn from new stylistic resources. Plates XVIII and XIX

The artist also widely applies the same formula in the second part of the vault. Contemplating the first section from below, he seems to have become aware of the contrast between the compositions done as if they were separate paintings and the necessity of the illusionistic "relief" which he was by now adopting rather broadly. This relief reaches its maximum effect in the colossal *Jonah* on the vertical of the main altar.

Michelangelo demonstrates in the development of his painting a more complete figurative synthesis in the considerations of the view from below. It is not, however, this that lessens the significance of the robust design which, modelling the forms, articulates the essential elements in a highly expressive fashion. The grandiose gesture of the Lord's hands seems to mold the two celestial bodies out of the void. This is not so much a reflection of the Holy text "Opera manum tuarum sunt coeli" as a palpitating transposition of the indicative movement of an artist who draws a circle on a surface with habitual, decisive firmness. The forefingers of both hands tensed in space from one hand to the other create the two spheres in space. One is seen suspended with an ingenious relief effect against the heavens. The second to the far right, indicated as a mass still in the process of formation, is so clear as to permit the separation of the arm and the hand of the Lord profiled in a halo of light.

To the left, in a purposely planned mirror image, Michelangelo paints the same image of God (this time without the genii). He rapidly departs in space, pointing His creative hand to the earth and bringing forth the green mass of trees.

Plates XX and XXI

In the final square of smaller dimensions, which returns to the beginning of Genesis and depicts in synthesis the *Creation of Light*, Michelangelo seems to be executing a theme which he chose as a test of his possibilities. He leaves us dumbfounded by the modern spirit of his solution which anticipates the artistic effects of late Titian or Tintoretto, and those of Impressionism and Expressionism. It appears to be almost Dionysian in nature.

In the exceptional image of the Lord, who moves almost as if dancing through the Chaos, Michelangelo has expressed the mysterious state of the creative inspiration with a revolutionary "élan." He depicts the moments in which the Lord gives order and clarity to formlessness. Michelangelo has purposely imagined the *Creation of Light* as a synthesis of the first moments of the Lord's mysterious opus; the lonely rapture of that act which provoked the vital throb of the Cosmos. He frames the event in a tumultuous form. The Lord's figure, molded in a luminescent substance, flashing with yellow gold and pinkish reflections, seems to be modelled out of a mysterious fluid matter. With vigorous strokes which make the heroic power stand out in relief, the serpentine pose (as it might be called by the Mannerists) is resolved in an unending spiral. The forms of the figure receive their sculptural relief as a result of strange and almost instantaneous reflections. The fascination which is engendered by such an exceptional pictorial solution (although altogether new and the product of a rapid conclusive moment of the enormous task, left almost as an ingenious sketch) owes its birth to a sculptural conception at the borders between the undifferentiated mass and the definition of the forms. We may compare it with an unfinished sculptural work of the artist which already demonstrated those disconcerting effects, the dynamic *Saint Matthew* in the Florence Academy. The latter work, as Bertini says, is extremely close (also typologically) to this unforgettable painting, in its taking form within a barely sketched frame.

We review the grandiose episodes of the Creation in which the Lord is the superhuman protagonist, and feel that the Biblical text is adhered to not as a source to be "illustrated" but profoundly interpreted in a manner faithful to the spirit of the Old Testament.

The austerity of the Biblical verses which mark the birth of life in the Universe stimulated the artist to develop them with noble simplicity in an equally severe and spiritualized painting style. This makes us unfailingly think of Michelangelo's paintings whenever we hear the ancient, sacred words "In principio creavit Deus coelum et terram. Terra autem erat inanis et vacua . . . et Spiritus Dei ferebatur super Aquas . . . ." The solemn majesty of the verses seems to be transferred into the alternating pauses of Michelangelo's painting compartments. They are like episodes linked to the powerful structure of the frames and pillars defining the spaces which, in turn, act as time intervals.

As for the progression of scenes along the central axis of the vault (although the artist was not conscious of the fact), a happy set of circumstances occurs. The episodes, therefore, unfold pictorially in an inverse order to the chronology of the facts. Michelangelo has painted with greater analytic truth the scenes in which Humanity takes over as protagonist of the "stories" from the Lord. He displays greater powers of synthesis (also due to his increased mastery of fresco techniques) in these initial scenes of the Creation through which the Lord moves as a solitary figure, in an undifferentiated ambience, like a mysterious, sovereign, and terrible force.

At the same time that he worked on the Creation episodes, the artist painted the monumental marble-like thrones. These were flanked by pairs of imitation-sculpture children's figures, and by the majestic seven Prophets and five Sibyls who, in their gigantic proportions, animate the great idealized base out of which the vault is born. These severe, mobile images, which are placed where the artist originally had planned to put the twelve Apostles, acquire a decisive relief from the fact of their position in relation to the entire painted surface. Each one occupies the curved skull-like space of the twelve small pedestals and is, therefore, nearer to our vision. The artist augments the relief of these images with his vigorous painting. He insists upon a strong chiaroscuro treatment which pays strong attention to the direction of the light which penetrates into the chapel from the window and projects the shadows against the imitation marble surface. It is almost as if the figures really stood out from the walls. In contrast he deepens the spaces in the intervals. The images here are only barely seen in shadow, emphasizing instead the brightness of the frames and the pillars. In addition to the joy of modelling in chiaroscuro the pensive, expressive seated figures, Michelangelo expanded his gifts towards the maximum efficacy of color. This adheres to the reflections of the material, becomes soft and velvety in the flesh tones and luminous in the whites, in a continually contrasting scheme.

When, therefore, one defines Michelangelo as a "sculptural" painter, such a definition (fundamentally correct, but insufficient) must be examined in the light of the extraordinary liberty which the artist shows in his execution of the monumental *Sibyls* and *Prophets* which are infused with such an intense and full life that even the unshakable sculptured structure palpitates. This is also the fruit of an intense maturation in his painting style which took place as this work developed (as we saw in the Creation scenes). The *Prophets* and *Sibyls* appear to be painted with a greater nimbleness of the brush and more coloristic variety. This takes place as the artist proceeds from the beginning to the conclusion of the task. He worked on successive sectors of the vault at a time when each contained three or four principal figures and two or three central scenes linked to these by the architectural structures.

Developing the pictorial decorations in this fashion, the artist also improves his powers of synthesis in the *Prophets* and *Sibyls*. He invests them with a greater coloristic vitality so that, in speaking of these great "human pillars" that ideally support the entire composition, we must keep in mind the differences between the first and last figures which are concluded in the triumphal figure of the prophet Jonah. This is the masterpiece of the whole in which Michelangelo, in full mastery of the placement of such a difficult foreshortening, impresses the highest stamp of his personality as a painter.

As we consider the different characterizations of these grandiose images, each of which was certainly accentuated by the artist's idea of the individual personality, we must not forget that Michelangelo was always very careful about the connection between the various parts of the vault. He was like a composer who, while he creates apparently autonomous motifs, always links them to the total rhythm of the piece.

When we consider the space allotted to each of the principal figures, we see that the artist has composed each of their thrones as large steps drawn from the same base of the vault. He has connected them in the upper part to the deep frames, to the medallions and to the very figures of the nudes. To the sides of the severe personages, the pillars are animated with pairs of children's figures, caryatids for which the artist used a mirror image of the same design. He thus obtains a return to the symmetry which is echoed in the young athletes who (at the end of the pillars, painted in vivid tones in contrast to the architectural portions of the decorations) respond in a similar symmetry. They conclude the whole of the composition which frames each of the Prophets and Sibyls.

Michelangelo certainly conceived his vast pictorial composition in such a fashion that, after having gained an overall impression, the viewer could observe it from two principal points. These points are the mean axis for the Creation scenes, and then turning towards the walls for the Prophets and Sibyls series.

This proceeding closely reflects the organization of the various parts and the relation between sculpture and architecture in the first project for Julius II's tomb. *Moses*, the only surviving figure which would have represented the Prophets in that monument, is akin, in its expressive intensity and the vigor of its movement, to the painted figures in the Sistine Chapel, which lacks a Moses. This fact, however, can also be ascribed to the *Moses Stories* which the fifteenth-century painters had executed on the Chapel walls in symmetry with the *Christ Stories*.

As Michelangelo executed the single images, among which some of the highest physical and moral ideals of Humanism are affirmed, he gave autonomous life to each one of them. He concentrated to the maximum on their costumes, gestures, and faces, their interior lives which are either closed within them or clamorously expressed in the knowledge of the possession of a superior truth destined to be revealed.

Possibly because their meditative solitude or contact with the Divinity becomes more intense and humanized by the dialectic established by the presence of the other figures, Michelangelo places two genii next to each image as he did with the figure of the Lord in the Creation scenes. They become participants in the moving agitation of the prophetic spirit, either in the reflection of the excitement of the eloquent gestures of the ancient wise men, or in their frightened withdrawal engendered by the impetus of the Prophets' and Sibyls' spirits.

Zachariah was among the first figures which Michelangelo painted on the perpendicular of the entrance to the chapel in sharp profile. He is draped in wide folds struck by sharply slanted beams of light and stretched forward as he leafs through an old book which he holds in his hands. He begins the list of the "Dramatis Personae" in the attitude of a calm and placid scholar. Behind him, the two small genii seem to observe with great attention his prophetic gaze on the chosen page.

Plate XXIII

Joel was also done at the beginning but is an entirely different type. We deduce this from the clarity of the outlines and the crudity of the folds which are almost schematically imposed by the contrast between light and shadow. The frontal pose is animated by the turning of the upper part of the body towards the lectern on which he rests his right arm. His face, chiefly characterized by a strong modelling and accentuated by the sharply slanted light, is crowned with flaming reddish white hair. The hair covers his great brow which is illuminated as if by divine knowledge.

Plate XXIV

64

Fig. 9 — MICHELANGELO *autograph drawing. Pen sketch for the composition of the frescoes on the Sistine Vault and studies in charcoal for Adam's hand in the scene of the "Creation of Man" (London, British Museum)*

The Prophet has opened a parchment roll and reads intently with a broad, decisive gesture. This is emphasized by the hooked folds of his mantle thrown over his shoulders and gathered at the bottom in a beautiful cascade of material, studied from life. There is something in the placement of the figure in the act of moving nervously which recalls the structure of the marble *Moses* with its unstable movement. The face of the strong model, however, seems to refer to the willful expression of Bramante, whom Michelangelo must have often met near the Vatican where he was at work on the new basilica. Bramante, as described by his contemporaries, was always choleric and meditative.

Plate XXV

The *Delphic Sibyl*, in symmetry with the *Prophet Joel*, is among the famous images in the Sistine Chapel. Artists, writers and critics of every age have gazed upon her strong and harmonious visage and her large eyes, full of presentiment. Few of Michelangelo's female figures express such an energy and pride in the illumined knowledge, transformed into such firm, palpitating forms. She comes directly from the Virgin of the *Doni Madonna*, but seems to have matured through a deeper experience of the interior world. The fine idea of that arm which is extended in front of her bust to unroll the manuscript which she weighs in her hand so cautiously in space is the development of the same pose which the Madonna assumes to take the Child to her bosom. That gesture engenders the deep fold of the mantle from which the beautiful body derives, modelled with a breadth of chiaroscuro and emphasized by the light that molds the well-rounded masses. When one considers her unforgettable face, it seems to appear from the material which frames it, com-

Plate XXVI

ing from a single block with consummate sculptural skill. The varied and sometimes silvery coloring penetrates the form and enlivens it, reinforcing the impression of palpability.

The *Eritrean Sibyl*, with her measured rhythmic pose, is like *Zachariah* seen in profile. The artist also justifies her gesture with the commencement of the reading in the large book on the lectern, covered by a linen cloth as if it were an altar. A child with sun-tanned flesh is intent on lighting with a torch the oil lamp suspended over the smooth pages which are cut at the margins as if they were precious marble. Much later, the artist recalled the sculptured motif of this figure when he sculpted the *Virgin and Child* in the Medici Chapel in a marble block. Such relationships, which indicate the echoing of analogous motifs in Michelangelo's works, emphasize that which his contemporaries said about him. Vasari observed that the possibility of memorizing certain cadences and structures was useful to the artist as a musician (in our personal simile) or poet makes repeated use of preferred harmonies and cadences.

In the variety of poses and gestures which Michelangelo conceived for these figures, he sometimes seems to wish to utilize the instantaneous movement suggested by a brusque thought or unforeseen action. Even in those cases, however, Michelangelo succeeds in blocking the form in a definitive manner.

This is the case in the *Prophet Isaiah*, whose vitality is born of an interior movement the exigence of which is happily

Plate XXVII

tempered by the composure and control that come with age. Seated in a frontal position, the Prophet is perhaps plunged in deep thought over that which he has read in the Holy book now held in his right hand, marking the page.

The arm on which he rests his head is still bent with the hand suspended in space. The face, which expresses the reflection of a new, unforeseen motif of attention in its agitated and vivid modelling, is brusquely turned to the side.

This, combined with his lowered, serious eyes, makes his face the reflection of an inspired idea. One of the genii behind him, standing beyond his gigantic shoulder, gestures downwards, thus emphasizing the gesture with his puffy, joyful face. His eyes are opened wide, and perhaps he has arrived running. A piece of material blows in the wind as if to direct our eyes to the mysterious distances. It is a situation determined by an instantaneous movement, as in the *Battle of Cascina* cartoon. Notwithstanding that the whole acquires a complex, dynamic life, everything tends at the end to fuse into the monumental firmness of a clearly sculptured effect.

The *Cumean Sibyl* descends from a race of giants who lived in a fabled age. According to Longhi, she displays a distinct relation to the figure of the decrepit Eve who is present at the death of Adam in Piero della Francesca's fresco in Arezzo. Something Etruscan seems to have filtered into this image with the muscular flesh of brown terracotta. The enormous body, molded into a titanic form, is slightly bent in the act of opening the book of ancient wisdom whose ivory pages define its geometric structure. Other papers and books come out of a bag which has fallen to the ground.

Plate XXXI

From behind the still powerful limbs of this hundred-year-old gypsy figure, we see the two embracing children who are ready to furnish her insatiable desire for knowledge with another book secured with clasps. In the colors, sometimes warm and sometimes marmoreal, we feel that Michelangelo gives us something new. The Sibyl seems to be a Hellenistic bronze rediscovered after years of oblivion.

The *Ezekiel* is the most animated of all the Prophets. He abandons the roll of sacred writings to turn towards the child's figure which points out to him the celestial truths. His almost wild face, clearly profiled against the light background, shows that he is following the boy's words, but his right arm points, instead, with an expressive and quick gesture, downwards towards the interior of the Chapel. The beautiful hand (on which Michelangelo lavished special care because he knew it would be a focal point) modelled from the real light of the ambience is detached from the painted surface with a prodigious effect of evident relief.

Plates XXIX and XXX

This figure, conceived with such accentuated dynamism, occurs at the halfway point of the fresco sequence. Michelangelo, perhaps imagining it almost in appellation to the visitor who enters the chapel, sought a greater effect of movement at the point where the figurative series is taken up again in the balanced and severe architectural rhythm. The figure, however, is one of those unforeseen Michelangelesque inventions which confirm the richness of the artist's exceptional imagination.

Ingeniously divided between light and shadow is the *Prophet Daniel*. He is intent on transcribing observations on pages which are placed on a tablet to the left. The material is drawn from the large book lying open on his knees and sustained (a new motif) by the child who seems to be a caryatid between the grandiose folds of Daniel's robe and who supports the book's weight. A beam of light shines on the limpid material and shapes the vast thorax of this hero of knowledge with the poetic visage. His face is emphasized with quick, clear brush strokes, barely foreshortened on the brow which is left free of the dense, almost flaming, hair. The semi-nude arm, with the hand abandoned beyond the border of the book, brings us back to the unity of the whole. The folds bring us in a sinuous movement to the whirlpool of shadow in which the child, almost crushed by the weight on his shoulders, hides.

Plate XXXII

The shadow covers the colors of the *Persian Sibyl*. The small book whose pages seem to be grazed by a late sunset light is brought near her gaze. The tonal decline, which becomes one with the full modelling of the robe and the mantle of a heavier material, enlivens the luminosity of the linen which is wound around the old Sibyl's head like an oriental turban. From a painting standpoint, everything is a function of this clear mass. Her profile, lost in shadow, also appears more mysterious as she gives her attention to her reading. We are even hard put to find the two small genii, who are so active and vivid next to the other figures. They are quietly absorbed into the ambience and immersed in the inertia which seems to exclude them from the concentrated thought which pervades the atmosphere around the old wise woman.

Plates XXXIII and XXXIV

In the stupendous figuration of the *Libyan Sibyl*, Michelangelo returns to his "science of opposites." The figure is surprised in the gesture of extending her arm to take the open book towards which she has turned in a twisted movement. This brings into the light and shadow the palpitating modelling of her shoulders and her limpid face which looks downwards, crowned with plaits of hair past the bands which restrain their serpentine vitality. The shoulders and arms

Plate XXXV

emerge from the upper portion of the body which emphasizes the elastic movement of her sides. The robe swathes the leg nervously placed against a step, determining the youthful thrust which animates the entire image. It would almost seem that Michelangelo wanted to test his capacity to overcome the compositional difficulties of the figure in space. The nervous life of the bodies, which signifies their latent energy, is unloosed here with extremely fine results, due no doubt to very acute life studies. This is demonstrated by an important study in the Metropolitan Museum of Art. Here, Michelangelo deepens his investigation of the Sibyl's shoulders and arms in a purposely accentuated modelling. He carefully follows the play of muscles and tendons (rather diminished in the actual painting). We marvel at his study of the left hand and the toes of the feet which jut out from the robe in the fresco. The artist certainly employed movingly scrupulous life studies for every tiny detail in every figure in the fresco (the extant testimony of which, however, is extremely rare). This leads us to speculate on the reasons for the exceptional energy which Michelangelo's painted works release. We refer to the artist's craving for perfection in the concrete translation of his ideas. His continual use of the living model gave body and truth to those forms (although seeming to spurt from the idealistic imagination of a world of pure beauty in which their details become factors in a dreamed-of harmony). They provoke the stimulating vitality which prevents them from being lost in the labyrinths of Mannerism which befell the Michelangelists.

Plate XXXVI Conceived in the final phase of the painting of the vault, the *Prophet Jeremiah* towers above in his designedly realized isolation. The action and urgency of burning thoughts which the preceding figures celebrated is succeeded in this image by a profound grief, which moves us to tears and is barely contained in a great and virile spirit. It has been often said that Michelangelo painted this sublime human figure with particular affection because he felt, in a certain sense, akin to the Prophet. This may be partly true, especially when we recall that there are many proofs of his sad turn of thought while he was working on the Sistine Chapel (notwithstanding the fact that he is still far from the profoundly bitter conception of the world which he expressed in his old age). He demonstrated, even in the highest creative impulses, a necessary liberation from his mood.

It is not, however, necessary to view the *Jeremiah* as a self-portrait to appreciate its austere, profound beauty. The artist seems to point up the value of the image by marking out the abbreviation "Alef. V" on a piece of parchment painted to the left of the figure. Following Michelangelo's suggestion, we look in the "Lamentations" of Jeremiah. The dramatic prayer begins with the words, "Remember, O Lord, what is come upon us: consider, and behold our reproach." And also,

> "The joy of our heart is ceased;
> our dance is turned into mourning
> ....
> for this our heart is faint."

These verses also seem to have inspired the artist:

> "It is good that a man should both hope and quietly
> wait for the salvation of the Lord.
> It is good for a man that he bear the yoke
> of his youth.
> He sitteth alone and keepeth silence;
> because he hath borne it upon him."

68

*Fig.´ 10—*MICHELANGELO *autograph drawing. Study in black pencil for the figure of Adam in the scene of the "Expulsion from Earthly Paradise"*
on the Sistine Chapel vault (Florence, Casa Buonarroti, 45 F. See Exhibition of drawings by Michelangelo. Catalogue edited by P. Barocchi,
Florence, Holschki, 1962, page 2, illustration VI)

The figure of Jeremiah, immersed in its dark grief, seems to be cut out of one block. The face with its long beard is sustained and partly hidden by the right hand. He seemingly withholds the tears by force of will. The other hand hangs between his knees, inert. Even the genii, those inseparable companions of the Prophets and Sibyls, are dressed in mourning. The one to the left expresses in his dramatic face a reflection of the deeper tragedy enclosed in the great heart of the Prophet.

If, however, the sculptured values are dominant in the powerful figure, it is impossible to negate the penetrating and new manner in which Michelangelo has used these values to express a sentiment of universal bitterness, of purposeful immobility, of concentrated thought and of an unapproachable desire for isolation. The intensification of his imaginative life and the deepening of the artistic language are focused on the human body. The artist thus arrives at the point where he can translate into form the most intimate impressions of feeling.

To a certain degree following in Giotto's footsteps in Tuscan painting, Michelangelo finds himself next to Leonardo in the exploration of the human spirit and transfers its mystery to the surface. Leonardo, pushing forward in his subtle investigations, became a master of the most hidden vibrations and rendered them in an infinite variety of shadings. Michelangelo, who clarified everything he touched, succeeded in rendering that which might be reserved to the shadows of states of mind in grandiose sculptured forms. He changed ephemeral instants into images of a universal moment for mankind.

Plate
XXXVII

It is useful, in regard to the *Jonah* which is the last of the Prophets and hangs over the main altar, to reread Vasari's description: "Who will not admire and remain bewildered at seeing *Jonah's* terribleness. By force of art, the vault which by nature would jut out, turned by the walls and driven by the appearance of that figure which bends backwards, appears straight. It is won over by the art of the shadows and light. It really seems to bend backwards. Oh, our fortunate epoch! O blessed artifice!"

With these words, however, we are already at the threshold of the taste for wonders which characterizes the advent of the Baroque period. The biographer (and after him, the succeeding centuries) emphasizes in the figure of the Prophet who is thrown ashore by the sea monster the extreme finesse of the foreshortening drawn by Michelangelo. This reverses the very structure of the wall, making it seem nearer to the eye when actually it is more distant. This judgment is characteristic of Vasari the Mannerist painter, theoretician of virtuosity and those abilities of graphic invention designed to "amaze." His mentality could not conceive of art without artifice and he naturally ascribed to Michelangelo's austere and profound vision an uncontemporary significance. He misinterprets Michelangelo's directly significant style based on feeling through his own Manneristic bias.

This does not mean that Vasari was not very often a critic of keen acumen (sometimes in spite of his intellectual position) especially when he followed his own artistic instincts which were greater than he demonstrated in his painting.

Michelangelo's *Jonah* is, above all, intended to translate into the athletic limbs colored by the sea and sun the slow return to consciousness which the prophet experienced after his mysterious period in the whale's stomach.

Something fabulous animates this composition. It is all movement and rustling where the colors, suddenly warm and settled in their various beauty, prove the contest with the palettes of the Venetians.

Situated crossways and turned on the marble block as if on a smooth rock, the gigantic body is placed in a diagonal. It is almost in an oscillation which would make it fall without the weight of the muscular legs, rich with healthy, primitive life, serving as a base for the thorax bent over backwards. The hands still move in imprecise gestures in opposition to the vivid displacement of the shoulders. The Prophet's face, however, is turned upwards in full foreshortening to receive light and knowledge from the invisible but present God. Behind the large immobile fish which fills the remaining space, two children's figures seem to flee in fright. Their garments seem caught in the whirlpool of the wind, and next to them the barely sketched pale branches of the wild fig tree rustle. The sketchiness is typical in Michelangelo's landscape elements and is employed here to help identify the Prophet.

The Jonah, a symbol of the Resurrection, is here conceived by Michelangelo's free genius without reference to any preceding or contemporary example. The artist's conception, proceeding from a primordial feeling of wonder, assumes something of the ancient "sacer horror" in which the mystery of Nature and the voice of God were identified because of the extraordinary fullness of the image. From this comes the exceptional climate of the figure which seems, in its winding through space, to reach the value of the conclusion of a long story. The image, however, does not exist only in itself. It is linked in its reference upwards to the first episode of the Creation which the artist was painting at the same time.

Above, in a space which, in its limitations, makes the energy of the *Lord Creating the Light* even more towering, something mysterious occurs. Order is imposed on Chaos and the great pictorial work begins from here. If Michelangelo desired such an evident rapport, he also intended, in our opinion, to direct the viewer's eye from the clamorous figure of *Jonah* (right there at the chapel entrance and in front of the observer; it is far away and at the same time near, due to the unforeseen composition in space), to the initial Creation scene. This indicates the sense of the "reading" of the entire vault which must proceed from the figures over the main altar towards the scenes of the *Flood* and the *Drunkenness of Noah* which are above us. It almost brings us back to earth after the contemplation of the Lord's great deeds.

Liberated, so to speak, from any symbolic or representative function, the twenty *Nudes* which crown the pillars of the Prophets' and Sibyls' thrones are intended as the most direct expressions of Michelangelo's sculptural imagination. One of these, to the right of the *Delphic Sibyl*, is lost. We can barely see the face and a fragment of the right leg. The others, rich with extraordinary vitality, display the most immediate designing and painting gifts of the artist.

As we have already seen in the nude youths grouped behind the Holy Family in the *Doni Madonna*, these figures speak the language of the forms in the various accents of gesture and pose. They are a concretization of the rhythms and rhymes of a poet's inspiration. It is also possible that the artist conceived this group of young athletes and their passionate, nervous, and sometimes indolent but always beautiful limbs with vague symbolic allusions.

That which more directly inspired him, however, was the joy of being able to insert, in a world rich with significance, an element of pure sculptural value. In others, this would have been purely decorative (as later occurred ad infinitum) but it was of deeply expressive value for him.

These young men are placed above and in pairs. They arrange the large shields with the golden reflections on which are depicted battle scenes or Biblical events which the artist paints with impressionistic vivacity. He outlines the images more or less distinctly according to the light conditions in which each is found. He keeps the tone of the colors low and raises them here and there with quick reflections as if they flashed in the shadow.

The metallic shields contain the various figurations as if they were ancient medals. This is a very able compositional execution in relation to the circular form. As always, the artist, parting from an apparently decorative pretext, transfigures the original intention through his overbearing expressive exigence which asserts itself everywhere. It is also evident in the less visible portions of the vault, in the agitated figures and rapidly sketched Biblical allusions in chiaroscuro.

These shields are painted in a style which is close to the illuminated drawings and monochromes already in use in the fifteenth century. The vigor of the improvisation, however, is transmitted with new force to the excited or calm

Plates XLII,
XLIII, XLIV

Plates IV, VII,
X, XV, XVII,
XX, XXII

Plate XVII

figures, which are often entangled, as if in reference to the *Battle of the Centaurs*. These figures are, however, always extremely clear. We note that Michelangelo, perhaps with the intention of varying the effects from the base, has painted them completely only to the halfway point of the vault (i.e., the shields which hang over the *Cumean Sibyl* and *Ezekiel*). He alludes to the others in a rapid chiaroscuro sketch. Among the more vivacious of these compositions are the *Slaughter of the Sons of Achab*, the *Death of Gioram, Elias on the Fiery Chariot,* the *Sacrifice of Isaac,* and *Absalom*, ensnared by his hair in a tree.

The artist illuminates the stirring images with clear and rapidly distinct brush strokes almost as if they were etched lines. This is reminiscent of the monochromatic tondos painted by Signorelli around the images of the Poets in the Chapel of San Brizio in Orvieto Cathedral, and principally, those images from the *Divine Comedy*, where the effect is obtained with strong, quick contrasts of light.

The full color *Nudes* justify their sometimes symmetrical, sometimes contrasting poses (occasionally derived from the same cartoon, with few variations) with the acts of fastening these large bronze shields with two ribbons. They pass them through splits cut into the edges of the shields and place heavy oak wreaths to the sides of the decorative tondos.

Michelangelo avoided placing pairs of young men on the pillars of the Thrones of *Zachariah* and *Jonah* (i.e., the Prophets at the beginning and end of the cycle) both because the space which they occupy is different in form and because the figures would have been badly placed in contrast to the adjacent nudes. This vivid motif, placed thus between the gigantic seated figures and the Creation scenes, gives life to the frame. It emphasizes the strong relief and the "sbalzo" in correspondence with the pillars. The movement of the youthfully energetic figures does not openly emphasize (as occurs at the end of the century and in Carracci's art—if we think of the decorations for the Palazzo Farnese) the external pleasantness of a figured decoration. It remains true to its naturalistic starting point and confers singular strength to the entire composition.

Michelangelo executed numerous studies from the model for these young athletes, as he had done for the Prophets (possibly a greater number than he had done for the latter since the former gave scope to a glorification of physical beauty in the vital joy of adolescence). There are, however, very few examples that have been conserved. These drawings are not limited to the bodily attitudes but inquire into the reactions produced on the muscles by sudden movements. They render the play of chiaroscuro extremely acute. One of the more complete studies of great sculptural effect is in the Haarlem Museum. It depicts the young man to the right, above the *Persian Sibyl*. This is one of the most intensely dramatic images conceived by the artist. The study is done in profile, with strong chiaroscuro.

Next to it is an investigation of the pose of the right arm which did not completely fit on the page. In the drawing, the anatomy is more accentuated, an almost crudely fixed phenomenon which occurs when the artist wants to use the study as he paints. In the figure realized in the fresco on the extremely firm anatomical structure of the body which is as tense as a drawn bow string, the light, which suddenly invests the proud image from the back, takes over. The face, in clear profile, is rough cut against the brightness of the marble. It is painted in flashing tones and the chiaroscuro fixes with extreme novelty this seaman's visage. He is shouting in the wind which tosses his thick hair onto his forehead as if during a storm. The expression is provoked by a dynamic situation. The artist has imagined that, in the placement of the large bronze disc, the ribbons have become relaxed. The model also seems to be slipping and therefore plants his legs with great energy to re-establish his equilibrium.

Elsewhere, he imagines dreamlike figures of young men with thick hair in headbands of an affinity, typologically, with the young men who joke among themselves behind the Holy Family in the *Doni Madonna*. These forms are either

72

*Fig. 11—*MICHELANGELO *autograph drawing. Study in pencil and pen for a cornice (at the left above) and for various movements of the "Nudes" on the Sistine Chapel vault (Florence, Casa Buonarroti, 75 F. See Exhibition of drawings by Michelangelo. Catalogue edited by P. Barocchi, Florence, Holschki, 1962, page 9)*

fleshier and more mature, or become thinner as if fused into the bronze. They are elastic and vivid, worthy of a Hellenistic sculptor. We should not exclude the possibility that the artist was inspired by the classical statues in the Vatican which he could not help but observe, and the collections of his Roman friends, so rich in ancient pieces (like that of Jacopo Galli). His nudes, especially, recall Alexandrine sculpture and dancing fauns (for instance, the sun-bronzed nude above the *Prophet Daniel*, who seems to snap his fingers in accompaniment to a frenetic dance). He imagines others for reasons of contrast, who seem to be pleased with their harmonious gestures or offer themselves in the clarity of their limbs to the admiring eye of the artist. All the figures, however, maintain something of the original pretext. They sustain the wreaths and stretch the ribbons, holding them in a new manner—with their feet. They push strongly against the marble so that their bodies always maintain a clear and decisive effect of necessity in their actions.

We cannot leave our consideration of this part of the Sistine Vault without recalling that Michelangelo had arrived at the full possession of the anatomic language of the human body through his youthful studies. In these nudes which seem without symbolic significance, he freely developed his favorite theme, which must have been extraneous to his arrival at this creative point. This was his practice in modelling small clay or wax models which were to suggest the boldest poses and sudden movements. The latter is borne out also by the traces of a little model which was widely diffused in prints and replicas. The oldest copy (note the word "copy," not the lost original) is illustrated in Brinckmann's *Baroque Sketches*, and this we have related (as has Biagetti) to the *Nudes* in the Sistine Chapel.[7]

It is possible that Michelangelo already exercised the use of such models in wax which, when softened in hot water, can continually assume new attitudes and suggest the most diverse sculptural and painting solutions. The double art of Michelangelo, painter and sculptor, would seem to point to a similar hypothesis. The existence of the little fifteenth-century model which has so much relationship to the Sistine nudes seems to already have been used by A. Dürer in an etching dated 1516. This should be considered as a possible part of the intense study which the artist made from the anatomy of living bodies. Michelangelo probably utilized his "artificial" models to sketch the first idea of the figures' movements. After having fixed the compositional scheme, he had recourse to the living model to determine the form more precisely. This procedure seems to be documented by a pen drawing in the Casa Buonarroti in which the pose of a virile, kneeling nude is rapidly sketched. It is limited to the pelvis and the upper parts of the legs.

The vigorous and sure sketch accentuates the anatomical investigation of the bent knee. This is typical of the artist's many studies of details which were later incorporated into the execution of the definitive cartoon. It has been conjectured that, as in other cases, this drawing is also a study from an ancient work, probably from the Belvedere torso. Comparing it, however, with the famous Vatican marble, of which Michelangelo was so passionately fond, the comparison does not bear up. If, instead, we refer this energetic sketch to the little sculptured model of which we have spoken, we find a much more certain relationship.

There is a supposition that these studies were made at the time of the Sistine frescoes, and more precisely, of the *Nudes*. We feel that the breadth and synthesis of the pen strokes which Michelangelo always achieved in this medium (which he had always held so dear) does not in any way contradict it.

As for the use of the "artificial" models (of which Michelangelo, if not the inventor, was at least one of the first practitioners) the artist's contemporaries offer us interesting proofs. Vasari, for example, in the preface to his *Lives* explicitly says that Michelangelo "first, made the models of wax or clay . . . from those models which, unlike real life models stand still, he obtained the contours, lights and shadows."

Vasari must have been asked very often himself, due to the intimacy of his life with that of the artist, the reasons for the fertility of sources and inventive ideas demonstrated by Michelangelo (of whose drawings Vasari had a far better knowledge than we can possibly approach). Michelangelo was accumulating a very wide range of experience by contact with ancient art, real life models and paintings of the past.

It was difficult to ascertain the sources of Michelangelo's inspiration when he inserted these details into the whole of the work. They had by then acquired such a heroic sense and such great intensity that they were no longer recognizable.

Certain singular inventions offered by the Sistine nudes, for example, refer to rather unsuspected prototypes. The idea of the youth agitating dramatically on his pedestal in the act of shouting in the face of the wind recalls the early masters of the fifteenth century. Michelangelo had studied them and certainly remembered clearly, having drawn from them in his youth. He drew from the *Flood* of Paolo Uccello for his own Flood scene as we have seen. This contains a young nude with disorderly, wild hair splashing over his forehead in the fury of the tempest.

The very contrasting movements of these studies of young athletes in rapid pen sketches (now in the British Museum in London) almost certainly were initially inspired by a precise memory of Signorelli's figures in the Chapel of San Brizio. These figures are nervously composed among the decorative motifs. We should not be surprised at this inspiration since the famous chapel had a great impression on Michelangelo.

Plates XXXVIII to XLI

Completing our consideration of the Sistine Vault, we must discuss the remaining four large cloister vaults at the corners of the ample surface and the triangles with the Hebrew families. The triangles are conceptually and compositionally linked to the lunettes around the windows with the *Ancestors of Christ*.

We note a significant difference in style (analogous to that which we have already seen in the procedure with the rest of the painting) between the two scenes of *David and Goliath* and *Judith and Holofernes* and the other two scenes above the main altar with the *Crucifixion of Amman* and the *Brazen Serpent*. These great compartments were, in fact, executed by the artist at the same time with the Creation scenes in those sections. The difference can be best noted if we consider that they represent the two fundamental moments in Michelangelo's style—his beginning style (1508) and his concluding style (1512). David has unhorsed Goliath who has fallen to the ground as a vanquished combatant. Here, the artist has modelled the group in sometimes strident, sometimes gloomy colors against an almost cubist background of the camp tents, as if he were doing a piece of sculpture.

In the *Judith*, where Michelangelo studies an almost geometric partition of the background in three fields, the two figures of the heroine and the maid-servant are rhythmically executed in the clarity of form and color. This borders on a sharp style, very dear (though later) to Mannerism. Almost by contrast, the body of Holofernes seems to writhe on the fatal bed before every vital movement has ceased.

The two final scenes revealing a more mature articulation and experience arrived at during the course of the gigantic work are more important.

The *Crucifixion of Amman* is also framed in spaces seen in perspective. They remind us of the circular painting of Filippo Lippi with the Madonna and her deeds. Here, however, the nude Amman, the tragic protagonist, seen in a very difficult foreshortened pose, is the most surprising accomplishment by Michelangelo in his drawing of the human body. The "posa di taglio," which follows a perspective plane of risky novelty, anticipates a much later development by the artist in the nudes of the *Last Judgment* which populate the lower wall.

The concatenated, moving composition in which the images twist themselves in serpentine motions becomes complex in the *Brazen Serpent* (from which Florentine artists like Pontormo, Il Rosso, and Bronzino were to derive ideas and motifs).

The central idea of the serpents which coil around the terrified persons, gathered in tragic groups, stimulated Michelangelo's imagination. He thus drew his principal starting point from the major archeological discovery of the times in which he had participated by giving his precious advice—the *Laocoön*.

The famous group, which appeared to the eyes of the Renaissance to be a mysterious gift offered by Classicism to their renewed admiration of the antique world, was discovered in 1506. Bramante had placed it for Julius II in the Belvedere. Michelangelo studied it carefully, together with Cristoforo Romano, and recognized that the group was not sculpted out of a single block as had been traditionally believed. It was executed in various pieces whose joints were very carefully hidden.

Certainly, from this famous and anguished Hellenistic work was born the spirit which agitates the scene depicted in the *Brazen Serpent*. The figures in difficult foreshortenings and contortions develop in many details the studies which Michelangelo had taken from the classic group. It was the nature of the theme itself which brought him back with a new interest to the famous masterpiece. The battle of the nudes with the serpents causing a swelling of the muscles and the desperate effort to keep the reptiles away from their heads to avoid the mortal wound; the contrast between the snakes' coils and the variety of the victims' gestures; these are all motifs which must have aroused the most acute interest in Michelangelo. It must have also re-evoked some details of his youthful *Battle of the Centaurs*. The theme itself, however, and its development in his vast pictorial composition, stimulated him to effects of disconcerting boldness in the union of the dramatic gestures with the courageous and unusual foreshortenings. In the right section, which is the most singular and important, we see drawings "sotto in sù." These suggest, with the contracted limbs, impressions of realism only comparable to the ostentation of veristic details which we find in seventeenth-century painting. The gloomy color, barely heightened by flashing lights and strident tones, transforms the recollection of antiquity into a convulsed human knot. Here too, we note vivid anticipations of the painting style in the *Last Judgment*. We are, therefore, led to believe that Michelangelo might have referred to these two scenes which are directly above the wall on which the *Last Judgment* is painted.

Plates XLV to LVII In the eight triangles enclosed between the Sibyls and Prophets, on the lunettes on the upper part of the walls, on the windows and in the less illuminated, secondary portion in front of the surface of the vault, the artist conceived a theme which (in its archaic imprecision and its links between the Old and New Testaments) lent itself to a very free treatment of the families of the Hebrew people—the *Ancestors of Christ*. Michelangelo refers to the Gospel of Saint Matthew, and generically, to the medieval tradition. He indicates at the center of the lunettes in lapidary characters the names in the genealogy which resound in their Hebraic forms as if to suggest mysterious personages. He interprets the theme in a completely personal style which becomes vividly real.

He sees, in the families which for so many generations gave credence to the presentiment of the Messiah's coming, a humanity evoked from the past and projected into the future. This is the impending sense of fatality and expectation forecasting the destiny of a superhuman event. It is beyond the clear understanding of men, since only the Prophets and Sibyls could occasionally announce the great Event.

The human material from which Michelangelo created this disconcerting story is that of the Hebrew people in its physical and psychological characteristics. This is made touching by direct, dramatic participation of the artist in that

Fig. 12—MICHELANGELO *autograph drawing. Schematic pen sketch for a figure on the Sistine Chapel vault or for one of the Popes (Florence, Casa Buonarroti. See Exhibition of drawings by Michelangelo. Catalogue edited by P. Barocchi, page 35)*

world of sacred legend and history. He relives this in his imagination as a spectacle of contemporary experience.

Because of this, we do not feel ourselves very far from the truth when we say that the section populated by the *Ancestors of Christ* reflects, in the unforeseen curiosity on the part of the artist for life in its concrete reality, a series of sketches and notes taken from life. They may also be from the populous sixteenth-century Roman market-places where he easily found those strongly characterized types which we see in his surprising painting. There, one could catch a glimpse of those families almost slothfully grouped together on the thresholds of the houses.

Michelangelo's imagination invested them with the reflections of their nomadic fate and the imminence of their age-old destiny. He knew how to transfigure this destiny into painting of a modern and unexpected manner. This is especially true in light of what we know of Michelangelo's art which tended towards an overbearingly heroic vision. Many rapid but incisive sketches at Oxford, published by Frey, show Michelangelo's interest in studying these compositions for the pungent definitions of the poses. The poses seem to come from daily life rather than from the model. Only Leonardo has offered us similar examples, although with different intentions. In Michelangelo's sketches, he tries above all to fix the gestures of the persons. They acquire for him an immediate compositional value and conserve the immediacy of the observation at the same time. We should then consider how the artist translated these quick sketches onto the Sistine Vault (certainly filtered through more definitive drawings from the posed model). We are surprised at the extraordinary adherence of the colors and wide brush strokes to the idea of representing a world "in penombra," almost condemned to the anonymity of a life without light. This is a world in expectation of something to make the passing centuries shine, devoid of dramatic deeds and clamorous gestures.

The condition of these *Ancestors of Christ*, according to Michelangelo, is that of a humanity which passes its days in a fatal immobility; a humanity whose daily life is burdened with the dark presentiment of that which must happen. Present is the latent conviction that the final event will not occur in their times but always in a succeeding epoch.

We think that these were more or less the sentiments which Michelangelo nurtured in his spirit as he executed such an ancient theme into such a new and modern vision. If we carefully observe each of the spaces in which the families of Christ's Ancestors are depicted, we can deduce that the artist wanted to conclude his enormous task on the Sistine Vault (where the prophetic thoughts are exalted and the Creation story is heroically unfolded) with a more intimate and free evocation of reality. From this grows a bitter condition of destiny, out of which this melancholy world emerges from the artist's spirit. It is timeless but derived from the surrounding reality.

The compositions, dictated by the limited space in the eight triangular compartments, are grouped in pyramids. These are dominated by a principal figure sometimes isolated on the smallish surfaces. They are painted in low tones, molded in broad chiaroscuro sections, with some slight hints of more vivid harmony which are immediately extinguished in the shadow of the background. There are women sitting on the ground, dressed in simple, peasant-like garments, intently gazing into space as if seeking to pry into the future. Behind them semi-nude children seem to try to distract their mothers from their obsessive thoughts. When the men appear, they are old and tired, bent over the poor goods scattered on the ground, or dominated themselves by an accepted but unknown destiny. From these groups, beautiful realistic motifs spring forth. Sweet and melancholy female figures with wide open eyes are seen from the front.

Plates XLV to XLVIII

The more ample lunettes contain two groups of persons which are almost always set apart. They are separated from the tables where, against a clear background, we distinctly read the names of the genealogy in rhythmic succession. It is almost a commentary on the images: Eleazar-Mathan; Achim-Eliud; Aminadab; Ezekiel-Manasses; Amonn; Asa-Jehoshaphat-Joram and Jacob-Joseph.

78

The mysterious feeling which arises from reading the Hebrew names reinforces the image. From the sound of the ancient words, it is projected into a distant time. The gestures of these figures and their unadorned clothes, often indicative of the popular sixteenth-century world, keeps them (certainly in accordance with the artist's will) in a state of limbo. They are suspended in a legendary atmosphere, since even their most spontaneous movements taken from life acquire a mysterious, grave, sometimes ritualistic significance.

In the lunette of Achim and Eliud, a young mother has prepared something in a bowl for her son and seems to get ready for an ancient sacrifice. In the lunette of Aminadab, only two figures fill the space, a young man who stares ahead with his arms hanging between his knees and a woman who combs her hair. She makes a sweet, melancholy and true gesture, crossing her legs and almost beating time to a song with the beautiful bare foot suspended in space. We feel like participating in her action with a movement of spontaneous assent.

In another lunette, the artist has also painted only two figures. The woman is reflected in profile in the shadow and the man is seated before a simple desk. He has stretched out his leg and placed it on a small base. He seems to be riveted to a fixed thought which he finds in the pages which are before him. Here, the background wall reflects his enlarged shadow so that we find ourselves before a surprising painting of modern intentions, almost luministic.

Groups of mothers with children at their bosoms occur frequently. Some of the women contemplate their sleeping children while others seem to protect them from unknown threats. One woman reclining her head on the swaddled child closes it in an embrace. Bent to one side, she seems to be singing a lullaby. This is an exceptional image for its penetration of feeling. It echoes the Madonna sculpted by Michelangelo in his youthful period and the marble Bargello "tondos" in London.

The lunette with Asa, Jehoshaphat and Joram opposes two contrasting figures. To the left is a strange, thin, male figure, almost a caricature, who bends over in the act of writing, balancing his folio on one knee. To the right is a woman who is almost suffocated by three children who besiege her. She breast-feeds one and gathers up the other two in her great arm. This is an image of Charity in a very new aspect. Inspired from life and animated by such maternal warmth, she makes the symbolic idea seem almost useless and cold in comparison with the great and generous inspiration of the painter.

Wherever our gaze travels in the shadows of these lunettes, we discover singular and unsuspected realistic moments in Michelangelo's art. No figure is more interesting, however, than that seated figure which appears in profile to the right of the space ascribed to Roboam Abias, almost broken with unforeseen grief. In order to paint her, the artist, fascinated by the pose (which culminates in the right arm abandoned as if it were a dead thing, hanging from the inert shoulder), must have executed various studies of which the Oxford paper contains two rapidly sketched examples in ink. They are very indicative of the accent on which Michelangelo wished to insist—the lifeless arm, suspended in space.

In his careful, although necessarily synthetic evocation of these lunettes depicting the *Ancestors of Christ*, De Campos says that the figure doubled over with grief, which seems so new and important, is singled out as a "derelict" with an athletic body and depressed like a dead thing.

Because of the abandoned hair (which hides the head) and the long robes, it is, in our opinion, a female figure. Accepting equally the psychological interpretation, we can easily refer, by way of analogy, to the female derelict of Sandro Botticelli. We recall the mysterious figure in the Florentine master's famous little painting which was executed in his late period when he was dominated by the thoughts and examples of Savonarola.

The influence of Botticelli on Michelangelo's art was not only episodic. Besides the above reference, it would not be difficult to invoke other examples in which Michelangelo shows acute comprehension of those aspects of Botticelli's painting in which his dramatic energy, very often hushed but always present, is most vividly demonstrated.

On October 31, 1512, as we have said, the entire work was unveiled and immediately attracted a multitude of young artists from everywhere. They continued to draw from the composition for a long time. This had occurred for the Brancacci Chapel at the Carmine di Firenze and for the cartoons destined for the Hall of the Great Council in the Palazzo Vecchio. This moment, in which the vastest and most profound pictorial work ever dreamed of was offered to the eyes of the world, was fundamental to the history of Renaissance painting. In these years, in consequence of Leonardo's new painting and Raphael's affirmations in the Vatican rooms, the "grand manner" was launched. After this, which includes, in the spirit of the early sixteenth century, a more ample and plastic vision of reality, a more conscious conception of reality occurred. Nurtured by deepened experiences of classical art and culture, it was also re-invigorated by a more human perception of reality.

The total effort with which Michelangelo faced the huge task after his initial hesitation was such that he worked with incredible intensity in a dramatic solitude, dissatisfied with any collaboration or help. Benedetto Varchi, in his funeral oration, recalled that "in the painting, not only did he do all the priming and [see to] all the other preparations and necessary tools, but he also ground the colors by himself, not trusting it to workers or apprentices." The fresco technique, which the artist treated rather timidly at the beginning, immediately acquired a new breadth and force by dint of the experience which the artist gained by painting.

According to the common taste of the times, the Sistine Vault, which is in reality the greatest revelation of that age, lacked in its coloring that final preciousness which was usually superimposed at the end to lend more gracefulness to a work. From Condivi's words (which so often reflect Michelangelo's thoughts) it would seem that the artist himself wanted to refinish the vast painting with additions of blue and gold, elements of which certain artists like Pinturicchio had made immoderate use. The biographer says: "It is true that I heard him say that it was not finished as he would have liked." He had been prevented by the haste of the Pope who, according to the biographer, constrained the artist with his impatience to demolish the scaffold before All Saints' Day. Condivi adds, "It lacked retouching with dry ultramarine blue and gold in some places so that it would appear richer."

The reason for the latter did not pertain to painting, in the strict sense, as much as to decoration. We like to think that the artist, who was so disinterested in such tinsel, took the opportunity to add nothing and leave the work in its severe majesty. This would adhere to the Biblical theme and also intimately reflect his proud spirit.

A detail noted by Condivi refers to the exceptional conditions in which the artist had executed the work and confirms (if it were necessary) Michelangelo's furious attachment to his masterpiece. We are speaking of a section of the *Life* which, according to popular conception, has been considered as one of those anecdotes which Vasari loved to include in his book. When mentioned by the affectionate friend whom Michelangelo had called upon to write a more truthful biography, it assumes all the characteristics of a story told by the artist himself.

"Having finished this work," writes Condivi, "Michelangelo, having painted for such a long time with his eyes continually raised towards the vault, saw very little when he looked downwards. When he, therefore, had to read a letter or other small things, he found it necessary to hold the material above his head with his arm. Nevertheless, little by little he began to read again looking downwards."

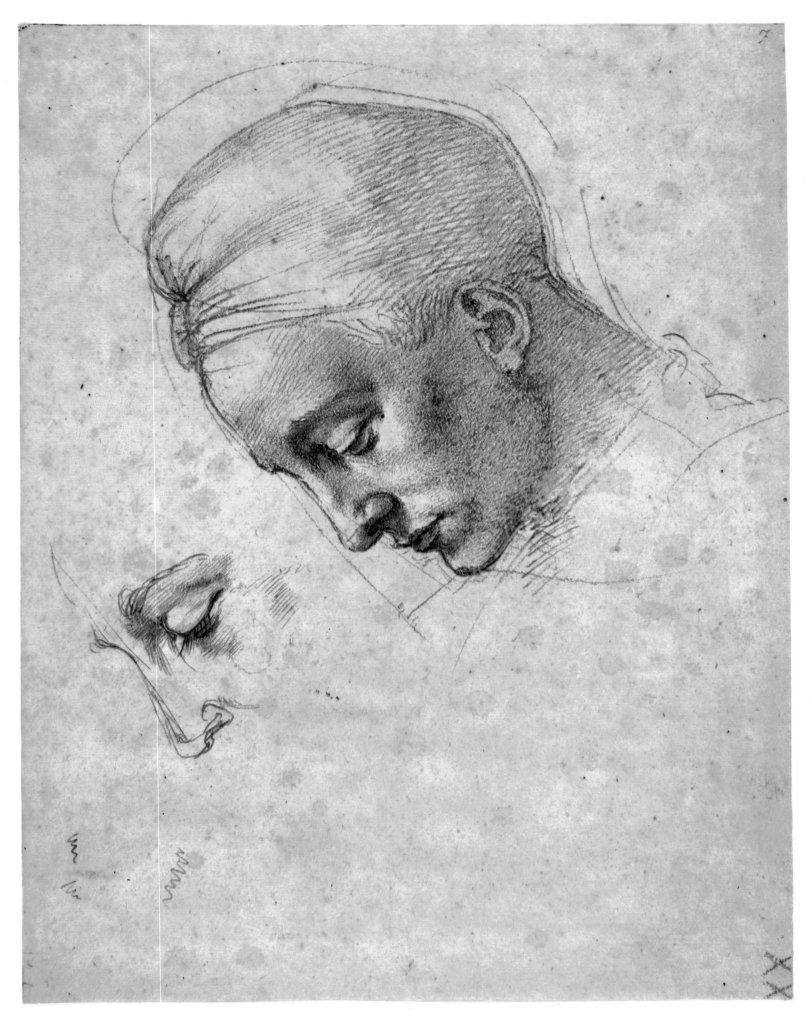

*Fig. 13—*MICHELANGELO *autograph drawing. Study of a head in red pencil. To the left, the detail of the eye and nose. It is one of the most accurate and sensitive drawings by the artist in which the geometric proportions of the face are also indicated (Florence, Casa Buonarroti)*

The result of an exceptional combination of creative inspiration and physical effort, the Sistine Vault represented that historic necessity which is only the province of masterpieces. It determined a fundamental moment in the realization of that "plenitude temporum" which Rome of the early sixteenth century offered to the world of art and culture.

The influence of Michelangelo's work was enormous, not so much because of the judgment of those who consider it a type of new painting "text," but in its power which established a different standard from that of the fifteenth century. It gave the model for the monumentality which invests every manifestation of the art and life of the sixteenth century. The painting of the vault indicated the ideals of those times which Aretino so acutely discussed when he indicated the tapestries of Raphael (consequences of Michelangelo's new style in the Sistine Vault) as the beginnings of a new age in which the "dryness" of the fifteenth century was overcome and everything was seen and felt "in grande."

This different standard determined by Michelangelo's work was understood in various ways according to the artist who thought about its advances in composition, chiaroscuro, and color. Michelangelo's painting acted as a stimulus for a freer, more robust and more expressive conception. Among the very first to interpret Michelangelo's lesson in his own fashion was, as we have said, Raphael.

We cannot, however, unreservedly believe the following statement of Condivi: "Raphael da Urbino, although he might have wished to compete with Michelangelo, said many times that he thanked God for having been born at that time, having learned from him [Michelangelo] another manner of painting than that which he learned from his father who was also a painter [Raphael's father] and from Perugino, his maestro." We cannot completely insist upon the validity of the affirmations which Michelangelo himself confirmed and which were taken down by the same biographer: the relationship between the two artists (certainly anything but friendly) was purposely changed by the supporters of one or the other into an incurable rivalry. We have numerous proofs of this rivalry even after Raphael's death. According to Condivi, Michelangelo was magnanimous towards his presumed rival because "he always universally praised everyone, even Raphael da Urbino, even though a competition in painting existed between them as I have written. I only heard him say that Raphael did not have this art by nature, but by long studies." It is an opinion which, although attributed to Michelangelo in whom art was a natural instinct (overbearing, exclusive, so strong as to occupy the entire genius of the artist and, therefore, opposed to the classical contemplative development of Raphael's pictorial creations), should not be taken literally. This is also true for the episode narrated by the biographer and accepted by some of the modern critics: it says that, after the unveiling of the first half of the Sistine Vault, Raphael sought to execute the second half, using Bramante's influence to convince the Pope.

It is true that Bramante often tried to keep Michelangelo from Julius' favor (especially to keep Michelangelo from commenting on his precipitous demolition of the old Saint Peter's). Michelangelo alludes to this fact in a letter to Monsignor Vigerio in 1542 in which he says, "All of the discords which existed between Pope Julius and myself were due to the jealousy of Bramante and Raphael da Urbino. This was the reason that his sepulchre was not executed in his lifetime, to my ruin." He adds, ironically, ". . . and Raphael had good cause, because everything that he knew about art he learned from me."

This is a peremptory and argumentative assertion brought forth from the embittered spirit of the artist because of the unfortunate affair of Julius' tomb. We should not hide the real reason for Michelangelo's insensibility to Raphael's painting beyond their personal argument, or beyond the fact of Michelangelo's own nature, which rests in his profound conviction that painting is best when it approaches sculpture. He must have, therefore, considered Raphael to be a real painter in those places where, assuming a new breadth and fullness of form and a vaster compositional impetus, he participated in the new, sculptural sixteenth-century style. This occurred when Raphael demonstrated his fascination with Michelangelo's vigorous art. It was only natural that Michelangelo considered Raphael's mature style to be little less than a plagiarism of his own art.

In the work on the Vatican rooms, closely parallel to the task of painting the Sistine Vault, we can grasp the limits of Michelangelo's influence on Raphael. It is interesting to reflect on the contemporaneity, in the same ambience, of two fresco cycles of such exceptional importance, especially when we think of the enormous broadening of horizons which these works represent in the history of painting. As we have already said, Raphael had already become aware in Florence of the potential value which he could derive from the study of Michelangelo's works (as he had also found in relation to Leonardo) not only of painting, but also of sculpture. Michelangelo's colors probably did not interest him, being so extraneous to his own chromatic taste; Michelangelo's draftsmanship, however (especially in the study of the nude and the new compositional "inventions"), quickly started an amplification of form and a broadening of his own painting world towards sculptural and monumental solutions.

In the *Deposition*, the references to that portion of Michelangelo's work with which he had become familiar in Florence are very evident and well known. From the period in which he began to work on the Vatican rooms with the frescoes of the *Segnatura* (1508–1511) until the composition of the *School of Athens*, the reflections of Michelangelo's art had already been absorbed into the complex of his Florentine experiences. We cannot, however, trace Michelangelo's influence as a determining factor. Raphael composes the *Dispute* in a special sense. It is in partial adherence to the great fifteenth-century models. In the *School of Athens* it joins with an ingenious absorption of Bramante's monumental ideas and his new compositional articulation. At a certain point, his new contact with Michelangelo's art and precisely the Sistine Vault enters into play. His contact with the great painting by Michelangelo is so singularly expressed that it cannot be passed over in silence. Raphael's great painting, together with Leonardo's *Last Supper* and Michelangelo's Sistine Vault, is one of the highest achievements of the Humanist Renaissance. The pensive, isolated figure of the philosopher Heraclitus, seated in the foreground and leaning on a square marble block in the act of momentarily suspending a piece of writing, certainly is an impersonation of Michelangelo as Raphael could have seen him in those days. This invocation of Michelangelo was not foreseen in the Brera cartoon and was, therefore, a later addition. It must have been done by Raphael when the painting was already complete, almost certainly after 14 August 1511. This is the date on which the first half of the Sistine Vault was unveiled. Raphael could have been among the first to contemplate the new vigor revealed in Michelangelo's work.

Although the ideal portrait of Michelangelo (which strives to present him in his typical, sullen solitude) depicts a different mood, it does have some analogy with the *Prophet Isaiah* on the chapel vault—one of the prophets that Michelangelo completed before 1511.

Raphael's allusion to Michelangelo, while it completes the various portrait characterizations of other artists (Bramante, Leonardo and his own self-portrait near Sodoma) in the *School of Athens*, also indicates a clear stylistic "homage." The figure is already painted in Michelangelo's new sculptured manner, in the deep chiaroscuro and the more balanced and full proportions which Raphael saw in the gigantic images in the Sistine Chapel and purposely wished to reproduce in his fresco.

The effect of the Sistine painting on Raphael's art is henceforth visible not only in the following frescoes in the Vatican rooms, but also in his own *Prophet Isaiah* in the church of Saint Augustine. This was almost certainly executed after the unveiling of the first half of the Vault (because it can be dated from 1511–1512). His intention of emulating

Michelangelo is overcome by a sweet and pathetic interpretation of the pride of Buonarroti's prophets, by the atmospheric version of the chiaroscuro (which, losing its adherence to the form, is diffused around the figure) and above all, by the tonality of the colors which in Raphael makes the shadows light and velvety and penetrates into the flesh. This is even more visible in the *Child with Garland* in the Academy of San Luca. Its moist eyes and limbs are saturated with vital color (a fragment which is, in our opinion, completely original to Raphael). It is also present in the *Sibyls* of S. Maria della Pace, in which the influence of Michelangelo is resolved in rhythmic fluidity and compositional breadth.

Raphael's classical spirit reacted to Michelangelo's art as to a fully conscious experience; an enrichment of his expressive means in a sense completely opposed to Michelangelo's. It is inserted as an immediately balanced but necessary element in the context of his miraculous polyphony. The solemn Arazzi cycle (from cartoons by Raphael) destined for the Sistine Chapel is the highest result of the encounter between Michelangelo's artistic world and that of Raphael (the two poles between which oscillates such a great part of the painting of the times).

This famous series of compositions does not only mark a fundamental episode in the history of tapestries, but is, above all, the realization of the new, monumental sixteenth-century vision. It is the fruit of penetration and alert absorption of Michelangelo's heroic style by Raphael, all the more since the tapestries, which were designed to enrich the ornamentation of the Sistine Chapel in solemn functions, were completed a few years after the unveiling of Michelangelo's vault. The tapestries take the evidently more tranquil reflections which are seen in Raphael's calm and almost Olympian conception. They were to animate the lower part of the walls with their ample figurations, where the painted draperies seem to have foreseen their function.

Notwithstanding the recognizable and documented collaborations, these sumptuous and noble tapestries demonstrate (as we can better see in the original cartoons in London) a breadth of plan, a classical seriousness of gesture and a grandiose simplicity of modelling. This furnishes clearer evidence of the new spirit which Michelangelo's masterpiece had instilled into painting, calling forth "classic" interpretations of his dynamic world and reaching towards the celebration of Man beyond the limits of the fifteenth-century standard.

We may also add another great painter to the group of those who, instead of falling victim to Michelangelo's overpowering vision, knew how to draw out a more spacious form in the development of their own art: Antonio Allegri, called Correggio. Although there are various opinions as to the probability of his journey to Rome, we must give credence to Roberto Longhi's persuasive deductions of a direct experience with the Sistine Vault in 1519. It does not seem possible that he could have arrived at such a broadening of horizons as he demonstrates in the domes of San Giovanni Evangelista and Parma Cathedral with only the influences of Mantegna and Leonardo.

His situation in relation to Michelangelo is analogous, though different, to that of Raphael. He too, without the "direct" vision of Michelangelo's work (especially in the art of the fresco), would not have stamped such fullness and grandiosity on his own compositions. Of a nature completely alien to the heroic one, Correggio was careful, in a modern sense of exquisite sensuality, to the point where he bore the law to seventeenth- and eighteenth-century painters through his canvases of the *Loves of Jupiter*. He was passionate and vibrant, always intolerant of the monumental thesis. Correggio, however, absorbed from Michelangelo the aspirations to the sublime, that impetus which ennobles the human image, that turgid fullness of the nudes (which he immediately resolves into suggestive, smoky apparitions in counterlight) without which he could not have overcome the sculptural relief of the fifteenth century.

On Correggio's reflections of his Roman "experience" the Sistine Vault certainly had a fundamental influence. One can find the total immersion of his painting world into a chiaroscuro which models the forms, emphasizes the foreshorten-

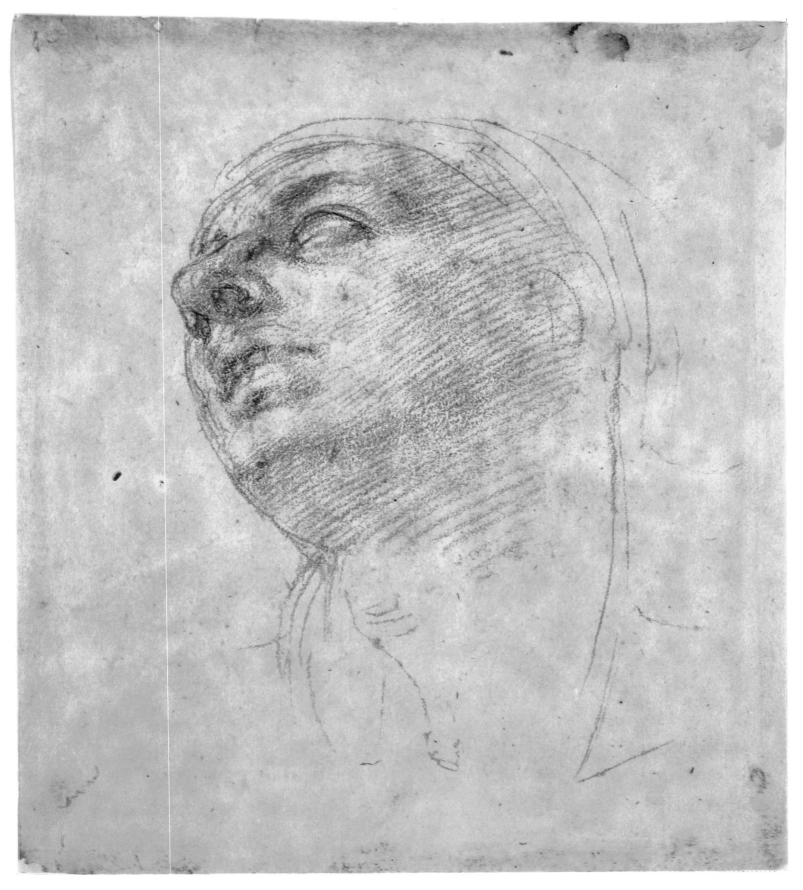

Fig. 14—MICHELANGELO *autograph drawing. Study in red for the foreshortening of a head turned to the right. Refers to the "Doni Madonna" or the "Prophet Jonah" in the Sistine Chapel. It is more probable that the first hypothesis is correct, even if, as has been often noted, the study is drawn from a male model (Florence, Casa Buonarroti. See Exhibition of drawings by Michelangelo. Catalogue edited by P. Barocchi, Florence, Holschki, 1962, page 7, illustration V)*

ings and tends to expand in space, but conserves its mysterious poetic fascination. This does not seem the place to document the other numerous and often determining circumstances in which the vision of Michelangelo's masterpiece produced efficacious consequences in single artists who were fascinated by it. It is enough to say that in the development of the problems in painting, there exists an "ante" and a "post" Sistine Chapel period. This always occurs to those works or deeds which, for their implicit value, assume decisive importance in the history of the human spirit.

(1) An essential bibliography of the Sistine Chapel is to be found in D. REDIG DE CAMPOS: *Itinerario pittorico dei Musei Vaticani*, Rome 1954, page 274.

(2) Pertaining to Julius II's tomb, one may find particular information in "Michelangelo" in the *Enciclopedia Universale dell'Arte* of Charles de Tolnay (1962).

(3) *Lettere di Michelangelo Buonarroti* with preface by G. PAPINI. Lanciano 1913, pages 121, 123.

(4) *Lettere di Michelangelo Buonarroti:* op. cit., page 37.

(5) CHARLES DE TOLNAY, op. cit. F. HARTT: *Lignum Vitae*, etc. in "The Art Bulletin," vol. XXXII, 1950, numbers 2–3.

(6) MICHELANGELO BUONARROTI. *Rime*, by ENZO NOÈ GIRARDI, Bari 1960. Page 4, 158, 159. For the *Rime* of Michelangelo, this critical edition supplants the preceding ones in its accuracy of information as well as in its philological interpretations.

(7) V. MARIANI: *Anatomia,* in "Michelangelo Buonarroti," on the 400th anniversary of the *Last Judgment* (1541–1941). Florence 1942, page 133. Also, D. REDIG DE CAMPOS—B. BIAGETTI: *Il Giudizio Universale di Michelangelo*, edited by Pontificia Accademia Romana di Archeologia, Rome 1944, vol. I, page 89; vol. II, plate CXXIV, 3, 4.

CHAPTER FOUR

THE *LAST JUDGMENT*

THE PERIOD which follows the unveiling of the Sistine Vault was characterized for Michelangelo by an intense return to sculptural activity. He turned towards the task which he always considered his highest: the tomb of Julius II. Because of adverse circumstances, however, it slowly became the nightmare which kept him chained. It became complicated through infinite material difficulties until he was put into a bad light before the Pope's heirs. In the meantime, other vicissitudes occurred. His hope of executing the S. Lorenzo facade was brusquely extinguished in 1520. In the same year, however, the artist was immersed in the work on the new Sacristy of S. Lorenzo and the Medici Tombs. This synthesis of architecture and sculpture determined, in the development of Michelangelo's mind, a strong plastic accent and, because of his meditation on the funereal theme, a deepening of his own thoughts in relation to Neoplatonic ideas.

He was completely taken by the concept of overcoming earthly life and arriving at the "Glory" which spiritualizes thought and action, forever fixing their value in the eternity of Fame. This we glean from the notes which he made next to his architectural studies for the work.

At the same time, he occasionally returned to the sculptures for the tomb of Julius II and the *Captives* of the Florence Academy which were left partly sketched. The power of the sculptured masses and the contrasting poses which illustrate the drama of slavery present us with an anticipation of that world of defeated giants who populate the *Last Judgment*.

The *Moses*, instead, can be linked to the *Prophets* of the Sistine Chapel for the rigor of its placement and its proud expressiveness (it had probably been conceived in the first plan for the monument and was abandoned and taken up again later). It is not so very different in its central idea from that which makes the painting on the vault so vital; the affirmation of a superior majesty, animated by a contrast of feelings which is absorbed into a vigorous formal synthesis.

The *Moses* (the prophet who is lacking in the Sistine group because his story is told in the fifteenth-century frescoes) can be considered akin to the severe figures which the artist painted as living links between the Divine truth and Humanity. This famous sculpture seems to be the translation into marble of that which Michelangelo painted on the Sistine Vault, just as the painted prophets may appear to be a pictorial evocation of the marble masterpiece. So intimately do ideas and stylistic values interconnect in his art, which in both fields interprets a single profound vision, that these interpretations seem most probable.

In the absence of documentation on Michelangelo's painting activity, and the presence of architectural and sculptural ideas and projects, we must deduce that, after the sovereign task of the Sistine Vault, he abandoned colors and brushes for a long time. We cannot, however, say the same of his drawings in those years. They often seem to assume their own character, not only as studies for works to be executed, but in their own autonomy. They are sometimes characterized by increased technical concern with the chiaroscuro of the bodies, of almost modelling the images and lifting them off the page with accurate effects of subtle relationships between shadows and light. These "finished" drawings are naturally accompanied by those more spontaneous and vigorous examples where the human body triumphs in its sculptural clarity.

There is a group of these drawings with the Resurrection of Christ as its theme, which the artist develops in various solutions. They are important because in a few of them, it is possible to perceive motifs which Michelangelo used in the left section of the *Last Judgment* fresco, where the resurrected are depicted.

There is a strongly sculptured, dynamic version in which the ancient sense of struggle, innate in Michelangelo's spirit, is transferred into the vigor with which Christ, having scaled the sepulchre, seems to take flight towards the heavens (as shown in a drawing in the Royal Library of Windsor and another of great dramatic force in the Louvre Museum). There is also another solution in which Christ's body, already soaring in flight, rises vertically from the sepulchre like an ancient, victorious hero. The artist oscillates between these two versions. The latter version is seen in three drawings in the British Museum.

In one of these, perhaps the last, and executed in pencil with extremely delicate chiaroscuro, Christ is depicted already risen in the sky with His arms in the cross position almost as if He were swimming in space. He is still partly covered with the shroud which accompanies His ascent. Another group of drawings is based on mythological themes. These are primarily, love motifs, almost all of which seem to have been executed for Tommaso de' Cavalieri. Among these are the *Archers* in the Royal Library of Windsor, elastic nudes, modelled as if for a bas-relief, the *Prometheus* chained to the rock (a sculptural nude which recalls Alexandrine sculptured art), and the three drawings for the *Fall of Phaëthon,* in the British Museum of London, at Windsor, and in the Venice Academy.

In these last drawings (which were widely diffused in the sixteenth century through copies and engravings), the scene is executed in a pyramidal scheme subdivided into three groups of figures: Jupiter with his thunderbolts, punishing Phaëthon, is above; the chariot overturned in the sky with the four horses which fall with Phaëthon is in the center; and below, we see the *Danaïdes* in despair.

The intellectual character of the subjects is also reflected in the quality of the rather statuesque drawing with the figures blocked in space. Their importance, however, emerges from the fact that, although they are motivated by themes dear to Humanism, by dint of their analogous dramatic situations and their compositional schemes they join the studies for the *Last Judgment* fresco where the theme of punishment is equally present, although transferred into a religious conception.

The times were ripe with disasters (the most serious being the Sack of Rome in May, 1527), and one might really feel the actuality of a reference to the *Last Judgment*, almost as a warning to those who had dared to break the age-old veneration for the See of the Vicar of Christ. It is logical, therefore, that the Pope, who had impotently had to watch the invasion of the city and the destruction caused by the sack from Castel Sant' Angelo, had in mind the execution of a theme which might remind the faithful of the extreme punishment reserved for reprobates on the day of Judgment.

Condivi's words, although they are rather vague, confirm that this theme originated with Clement VII and was later adopted by Michelangelo. Speaking of the artist's return to Rome, he says, "The Pope sought to occupy him with something else and to have him paint the face of the Sistine Chapel. Since he was of good judgment [the Pope], having meditated much on these things he finally resolved to have Michelangelo do the day of the Eternal Judgment. The Pope thought that the variety and scope of the material should provide this artist with the opportunity to exercise his powers to their limits." This passage seems to indicate that it was Clement VII's intention to engage Michelangelo again in the Sistine Chapel. It is uncertain, however, whether the Pope had immediately decided on the *Last Judgment* as the theme. This uncertainty is borne out in the words, "having meditated much on these things, he finally resolved . . . ."

From this passage and from a letter of the Venetian ambassador of February 20, 1534, which says that the Pope "has done so much that he has arranged for Michelangelo to paint in the Chapel, and above the main altar he will do a Resurrection," several critics have deduced that the Pope's original idea was to have the artist paint a Resurrection of Christ above the main altar (for which there would be drawings on the same theme, to which we have alluded). Others have interpreted the word "Resurrection" as referring to the "Resurrection of the Dead," in other words, the *Last Judgment*.

It is important to keep in mind that Clement VII finally ordered the artist to execute this grandiose theme. Michelangelo translated it, however, into the tempestuous fresco only after the insistence of Paul III. The date of these early talks with Clement VII and, in consequence, of the artist's first studies for the new task may be fixed the return of the Pope from his journey to France, December 10, 1533.

Michelangelo, as much as he could gladly accept this fundamental task which would keep him away from Florence (by now dominated by Alessandro de' Medici who certainly did not look favorably upon him), considered the new work as a serious impediment to the labor on Julius II's tomb because he had been engaged for so long with such difficulty on the latter project. We can, therefore, imagine that Michelangelo, notwithstanding the fact that the first temporary scaffolds were already being prepared in the Sistine Chapel, went very slowly about drawing not only the preparatory sketches but also the cartoons of greater proportions. As Condivi relates, with the air of one who has gleaned his information from personal contact, "Michelangelo, who was aware of his obligation to the Duke of Urbino, fled from this thing whenever he could, but since he could not free himself of it, he drew the affair out. He pretended to occupy himself with it, as he did in part in the cartoon. He was, however, secretly working on the statues which were to go in the sepulchre."

In the meantime Clement VII died on September 24, 1534. Paul III Farnese was elected to the Papal chair on October 13, 1534. This man had wanted for many years to utilize Michelangelo for some great work. The artist, who had hoped to free himself from the task, instead found it confirmed with greater peremptoriness by the new Pope who made himself intermediary to break the long, complicated question of Julius II's tomb. He thus facilitated its conclusion, which is still to be seen in S. Pietro in Vincoli.

At that time, Michelangelo could give no reason to insist upon abandoning the *Last Judgment* painting. The Pope and several members of his retinue visited the artist personally and wished to see the cartoon prepared for Clement VII. It would seem that the Pope also wanted the artist to paint the entrance wall to the Chapel on the inner facade with the *Fall of the Rebellious Angels* (a theme already suggested by Clement VII and probably allusive to the recent serious events which the Church had experienced). It seemed, however, a better idea to limit him to the large *Last Judgment* scene which was to have immediately caught the eyes of the observers for its greatness and "terribleness" all the way from the entrance. We should keep in mind this original idea. Michelangelo's gigantic composition, as it was actuated, possibly incorporates into the peremptoriness of the *Judgment* some reflection of the punishment of the Angels, combining the two great affirmations of the Supreme Justice in a unified and dramatic figuration.[1]

When Paul III went to visit Michelangelo in order to see what the artist had prepared for the preceding Pope, it is possible that he did not see anything but a cartoon of reduced dimensions. This was the result of detailed studies which were necessary to judge the whole of the future fresco from the point of view of content and adaptability for the wall of the main altar. On this matter, the records and the biographers have nothing precise to say. They do speak, in either case, of this cartoon which certainly must have been complete and in proportions such that it could be enlarged afterwards.

The vast wall on which the artist was to paint the *Judgment* was 17 meters high and offered a surface of about 200 square meters to be filled by a single pictorial composition. It was not, however, entirely free. In Sixtus IV's time, the paintings of the lateral walls were also developed on the wall of the main altar and arrived with the same division up to the lower edge of the vault. There were still, according to the architecture of the harmonious and vast ambience, two mullioned windows with two lights apiece. Above these, as he had done for the other walls, Michelangelo had painted two other lunettes belonging to the series of the *Ancestors of Christ*.

These paintings can be ideally reconstructed on the basis of old drawings which indicate the state of the Chapel before Michelangelo painted his *Judgment*. They are especially clear in a Windsor sheet where, drawn with a pen and spotted in chiaroscuro, the figures which compose Michelangelo's lunettes are sketched (under the vault with the two final scenes and, at the center, the *Prophet Jonah*). They are divided in analogous manner to the others. The lunettes to the left contained two seated figures, one of which was reading from a vertically placed book. Symmetrically situated, the other figure is that of a bearded old man, seated, behind which another image appears. The lunette to the right, also filled with four symmetrical figures, contained a sleeping youth and to the front a female figure, seated at a diagonal in a prayerful attitude.

This is only a generic copy but it is valuable anyway. It gives us an idea of what the artist had painted as well as what he was prepared to destroy in order to have his new work occupy the entire wall.[2] There were, however, on the lower portion, from the fifteenth century, four figures from the Papal series which completed those of the lateral walls. There were also two frescoes by Perugino, the *Discovery of Moses* and the *Nativity* which began the two symmetrical series of paintings dedicated to Moses and Christ—and the altarpiece of the *Assumption of the Virgin*.

All this was completely destroyed and the altarpiece removed. It was necessary, according to the artist's definitive plan, to completely fill the entire wall until the edge of the vault in order to avoid a strident contrast with painting of such different style. This was also necessary in order to create a unified, gigantic figuration which might evoke a single, powerful feeling of sacred awe.

Named by the Pope as architect, sculptor and painter of the "sacri palazzi," Michelangelo was even more linked to Paul III. The Pope showed himself to be as proud of having such an artist with him as he was impatient to see the quick realization of the *Last Judgment*. He wished to leave a mark of his strong, admonishing will also in the field of art.

The artist, by now sixty years old, was weighed down by so much work and thrown back upon his closed world of thoughts which were tending more towards profound religious conviction. It seemed that the days of Julius II had returned; the years which had been rich in glory but also in unexpected clouds which suddenly gathered on the horizons of his imagination and weighed upon his great heart. His years and his complex inner maturity notwithstanding, Michelangelo faced his new task with all the fruits of his experience and sought to take up his painting activities again under better technical conditions. These conditions would allow him the maximum certainty of resistance to time in filling such a large space, without the possibility of unforeseen deteriorations of plaster or color (as had partially occurred at the beginning of his experience with the painting of the vault).

Michelangelo, notwithstanding romantic versions of his personality, always had an artistic temperament so innate to his craftsmanlike and technical activity that he must be considered as kin to the great Tuscans of the early fifteenth century (Brunelleschi, for example). We need only think of his continual insistence on working directly with the material,

Fig. 15—MICHELANGELO *autograph drawing. Very important black pencil sketch referring to the first fundamental idea of the "Last Judgment" in the Sistine Chapel. Can be dated between 1533 and 1534. The extremely quick and impetuous drawing constitutes one of the rarest pieces of evidence of the immediacy of the master's compositional vision (Florence, Casa Buonarroti. See Exhibition of drawings by Michelangelo. Catalogue edited by P. Barocchi, Florence, Holschki, 1962, page 41, Illustration XXVI)*

of varying the quality of the marble and the colors, of his preoccupation as architect of San Pietro with the quality of the lime and earth. He reacted violently to any attempt at compromise which might injure the success of a work for which he had assumed full responsibility. This is not in conflict with his artistic ideal and the spirituality which he attained in his masterpieces. His great spirit proposed such a lofty goal, being stimulated by such an incapability of being satisfied, that everything contributed to augment his creative possibilities to the maximum. He gained from the continuous deepening of his artistic experience in relation to the technical difficulties he had to overcome, and the liberation from these difficulties which slowed up his poetic affirmation. No other artist has possibly felt with as great purity, in his daily life, the value of the Greek term "poiein," from which "poetry" derives, meaning "to make."

Michelangelo's concept that it is the work which qualifies the artist must have become proverbial. Even Bernini, in conversation at the court of Louis XIV ("le Roi Soleil"), referred to the fact that Michelangelo, when spoken to of the qualities of an extolled artist, would say, "What has he done?" This type of statement remained alive in the artistic circles of Rome almost as if it were a proverb.[3] We find it necessary to recall all this in order to more clearly focus on the care with which Michelangelo turned to the *Last Judgment*. This is also necessary in relation to his long but essential technical preparation.

He was able to have all the extant paintings on the wall, including his own two lunettes, removed by chisel. It was a necessary operation which he clearly showed by according the same treatment to his own work as he did to the work of the fifteenth-century painters, in their fatal destiny of being succeeded by new requirements. Michelangelo considered the vastness of the wall in relation to the visibility of the painting which was to have covered it. He considered with great acumen that such a large perfectly vertical surface would eventually become covered with dust and, therefore, darkened. He decided to have a lining executed on the by now chiselled wall, no longer vertically, but inclining downwards in such a manner as to serve both the exigencies of natural visibility (which would avoid the optical deformations of foreshortening) and conservation.

As far as this last worry goes, it was resolved after the completion of the painting by the institution of a new office, the "mundatur picturarum Capellarum Palatii Apostolici." This office was given to Francesco Amadori d'Urbino, that "Servant from Urbino" who was so dear to Michelangelo. He kept him at his side for a long time, engaged in the most diverse tasks, including helping on the preparation of colors and the "spolveri" (pounce) destined to transfer the drawings of the cartoons to the walls. He aided Michelangelo in the final execution of those decorative portions of which he received the life-size drawings.

At this stage of the work, the new wall was prepared and the wooden scaffold was raised in order that the artist might paint that wall, finally placing him in front of the surface on which he had to work and no longer under it, as during the execution of the vault. Michelangelo, having prepared the cartoons during 1535, began his work in the spring of 1536.

At this point, an episode occurred which was important to the development of this work. The episode relates to his rapport with the Venetian painter Sebastiano del Piombo, who, after having worked at the Farnesina for Agostino Chigi, next to Baldassare Peruzzi and Raphael, became one of the most noted personages in sixteenth-century circles. His beautiful portraits of monumental proportions were imbued with that warm, mysterious Venetian color that he had absorbed from Giorgione, and of which he was the first and most efficacious exponent in the art which he practiced in Rome in Raphael's and Michelangelo's footsteps. Sebastiano del Piombo vividly exchanged painting research with Raphael through which the latter brilliantly absorbed the Venetian color used to create that absolute masterpiece, the *Mass of Bolsena*. The former profited by Raphael's classicism and intensified his sense of grandiose calm and monumentality, which he had revealed consistently beginning with his Venetian works.

Sebastiano del Piombo became a competitor of that great artist at the time of Raphael's *Transfiguration*. He became linked to Michelangelo in friendship and was drawn into the arguments which raged over the priority of one or the other. The two geniuses shone in their own light in Rome during the first half of the century.

At the time of the *Last Judgment*, Sebastiano del Piombo, who had influence with the Pope, insistently expressed his opinion that the great painting should be done in oils on the wall, making use of an adequate preparation of the plaster. This opinion was a cause of hesitancy on Michelangelo's part. This hesitancy delayed his plunging into the work. Vasari shows himself to be the most informed of all his contemporaries on the matter. He recounts the episode as authentic. This seems possible when we consider that the art of fresco was especially employed by the Tuscan artists while the Venetians preferred the technique of oil painting. It would not, therefore, seem improbable that in his suggestion to his "friend" Michelangelo, Sebastiano del Piombo (who already had the privilege of availing himself of Michelangelo's drawings for his works) wanted to associate himself in the task as a collaborator. He probably wanted to execute the painted section, given his superior knowledge of oil technique.

The proposition seems to have been confirmed by a particular. Based on positive documentation, the scaffoldings were already completed in January of 1536. The plaster, already finished, was destroyed and substituted with another, evidently of a different mixture. According to Vasari, waiting for Michelangelo to begin work, "He remained thus . . . without putting his hand to the work, while the facade was being prepared in Father Sebastiano's style. When he was urged to take action, he [Michelangelo] finally said that he did not want to do it except as a fresco, and that oil painting was a woman's art and a rich man's art (and for lazy people like Father Sebastiano). Dashing to the ground the encrustment done at the friar's order, and having had everything prepared in order to be able to work in fresco, Michelangelo put his hand to the task."

We may wish to attribute a good part of this story to Vasari's polemic spirit and to his oft-displayed veneration for a Michelangelo who contained his impetuousness and fire badly. We can give credence to the assertion that Sebastiano del Piombo's interference was ended by Michelangelo in a decisive manner. He was fully aware that he would have to assume this second gigantic task of painting alone.

The return to painting the work in fresco, according to the old, glorious Italian technique, leaves us a moving documentation of Michelangelo's working days on the great opus. Fresco (or, as it was called, "buon fresco") renders to the utmost only if executed on a plaster which is still humid (no longer than one day old). Reconstructing the single plaster sections prepared each time, we can follow Michelangelo's daily progress. Sometimes this means complete figures modelled in color with extreme vigor and sureness of brush stroke, or sometimes a single head on which the artist worked with particular care or perhaps an arm or a shoulder with which he had been dissatisfied and the design of which he changed as he painted. These are all elements of a creative labor which, the more it indicates complex technical vicissitudes, the deeper it appears.[4]

The actual beginning of the work can be fixed in May of 1536 when a notable quantity of ultramarine color was ordered through a certain Messer Cesare, a merchant who had arrived from Venice. The work continued with some interruptions and in some periods with great alacrity, until October 1541. When it was unveiled, it left its first audience amazed and almost dismayed at the audacity of the conception and the "terribleness" which Michelangelo's art demonstrated. The Pope, ever since the beginning of the work, urged the artist to hurry and often came in person to check on his progress as is documented on February 4, 1537.

The composition of the *Last Judgment* (as we are led to believe when we look at the very beautiful drawing in the Casa Buonarroti; fig. 15) sprang impetuously from Michelangelo's imagination. It had at the beginning, however, some variations which we can only imagine and which must remain as likely hypotheses. We may consider the drawing as a sketch of the whole, a first idea, a thought destined to constitute a point of departure for the general placement. We can thus explain the rectangular space at the bottom center, subtracted from the painting (because it was destined to the conservation of the altar with the relative and existing "pala," in the absence of some allusion to the upper section in the lunettes' place). We must, however, suppose that the artist had not originally thought of destroying his own compositions, done during the work on the vault. This probably occurred immediately afterwards when the space for the painting of the *Judgment* was extended. It then included those two sections of the wall which, however, always conserved a certain autonomy in respect to the rest of the work. The singular form was anything but inviting to a unified treatment with a central focus on which everything else depended (the figure of Christ the Judge). Michelangelo preferred to cover the entire wall with his painting although he accentuated the spatial difference between the two extreme groups with the symbols of the Passion. The rest of the scene unfolds tempestuously and asymmetrically, almost upset

Plate LVIII by the whirlwind-like movement of the groups of figures.

The study for the *Judgment* composition, like that of the Vault, has provoked complex interpretations. They go from the form to the content, to Michelangelo's spiritual and intellectual movements. They have more or less acutely delved into the consciousness beyond art of the inner world and the culture of the artist. These things were often considered in parallel relation to those events which occurred in the years that were so important and decisive in the life of the Roman Church and of Catholicism.

The idea of having a *Last Judgment* painted on the wall of the altar in the Sistine Chapel aroused a vivid interest in the cultured men of the epoch. There is a clamorous bit of evidence to support this statement in the famous letter which Pietro Aretino, from his "throne" as moderator of the passions of his times (which adulation and his cunning diplomatic spirit had won him), addressed to Michelangelo on September 15, 1537. The artist must have already been rather far along with his work because the Pope had been able to observe the work since February of that year.[5]

It was customary in the Renaissance for men of learning, poets, and, naturally, theologians, to give counsel to artists (a concept inherited from the Middle Ages and transferred to the field of Humanistic studies). They sometimes even prepared "outlines" for the artists to help them in the execution of their compositions. These outlines were very often allegorical or at least allusive with didactic content. They corresponded to the idea that art should contain an "edifying lesson" or be the figuration of an intellectual content expressed in images.

Michelangelo himself, as a boy, had accepted Poliziano's advice for the *Battle of the Centaurs* and Raphael followed a plan which was firmly fixed, probably by Julius II, in the preparation of the "Stanza della Segnatura." We should not be surprised, therefore, to find Aretino in the capacity of conceiver of a pictorial composition. He was a man who was sought out by princes and artists for the drawing up of important letters which required an aulic form in the courtly style. Writing and publishing letters was for him one of the most genial of activities from which it is sometimes possible to ascertain the best qualities of his nature.

The letter to Michelangelo, although crammed with limitless praise ("And I must look upon you with reverence, since the world has many Kings but only one Michelangelo"), contains an extremely complicated, manneristic subject, developed with exasperating minuteness. The artist was to have executed it in painting. It is a theme which might have pleased a Beccafumi, a Salviati, or some Nordic engraver of a Mannerist type. Its allegories and subtleties came from a decadent sixteenth-century culture. It could certainly have no appeal for Michelangelo, however, whose spirit and deep imagination were made of sterner stuff.

Pietro Aretino wrote his literary composition as if Michelangelo would have executed his theme under dictation and in several phrases substitutes himself for the artist, imagining that he sees his inflated invention painted on the Sistine Chapel wall. Not being able to go to Rome, he consoles himself with what he believes he sees as if it were already realized. This is a rhetorical attitude, but rather typical of the writer.

Michelangelo's reply is of impressive strength and hardly veiled with an aristocratic tone, although he was well aware of with whom he was dealing. The letter is dated November 20, 1537, and begins with great homage to "Magnifico Messer Pietro, my Lord and Brother" but immediately declares that "having [already] completed a large portion of the history" he cannot, much to his regret, put Aretino's "imagination" into the work, which "is such that if the Day of Judgment had occurred, and you had seen it in person, your words could not represent it better." As for Aretino's regret that he could not come to Rome, Michelangelo advises him not to change his decision in order to see what the artist was doing because it would be too much to ask ("pur troppo").

In his reply, Michelangelo also allowed a dangerous invitation to escape to Aretino. He asked him which of his works was most favored and said he would offer it to him "wholeheartedly." Aretino did not need to be coaxed. He wrote other letters asking, at first politely, then almost as if it were due to him, for at least one of those drawings which Michelangelo habitually destroyed. The artist did not reply. Aretino's campaign against the *Last Judgment* under the guise of morality and respect for religion was most likely caused (in addition to the vexation of not having seen the artist accept his "invention") by the manner in which Michelangelo treated him. Michelangelo not only failed to send him any drawings in homage, but did not even answer his letters.

All this may seem extraneous to the vicissitudes of art. It did, however, cause notable repercussions in Michelangelo's work and in the significance that it assumed in Michelangelo's inner life.

In the meantime, on the scaffolding erected in front of the wall of the *Last Judgment*, the artist proceeded with the painting. He had begun with the two extreme groups of Angels which bear the symbols of Christ's Passion. In December 1540, the demolition of a section of the scaffolding is recorded. Later, when the artist had already completed three-fourths of the work, Vasari says that the Pope again wished to observe the progress of the work. He climbed onto the scaffolding where Biagio de' Martinelli da Cesena, the ceremonialist of the Vatican court, had also managed to slip in (perhaps stealthily). The latter criticized the artist's work so sharply that Michelangelo painted him into the same fresco with the figure of Minos (the infernal judge) near the fifteenth-century door of entrance open on the wall.

The anecdote is certainly authentic, in the midst of the controversy surrounding the *Last Judgment*, and aroused a furor in the Vatican court. The final phase of the painting was briefly but dramatically interrupted by an accident. Michelangelo fell from the scaffolding and seriously injured his leg. According to Vasari, "Because of his pain and anger, he did not wish treatment from anyone."

Luckily for him, a doctor friend of his, Baccio Rontini, ran to his aid. He overcame the obstinacy of the artist, who had locked himself up in his home, cured him and stayed by his side until he had recovered and returned to the Sistine Chapel. A few months later, the great painting was finished.

On October 31, 1541, the Pope, having returned from Bologna, had the fresco unveiled and personally (as we know from the records) celebrated the solemn Vespers. The official inauguration, however, in which an extremely large public was allowed to participate, occurred on Christmas Day. This was after the necessary removal of the material required for the scaffolding had been effected.

The first praises, even if they were sincere, expressed in the magniloquent sixteenth-century form by friends like Niccolo Martelli, were answered as if Michelangelo were speaking from a great distance after the enormous task which he had sustained: "I see that you imagine me to be what God grant I should be. I am a poor man of little worth that I wish to slave on in that art which God has given me to lengthen my life to the utmost."

When he conceived his *Last Judgment*, Michelangelo, just as he destroyed the existing painting on the wall where he was to execute his composition, seemed also to ignore the chapel's decoration. He barely alluded to it with a few echoes of details from the vault which he had painted. These allusions can, however, be considered as personal developments of embryonic ideas in his preceding compositions (especially the *Brazen Serpent* and the *Crucifixion of Amman*). His conception is of the single vast scene, brusque and peremptory, which is inserted into the complex of the pre-existing paintings and in the character of the ambience he seems to demonstrate a spontaneous and, perhaps, desired independence, as if the Sistine Chapel contained only one painting, the *Last Judgment*.

He was certainly pushed to such an exigency by the value which he attributed to the theme itself. It was not executed, as was customary in the Middle Ages (and in only rare examples in the Renaissance), on the inner part of the wall of the entrance to the edifice. It was executed directly on the wall at the end, above the altar, and thus becomes the immediate visual object for the person who enters the chapel.

It forces them to enter into the reality of the tempestuous and dramatic representation in order that their thoughts and conscience should be strongly impressed and shaken by the spectacle. The prime reason for the manner in which the artist treated such an austere and hieratic theme which he had culled from ancient tradition was to rivet the attention of the faithful.

During the preceding centuries, the *Last Judgment* scene had maintained its iconography almost without variants: Christ, the Judge at the center, surrounded by the Apostles on thrones as if in solemn review with the Elect and the Reprobates on opposite sides. The first group is accompanied by Angels, and the others are seized by demons and condemned to the Inferno. There were also clearly visible Passion symbols as evidence of Christ's sufferings for Humanity.

Michelangelo already had an example of his theme before his eyes in Rome, at S. Cecilia in Trastevere. This is a masterpiece of the highest dignity, already animated by a great inspired art which interpreted the feelings but which was respectful of the admonishing nature of the subject. We refer to Pietro Cavallini's *Last Judgment* which the great Roman painter did around 1293. From this Giotto drew his inspiration for that monumental scene on the same theme which he did in the Chapel of the Arena, in Padua.

Michelangelo could have also seen numerous other Tuscan versions, in Florence (the work of Orcagna, for instance) and Pisa (the Camposanto's frescoes). The Renaissance painters could have offered models of a more modern interpretation—Beato Angelico and the Luca Signorelli in the Chapel of San Brizio in Orvieto Cathedral, a work which Michelangelo always bore in mind. That which profoundly differentiates Michelangelo's work from its predecessors is the character of the upsetting and revolutionary vision of the *Judgment*. It sprang from his spirit, in which many different religious and moral ideals had matured during the tumult of passions which stirred around the Church in those years. Michelangelo did not wish to offer his gigantic image only to the contemplation of the faithful. He sought to ignite a more direct and profound spiritual participation in whoever contemplated the work and was profoundly affected by it. The fresco indeed appears to be a scene in which we participate. Having rejected the idea to frame the composition or link it with the architecture, Michelangelo imagined the tumultuous action as if it were suspended in the ambience of the Sistine Chapel. It is molded in an indefinable space, supporting its powerful masses by its own motion and spatial definition.

The artist did not refer to the tradition of representing the *Judgment* with the solemn celestial tribunal in the austere majesty of its contemplative calm. He re-evoked his constant motif of the struggle and contrast and made it the fundamental element of his gigantic composition. The hierarchies are destroyed and separated in sections and distinct spaces. The dark sky on which threateningly heavy clouds are suspended is populated by an indistinct crowd which rises from the ground and draws near to Christ the Judge, or precipitates, struggling fiercely, towards the livid marsh and the thresholds of the Inferno.

In this dramatic and swarming vision, the artist has purposely rendered difficult the task of distinguishing the Elect, the Saints and the Blessed, from the Damned and the Demons. He wished to convey the same sense of anguish and doubt which is only felt in very great earthly cataclysms of which, at first, we cannot measure the seriousness.

Many sources of inspiration have been attributed to Michelangelo (almost all of which are partly acceptable). We have the words of the Gospel of Saint Matthew pronounced by Christ, who was almost at the tragic conclusion of His earthly mission. They seem to come close to the central idea of the artist's composition.

The almost absolute nudity of the figures, the confused agitation of the groups herded together in a last hope of salvation, the lack of clear distinction between the various personages (who all seem to be on the same level in the moment of the final Judgment) confirm the idea that Michelangelo drew a new expressive liberty from these austere words. The Christ at the center is not to be recognized by the splendor of His vestments or other attributes. He is recognized only because He is placed on the clouds of Heaven with power and great glory.

The composition of the left section of the fresco shows the bodies rising with difficulty from the ground in various stages of decay although without the least hint of macabre intent which was, as the reader will recall, foreign to Michelangelo's taste. The artist must certainly have had in mind Ezekiel's incisive words which refer with such power to the *Resurrection of the Dead*.

The Prophet, who visualizes an immense field strewn with bones, hears the voice of the Lord who commands him: "Again he said to me, . . . O ye dry bones, hear the word of the Lord. Thus saith the Lord God unto these bones; Behold, I will cause breath to enter into you, and ye shall live: . . . So I prophesied as I was commanded: and as I prophesied there was a noise, and behold a shaking, and the bones came together, bone to his bone. And when I beheld, lo, the sinews and the flesh came up upon them, and the skin covered them above: but there was no breath in them. . . . and the breath came into them and they lived, and stood up upon their feet, an exceeding great army."

And again, with greater emphasis, the Prophet refers to the Lord's final words: ". . . I will open your graves, and cause you to come up out of your graves . . . ."

Here again, as with every motif which stimulated his imagination, the artist unites the various episodes into a synthetic vision which had taken hold both of the medieval mentality, and for reasons of realism, of Signorelli's. He animates the gloomy episode with a very different expressive force. The gestures follow no longer with tragic analytic clarity as in the Holy Scriptures, but in relation to the progressive consciousness of each of the reborn. They lose the squalid aspect of abandoned lifeless things, first seized by a sense of levitation extraneous to their own knowledge, then drawn upwards, conscious of salvation.

For this section of the *Reborn* Michelangelo referred to the drawings (1532–1533) which he had done for the *Resurrection;* in these he anticipated the theme of the reconquering of vital energy and the more or less decisive separation from the earth. The sculptural problem and the essential feeling are analogous—only the greater impetus given to the study of the Christ figure (the only Protagonist in the mystery of the Resurrection) is expressed in a distinct elaboration of the various succeeding moments, thus creating episodes of great expressivity.

In order to depict the tragedy of the great moment, Michelangelo imprints an almost fatal movement on the Humanity which swarms around Christ's figure. From the opaque, squalid earth rise the dead who slowly but surely acquire rapidity of movement. The groups of *Reprobates* precipitate in waves, falling like crumbling blocks. At the center of this ascending and descending movement, the Saints and Blessed who surround Christ seem to move in ever widening circles under the groups of Angels above who bear the Symbols of the Passion. They fill the space which has become insufficient because of the thickening of the agitated crowd.

The sculptured impression (suggested by the vivid relief which makes the gigantic nudes stand out of the wall) makes us think of a type of colossal high-relief, also because of the gloomy tonality which the painting has assumed with the passing of time. Taking into account the diverse proportions of the figures, we become aware that the artist also wanted us to imagine a space with depth. This was destined to determine the impression that the wall is completely abolished and that behind, in a timeless scenario, something irreparable and terrible is occurring. Here too, Michelangelo echoes, from the sculptural standpoint, one of his youthful ideas.

The artist, who had sculptured in relief the *Battle of the Centaurs* as an adolescent (in which the sense of the battle already overcame the literary stimulus, in an affirmation of overpowering energy, dominated by the grand gesture of the hero at the center), referred to the same dynamic motif when he conceived his *Last Judgment*. He articulated it in the painting in a more complex manner. This was stimulated by an analogous set of feelings, relived in his ignited imagination.

From the conception of the youthful relief springs the tremendous moment of accusation of Humanity. Christ the Judge is configured like the young hero of the relief. The battle between Good and Evil is executed in a tenacious scheme of interlacing bodies and violent reactions, like the battle among the sculptured figures. This entire world in tumult (which is broadened from the initial motifs of the battle and contrast until it acquires the fearful vastness of a superhuman event) contains elements and ideas which recall classicism.

The *Battle of the Centaurs* was a reflection of the scheme of the *Battles of Alexander* from Greek sculpture. In the *Judgment*, the ancient idea of Destiny and the Nemeses imprint on the tragic composition an archaic expressive value which renews, in an austerely Christian sense, the peremptory decision of the ineluctable Fates.

Among the various sources of inspiration which stimulated the artist in the conception of the "terribleness" which characterizes his fresco, we must recall a religious hymn which he was certainly fond of. It is born in the intense fervor of Franciscanism and reflects its most dramatic aspect: the "Dies Irae."

Many critics have indicated this as the stimulus to Michelangelo's imagination. This upsetting evocation of the *Last Judgment* numbers De Campos among its exegetes. He penetratingly demonstrates the relation between the sacred hymn and Michelangelo's fresco.[6]

The artist's painting contains a pictorial transfiguration of the most efficacious sections and the most influential images of the "Dies Irae." The same admonitory nightmare which is so effectively invoked in the religious text seems to hover over the fresco. We can also say that he relived in his imagination the great and austere evocative force of the "Dies Irae" (such a lofty interpretation of the medieval spirit). The artist was induced to impart to his work a character which, notwithstanding its new, disconcerting aspects, can be easily compared to the dramatic intensity of Cimabue. This colossal fresco seems shaken by a dolorous and passionate fatality. This results in the archaism of the gloomy color which Michelangelo adopted for this tragedy of Humanity (not only because of the length of time in which he had not painted, but also because he had an express purpose), the light flashing in the stormy sky, furrowed by livid lights, the lively gestures, the entreaties and, above all, the forcefulness of the irrevocable judgment.

In order to suggest the central axis around which the *Judgment* nudes seem to revolve, Michelangelo placed the figure of Christ directly below the corbel of the vault. This figure seems to contain in itself the sculptured energy of Plate LXV a Greek divinity and the profound humanity of the Christian God.

The severe image of the Supreme Judge was closely studied by the artist who concentrated all his gifts on it and, above all, a profound inspiration of feeling. It would seem that he wanted to portray (in that figure which seems almost chiselled in marble and raised from the luminous mass that surrounds it) the highest expression of his faith in a heroic form, animated by intense spirituality. We immediately think of the statue of *Moses* which was to have been done for Julius II's tomb. Here, the heat of anger seems to agitate Christ's limbs. He too arises from His throne of clouds raising His arm which is swollen with muscles and painted with infinite care as He lifts His hand in the fatal gesture. It is almost rounded off as if it were carved in marble. There is also a dynamic contrast between the lower parts of the body and the stupendous thorax, worthy of an ancient sculptor. The other arm and the brusque movement of the face are very much alike in both the *Moses* and the fresco. They both demonstrate feelings of proud rebuke, wounded justice and of implacable condemnation.

In order to increase the expressive power of the gesture on which the entire composition depends, Michelangelo reveals his intention by a technical device. In the shadowy section from which the profile so decisively stands out against the background of light, the powerful arm bears the traces of repentance. This consists in an increase of the sculptured mass of the muscles along the entire lower edge of the arm. Although already monumental, they seemed to Michelangelo too small in relation to the distance from the bottom and above all, to the essential function of the gesture of Christ the Judge, projected against the halo of light.

This is one of the most eloquent details of the artist's style in the *Last Judgment*. His is a style of absolute anatomic verity in the nudes and in the expressive value of their movements. It is a style which freely creates disproportions and dis-compensations made necessary by the expressionistic energy which interprets the passionate fullness of the feeling. Only a few years passed before Michelangelo seemingly re-evoked the fatal gesture which he assigned to Christ the Judge, in one of his most beautiful and profound poems (in which he renounces art in order to turn to God). This is an admirable translation of pictorially imaginative images into poetry.

He implores:

> Let not Thy holy eyes be just to see
> My evil past, Thy chastened ears to hear
> And stretch the arm of judgment to my crime. . . .

At Christ's feet, Saint Lawrence and Saint Bartholomew ride the clouds and herald the advent of the Savior. The Angels who sound the trumpets and show the books of the good and evil works to the astonished Humanity appear lower on the wall almost as if on a rock suspended in space.

"Liber scriptus proferetur

in quo totem continetur

unde mundus indicetur."

The Book of Merits is small but the Book of Faults is large and heavy. Further down on the wall, at the center
Plate LIX above the altar, projecting from the brown earth and molded in the mud, the artist has painted the entrance to a dark grotto. We indistinctly see Demons and the Damned, among which we find a rapidly and clearly sketched beastlike snout of impressive modernity almost scraped against the dark background. Michelangelo probably knew that, during the sacred functions, a canopy would be raised there. He, therefore, did not paint anything but these infernal hints from which, with a fine effect of luministic novelty, the chilling clarity of the endless livid marsh is distinguished. They are in a synthetic determination of space which is almost phosphorescent, as if in analogy with an impending storm over a countryside and the metallic light which would shine over the horizon.

This mysterious cave at the center divides the space into two zones. To the left, the *Reborn* arise with difficulty and from them we become aware of the most vivid references to Signorelli's *Resurrection of the Flesh*. To the right, Charon brings his black boat to shore (a clearly Dantesque reference) and strikes the wretched flock of *Reprobates* with his oar for being too slow in moving ashore. The contrasting relationship between the two parts, the Resurrection and the definitive Fall, is evident. The group of Angels who sound the trumpets represents a spontaneous reference to the motif in the foreground of the *Battle of Cascina*. This is not the only echo of that work to which the artist had given so much of himself in his first affirmation of the human nude as an expressive language in painting. The attitudes of many of the *Reborn* and the Angels who help the Elect climb to the clouds from below are closely analogous to those of the combatants who scramble up the river bank helped by their companions in the cartoon painted for the Palazzo Vecchio. To the right, the episode with the winged demon which carries its human prey on its shoulders is a new version of Signorelli's theme from the scene of the *Reprobates* in Orvieto Cathedral. It is transfigured by a novel anatomical realism and the strong, truthful energy of the great wings of the rapacious bird.

Thus, in the ignited fantasy of the artist, literary, religious and figurative references are fused from fifteenth-century works, from his own works and from classical and Renaissance statuary. All this occurs in the constant and profound study from life and in the impetus of a unified personal conception of jealous autonomy. This is translated into an individually sculptured expression, independent and vigorously polemic.

The nature of Michelangelo's inspiration is evidenced in singular fashion by that wonderful drawing for the *Last Judgment* in the folio in the Casa Buonarroti which we have already examined (fig. 15). It is sketched with feverish rapidity in order to fix the theme in summary but essential outlines, just as the idea was turning in the artist's imagination.

This drawing, which can only be compared to certain of Leonardo's sketches, also demonstrates with exceptional firmness the determination of those strong points from which the entire composition is unchained. The study of this rare document brings us back to the mysterious world of artistic creation in which the idea arises from the imaginative and confusedly deep impulse. It is, however, rich with a clarifying force which is only determined as it takes form.

The central motif is that of Christ's gesture. The Savior is depicted as a gigantic figure, almost a mythical hero. The gesture of punishment for the *Reprobates* presents itself immediately to Michelangelo's mind.

In the drawing (different from the painting which still exhibits a fundamentally pessimistic conception of the *Judgment*) the Virgin, kneeling before the Son, throws open Her arms to implore clemency for the Reborn. The Elect, meanwhile, crowd around the Supreme Judge as if saved from a shipwreck. The center lacks the definition of the groups of trumpet-carrying Angels, barely hinted at and flying across the sky. Instead, it contains the battle between the Angels (here too wingless, like "athletes" of the Faith) and the *Reprobates* who rebel at their sentence and try to climb to Paradise. They are sculpturally defined as a necessary and determinant element.

This reluctance to submit to their condemnation constitutes a strong motif of contrast. In the preparatory sketch, it is emphasized as being of "intentional" value. We would say that at this point in Michelangelo's imagination, the struggle assumed the character of a gigantomachy. At the center, on barely hinted steps which confine the space of the altar, the Angels proudly fight against the *Reprobates*. They are like true champions of Christ as they repel the invaders who try to scale this ideal fortress (just as in the *Altar of Pergamum*, the giants attempt to climb to the summit towards the sacrificial altar). It is possible that the artist might have thought that, having to respect the space for the main altar, he could produce a singular effect with the mass of nudes who climb up around the altar itself. We can observe that in that place had been Perugino's *Assumption of the Virgin* which Michelangelo at first had not thought of removing. In the general vision, however, and in its vertical movement and the crudity of its contrasts, there is an echo of the drawings which the artist had conceived for Tommaso de' Cavalieri with Jupiter who strikes down Phaëthon with lightning. In the sketch of the *Judgment*, we find not only the essential elements of those compositions but, above all, the concepts which motivated the dramatic expression. The principal concept is that of the pride of Man, punished by the Divinity.

Just as Jupiter makes Phaëthon's chariot precipitate, Christ punishes the *Reprobates*, abating their proud boasts with the great condemnatory gesture. The gesture is, therefore, a manifestation of the same thought which formed itself in the artist's imagination. This is true even if in the drawings of Phaëthon's fall the subject is mythical, and the *Judgment* more directly animates the tragic Christian image.

In the group of mythological drawings, the idea of punishment comes from an allegory which is complex in a different way and not yet "liberated" by a translation into a religious meaning. The constant feeling is that of an aspiration towards that which cannot be reached. It is a tension that inevitably clashes with the fatal condemnation. We therefore have the frequent analogies with slavery from which Man struggles in vain to liberate himself.

This entire world which Michelangelo reveals in this period is a dangerous literary atmosphere which seems to wind about his spirit and freeze his imagination. This confusion of concepts may be better expressed in poetry. This is resolved in the elaboration of the *Last Judgment* in the passage from vague heathenish aspirations to the dramatic religious conception. Even the most distant allegorical resonances are fused in a "memento homo" of choral power.

From the confrontation of the original idea for the fresco and its realization, we acquire a more profound awareness of its development in relation to the evolution of Michelangelo's thought. The variation which is most interesting for the understanding of the fundamental moment in Michelangelo's religiosity is the different function assumed by the figure of the Mother before the Son in the grand and terrible moment of the Judgment.

In the drawing, the kneeling Virgin is placed to the side of the Christ with His vigorous gesture. She is studied in the nude like the other figures in order to better establish Her movement. She is, however, destined to wear clothes as we note from evident hints of a careful examination of the details. The gesture with which She opens Her arms and turns imploringly to Her Son is full of moving ardor. Placed in relation to the crowd of the Reborn who try to gather together behind Her, it assumes the value of a warm intercession on behalf of Humanity which, reborn and already risen to the level of the clouds, awaits the final words of Christ the Judge with trepidation.

In the fresco, the situation is completely different. The Virgin is no longer the living path between the waiting of Humanity and the invoked clemency of the Supreme Judge. She is gathered in the shadow of the terrible, threatening gesture of Christ. She is almost frightened Herself at the anger of Her Son. Completely wrapped in the robes which emphasize the vitality contained within, She seems to bury Her visage in the folds of the mantle by crossing Her arms

Plate LXV

105

near Her face. This increases the expression of profound pity revealed by the closed lips and the large, lowered eyes that gaze with infinite compassion on the tumultuous ascension of the Reborn. It seems that even the gesture of turning the head from the opposite side to that of the *Reprobates* has a nuance of instinctive restraint, almost of horror at the spectacle of the guilt with which Humanity is soiled. From the intentional change in this important detail, we can better grasp the vastness and complexity of concepts, ideas, and feelings which revolved in the artist's spirit during the execution of his gigantic painting.

Many critics have occupied themselves, often with penetrating research, with the reconstruction of what must have been the artist's spiritual situation in this period. This has been done also in relation to the ideas that animated the profound revision of Christian thought in the years which preceded the Council of Trent.

We can construct a clear and authentic idea of the deep religious crisis which matured in Michelangelo's spirit and its influence on his art, from reading his poetry dedicated to Vittoria Colonna. This idea can be followed in the study of the *Dialogues* of Francisco de Hollanda and the writings of the other prelates and intellectuals who frequented the philosophical and religious gatherings of the "Marchesana" di Pescara. The artist has a singular importance in the history of the Christian spirituality of the Renaissance. He knew how to concretize, in his sculptures and paintings, his inner struggle, resolving it in formal aspects and creative inspirations of great dramatic power. He did all this, however, as an artist and not a theoretician. If we are to understand his spiritual world which determined the climate in which his creations were produced, it is as such that we must consider him.

If Michelangelo renounced the depiction of the Virgin interceding on Humanity's behalf with Christ, it is due to the fact that he wished to invest the Savior, in His terrible and solitary energy, with maximum significance. This significance in relation to the composition depends totally on the fatal gesture of that arm raised in the heavens, a gigantic symbol of strength. In order to obtain this end, and to reassume an expression of absolute firmness in the figure of the *Son of Man*, whose severe face is only slightly marked with bitter melancholy, the artist renounced his original intention of the intervention of the Virgin's *Pietà*. He placed Her next to Christ as a necessary and fundamental element. She is, however, certainly in the shadow in relation to the peremptory presence of the Supreme Judge. All this, even if resolved into a sculptural necessity, is in evident relation to that complex of ideas and thoughts which revolved in the artist's mind and spirit. There is an infinity of other episodes which demonstrate the complete adherence between feeling and form in Michelangelo's works, the *Last Judgment* included. We have the function of the Saints and Martyrs in the great crowd of the Elect pressing around Christ and turning to Him, almost calling His attention. In the various sections of the fresco emerge the anonymous figures of the *Reborn* bearing the instruments of their martyrdom. No other preceding artistic figuration of the *Judgment* had offered us a similar spectacle. Tradition had always insisted on the great majesty of the Apostles, Saints, and Martyrs, an almost ideal assembly convoked to be present at the final act of human vicissitude. They sanctify the implacable justice with their austere presence. These images of philosophers or old wise men were characterized by symbols of martyrdom or supreme dignity, signifying the victory won through the evidence rendered to Christ.

Michelangelo, however, who developed everything from his own kindled fantasy according to a personal dramatic conception, depicted the Saints and the Martyrs either nude or semi-nude standing around Christ. They are an agitated and moving crowd of giants who show the symbols of martyrdom or of sacred dignity to the Supreme Judge. It is their sign of recognition, on that awful day, of the fullness of their Faith and of that which they had suffered in life for that Faith.

It is possible to refer such an entirely new concept to the importance of good works in order to deserve eternal

glory. It is also correct to see this conviction reflected in Michelangelo's sculptural idea. It animates and motivates every- Plates LXIII and LXIV
thing, molding the material in constant ferment, linking the groups suspended in space like gigantic human clusters
and wandering masses like storm clouds, dense with images.

The space seems to resound with the heavy tramping of the Saints and Martyrs. They are legionaries gathered
around Christ towards Whom they show the symbols of the Faith just as Bertran dal Bornio says, showing his truncated
head: "Vedi s'alcuna è grande come questa" ("See if you can find one [head] as big as this").

There, the greatness of the punishment was recalled, here the greatness of acquired merits is invoked. The same
sculptural energy animates both the gesture which Dante conceived and that which Michelangelo assigned to his figures.
Saint Peter is an old man with the body of a Titan who turns towards Christ and stares at him, showing the heavy
keys, held up by his heavy, muscular wrestler's arm. Saint Bartholomew displays his skin (which is almost still dripping)
with his hand. This is his squalid trophy. He grasps the knife with which he was flayed and turns his proud face towards
the Supreme Judge. Similar episodes occur throughout the fresco wherever the composition is enlivened by figures
who are distinguished from the others because of their more definite characterization. They appeal to Christ so that
He may remember them in His pronunciation of the irrevocable sentence.

We believe that the artist wished to insert these personages among the crowd both to animate the tumult of the
nudes with elements of greater expressive efficacy, and to offer the Faithful an opportunity to eradicate the traditional
conceptions which he revised radically. It is not surprising that these images have given rise to many critical hypotheses
as to their identification. Michelangelo's work is so vast and complex in its conceptual nature and vigorously figurative
execution as to place it among the greatest creations of the Human spirit.

One group is composed of figures who are more clearly identifiable. Saint Catherine has a piece of the rack of her
martyrdom (one of the images which was completely redone at the time of the covering of the nudes). Saint Sebastian
next to her, on the right side of the fresco, is depicted as an archer who in his heroic gesture and the beauty of his limbs
seems to evoke the overcoming of the martyrdom which he suffered. Higher on the fresco is the Cyrenean whose splendid
body and gesture of sustaining the Cross vividly recall the slaves for Julius II's tomb. In the central section below the Plates LXIII, LXIV, LXVI, LXVIII, LXIX
Christ and symmetrical to Saint Bartholomew, Saint Lawrence clasps the gridiron like a soldier on the march. The
gigantic figure of Saint John the Baptist, whom many critics have (following Vasari's suggestion) interpreted to be
Adam, is more logically identified with the Harbinger. This is borne out by the characteristic hide which he wears and
by the absence of Eve, who is always depicted next to Adam in the *Last Judgment* scenes.

There is a monumental female figure, strongly modelled on the clouds to the left. She turns toward Christ the
Judge and seizes a young girl who clasps her around the waist as if in an act of protection. They form a clear statuary
entity because of the vividness of the chiaroscuro and colors which the artist employed to cleanly separate the group
from the figures which surround it.

The two figures are at the edge of a cloud strip which serves as a sculptured base. The affectionate but sudden,
almost primitive gesture of the woman whose powerful hand grasps the young girl at the waist is the gesture of one
who extends herself to save someone else who is about to fall into space. The woman's instinctive gesture, translated
with such strength and immediacy, recalls the statues of the *Niobids*. We especially think of the group with Niobe who
seeks to protect her adolescent daughter from the thunderbolts of Apollo and Diana, already well known in the Renaissance. It is, therefore, clear that here the reference to classicism is caused by a deeper reason.

It goes beyond the undoubted admiration of the artist for similar examples of ancient art. This reason is translated
into a penetrating interpretation of dramatic sentiment which is born from a new movement of the spirit. It is trans-

figured from myth into human reality, although conserving its ideal symbolic value. These two female images have been interpreted in the most diverse manners. Considering the intentional nudity of the turgid bosom of the woman who affectionately protects the young girl, and the immediacy of her gesture to which the latter responds with such devotion, the group obviously depicts a mother and daughter. We would say that the artist intended it to represent the centrality of maternity to human destiny. This is the essential life principle which is affirmed even in the supreme moment which invests the condemnation of Mankind with its value. We should not be surprised that the artist actuated the treatment of the figures in a different manner. He alternated the anonymous vigor of the nudes and the beauty of the types to the most emphasized characterization. The sculptured evidence of this concept takes concrete form in the human body. His natural idealism rooted in the admiration of ancient statuary is not separable from the intensive realistic knowledge which he gained from his life studies. In his studies, one can find an allusion to life in its determination of character in some portrait-like attitudes (rather rare, because they were so foreign to his feelings). He was, however, stimulated in that direction by concrete references to life in its actuality of sentiment.

If we, therefore, were to seek out personages of the times in his fresco (such an obvious and easy task in much Renaissance painting) we would be hard put indeed. His art, and above all, the *Last Judgment,* moves in a sphere of high tragedy where there is no individual who is not absorbed into the unity of the vaster concept of Humanity.

This is an entirely coherent attitude on the part of the artist. Thirty years before, he had already produced on the Sistine Vault the great poem of the Creation, the Fall, and the announcement of Salvation by means of personages who were characterized by their expressive power and sculptural concreteness.

Among the portrait-like hints, omitting the many problematical identifications (which include Dante, Vittoria Colonna, Julius II, Tommaso de'Cavalieri, the servant Urbino, etc.), there are at least two which have singular importance. The first refers to the Vatican ceremonialist Biagio da Cesena, whom Michelangelo punished in Dantesque fashion in the Plate LXXIII   grotesque portrait of Minos. The anecdote which explains the origin of this allusion is well documented and we should not be surprised that Michelangelo wanted to nail this critic to the wall as Minos, the Infernal Judge with the long ass's ears (like the evil judge in the *Calumny of Apelles* by Botticelli).

Such transpositions were common to Renaissance artists. We need only think of the number of contemporary personages whom Raphael painted into the frescoes of the Vatican rooms. Michelangelo, with the typically ironic attitude which so often characterized him, pushed the allusion towards the grotesque and beyond the person in effigy, since he situated him on the door of the chapel entrance. This is where the personalities of the Papal Court usually entered.

The other allusion was not documented by the artist's contemporaries but was discovered by F. La Cava in his study in 1925. It refers to the famous self-portrait of the artist in the skin of Saint Bartholomew. This is technically a dramatic and exceptionally modern portrait in its invention and significance.[7]

The artist, always consistent with his temperament which very often turned on himself with bitter irony, hides his own visage in the folds of the upheld skin of the Saint. It is broadly sketched, as if improvising on an idea which occurred Plate LXVI   to him while he was completing Saint Bartholomew's gigantic figure. The correspondence with the existing portraits of Michelangelo is evident. He adds, however, a certain air of strange desperation, availing himself of the flaccid folds Plate LXVII   of the skin to distort his face even more. His visage follows (like a tragic "veil of Veronica") the inconsistent material in which it is molded.

The exceptional self-portrait corresponds very well to the tone which the artist employed in the sonnet addressed to Giovanni da Pistoia (when he was, with difficulty, painting the Sistine Vault). This seems to be illustrated by several verses of a grotesque flavor written about his own figure, almost as if seen in a trick mirror:

> "Bloodshot eyes, pounded and crushed,
> teeth like keys on an instrument . . ."

The latter verses seem to match the portrait painted in the *Judgment* perfectly:

> "My face is frightful to behold."

Such testimony certainly sheds vivid light on the autobiographical value of his painting. Besides constituting an index to his state of mind, it can be linked to the fact that even then the artist was conscious of how hard it was to find acceptance for his singular vision of the *Last Judgment*. It was difficult to overrule the still timid but insistent voices which criticized the spirit and the entire free composition. The nude assumed the role of protagonist as a symbol of Man stripped of his hierarchical privileges—and was a sculptured image of Humanity.

It would be more exact and legitimate to argue that the detail had a clear relation to Aretino's protests against the "impiety" of the work. He clamorously expressed this in his famous letter of condemnation of Michelangelo's famous work. It is inconceivable that the artist retouched the fresco just when he had already completed the work (when the criticisms showed themselves to be more harsh and diffuse). One is led to believe that some rumor of this sentiment reached the artist's ear when he was about halfway through with the painting of the wall. It seems almost impossible that Michelangelo used Aretino's face for Saint Bartholomew. The resemblance, however, is as vivid as is the artist's face in the skin displayed by the Saint. It would be exceedingly important to be able to accept the idea that Michelangelo wished to depict, in the Saint Bartholomew, that person who was flaying the artist with his criticisms. The artist had, however, answered Aretino apropos of his complicated suggestion for the *Judgment* composition. He almost anticipated what he would paint: "If the Day of Judgment had occurred in your presence, your words could not describe it better."

This would all seem to be due to Michelangelo's profound reaction to Aretino's first letter. While seemingly elevating a monument of glory by placing him so close to Christ the Judge, Michelangelo gave him those attributes (the knife and the skinning) which he merited just as the ass's ears and the function of Infernal Judge fit Biagio da Cesena so perfectly. (Biagio da Cesena had already listened to the criticism against the artist!)

We must frankly say, however, that it is better to avoid too many hypotheses which tend to transform the painting of the Judgment into a gigantic autobiographical page. That which really mattered to the artist, even if he did resort to these and the other references to the ambience which surrounded him, was the supreme synthesis of the whole. To this point he arrived with the tenacity of a builder, placing one gigantic sculptural block on top of another although he felt that the almost superhuman effect would have suggested the collapse rather than the safety of his immense architecture.

The overhanging of the upper section of the fresco on the lower part (given also the larger proportions of the figures) clearly shifts the equilibrium of the masses, which gravitate downwards creating a painful sensation of dread. This is the same sensation we experience before his architecture when he has reversed the relationship between the upper and lower sections (with increasing clarity in his later years). He arrives at (in his drawings for the Porta Pia) the suggestion of a pressure of the sculptured elements from above, as if form were enmeshed in a fatal slavery within the incumbent material.

The idea of the left portion of the fresco with the *Reborn*, where the problem has been faced and solved with such inspiration and such imaginative force, assumes the significance of self-comparison for a sculptor like Michelangelo.

Signorelli's *Resurrection of the Flesh* in Orvieto was certainly borne in mind by Michelangelo. We can find this in a skeleton or two which rise from the ground with an astonished mien, or in some other figure which is still burdened with mortal sleep. We are, however, in an artistic world of a different scope. Signorelli glorifies the proud firmness of the bodies which reconquer life and places them on an almost marmoreal plane of perspective which still recalls Piero della Francesca. Everything is definite, modelled, robust and sustained by an energy which is born from the concept of Man as master of space.

In Michelangelo's work, instead, the bodies pass from the inertia which joins them to the earth from which they rise with difficulty, almost painfully. The ascent is carried out as a rescue in a linking between the colossal nudes. They are still heavily wrapped in torpor and falling backwards, held up by their reborn companions and by the Angels. They are like lifeless bodies in the conquest of a full, sudden new consciousness which projects them upwards. They seem
attracted by a force similar to the desire which, in Dante, stimulates Paolo and Francesca. This is certainly not, however, because of "the tender cry," but because of the Divine Will which calls them unto Him.

As a great master of modelling, Michelangelo molds the nudes (which still drag along on the earth with faces untouched by Grace) in broad strokes, drawing them in the shadow of the terrain. In the three groups which raise themselves in a pyramid, the artist knots the figures among themselves. The effect is that of drawing the colossal bodies upwards as if they were shipwrecked victims saved from the storm and pulled to shore. He then arrives at the stupendous image
Plate LXII
of the young athlete who raises up the two reborn figures who are desperately clutching a large rosary as if it were the only means of salvation.

Ideally linked, these groups all display various aspects of a single motif, that of fraternal aid in order to acquire celestial blessedness. In several of these figures, modelled on gigantic proportions, the study from life has suggested to the artist profound anatomical effects. The bodies, which are barely delivered from Death, conserve something of their inert mass. In comparison to the Angels and Reborn who sustain and lift them, these Titans' bodies, torn from the devouring energy of the earth, seem burdened with a weight which is not only material, but which is nevertheless manifested through the physical impression of the material.

In such a progressive return to consciousness, these human knots (in which the bodies raised with difficulty are still inanimate) reveal the deep meditation on a theme typical of the artist (which he expresses contemporaneously in sculpture—the *Pietà*). This is no longer a figuration of the Mother who holds the fragile and precious body of the Son on Her knee. It is (as in the *Palestrina Pietà*) the figuration of one who has the weary task of sustaining and showing to Mankind the gigantic body of Christ, the temporary but fateful prey of Death. The analogy between this sculpture (which several critics still inexplicably exclude from the catalogue of Michelangelo's works) and the groups of Reborn who begin their difficult ascent into space is extremely significant. It serves to confirm the authenticity of the marble and fixes the date of its execution contemporaneously to or immediately after the great fresco. It also helps us to understand the profound change which occurred in the artist's spirit as he faced the same theme, from the serene melancholy of youth to tormented maturity on the threshold of old age.

The immense painting, also because of its reflections on the artist's contemporaneous activity, is thus articulated in a complex and profound manner, even if dominated by a lofty power of synthesis. The episodes which reveal Michelangelo's richness of thought and feeling are infinite, and find singular correspondence in the variation of the sculptural effects, the colors and the light. Next to groups of very strong sculptural distinction (like the group to the left, dominated by the nude of the Cyrenean and developed in an upward direction by a harmonious connection of gestures) there are other groups modelled in shadow. They are no less expressive and are more intimately linked to those manifestations of sentiment which, in Michelangelo, seem to emerge with difficulty, struggling against his lonely austerity.

There are, for example, those nudes who, having reached the state of Blessedness, recognize each other and embrace like comrades in arms who meet again after the battle. In these, as in so many other figures which can only be discovered with careful study, the artist spent his energy in creating effects of broad shadow as he had done in the lunettes with the *Ancestors of Christ*. He diminishes the relief of the heroic forms in a de-emphasis of tones which often renders the colors sensible to more subtle changes than those he employed in the painting of the vault.

Certainly, from the painting point of view (in the narrow sense as a coloristic vision), the *Last Judgment* brings his idea to its maximum development, always tending towards a sculptural effect which absorbs the colors within itself. This corresponds to that which the artist wrote to his friend Benedetto Varchi in response to the "referendum" on the pre-eminence of sculpture over painting or vice-versa. Theoretically, this is not a very rigorous question, but quite significant because of the moment in which it was proposed. That moment was the final phase of Florentine painting, which reached its culmination in Michelangelo.

The letter to Varchi contains important statements from which it is clear that the artist entertained the firm conviction of the priority of sculpture. This is weakened by his intelligent consideration of the theoretical arguments which Varchi himself had developed. The artist wrote this letter several years after having finished his great work and also after having completed the frescoes in the Pauline Chapel (which are the final examples of his painting style). His recent experience, in which the sculptured effect is developed to the maximum, must also have confirmed his instinctive certainty. He says, "I say that painting seems to me best when it tends towards relief, and relief is worst when it tends toward painting. I used to hold the opinion that sculpture was the beacon of painting and that one is different from the other as is the sun from the moon." He adds, however, that his friend's arguments have convinced him and that sculpture and painting are "the same thing," so that originating from the same intelligence "they can arrive at a good peace."

He says this above all because being so alien to theoretical disquisitions and so profoundly immersed in his work, he considered such discussions little more than time wasted. He concludes thus: "Leave such disputes, because there [in these disputes] more time goes than [it takes] to execute the figures."

Here it is opportune, as we have already discussed regarding the *Nudes* of the vault, to recall his use of the models in clay or wax. This was a practice which he frequently employed and which was also widespread among the painters of the sixteenth century and later.

We make use of G. B. Armenini's *Precepts of Art*, which record with a precision due to direct information these little models for the *Last Judgment* nudes: ". . . it can also be seen, from whatever point one may consider the Judgment painted by Michelangelo, that he made use of the means I have described. There have been many who have said, in this respect, that he had made several figures of wax and twisted their limbs in his manner, wetting the joints first with hot water so that they became soft again."[8] It is important to note how (probably due to Michelangelo's example) the artist who belonged to schools of painting which were less linked to drawing made use of such wax models. Tintoretto used models which he illuminated in different manners in order to draw successive studies from them. The result of this practice is his way of drawing on paper of grey and bluish tints. He heightens the chiaroscuro with rapid strokes of white chalk which reveal the artificial illumination. It is clear that this practice of Tintoretto was passed on to El Greco, and it is a part of the "Michelangelism" expressed in various ways by the two great painters.

With the reference to the custom of utilizing artificial models, we should also make note of the intense study which

Michelangelo made of anatomy during these years. This fact is documented by numerous drawings and by an important page in Condivi in which he explicitly speaks of a treatise which the artist was compiling as a summing up of his own experiences. This compilation dated from the youthful days of his friendship with the Prior of Santo Spirito in Florence.

These studies, as the biographer clearly confirms, differed in their anatomical manner from those of Leonardo's investigations, which went beyond an artistic scope in a scientific search (a manifestation of Leonardo's insatiable thirst for knowledge). Michelangelo understood anatomy to be the possession of the secrets of the movements in his nudes, and his drawings do not go beyond an inquiry into muscular bundles, tendons and bone as the essential scaffolding of that masterpiece of Creation, the human body.

In Condivi's words, which in relation to Michelangelo's anatomical studies are especially valuable, there is a close relationship between the artist's passionate research on the structure of the human body and its function in action as an expression of feeling.

Michelangelo did not hide a certain irony which he felt towards Dürer's anatomical principles. Michelangelo's studies were animated by a reflection of the ideal which was much different from that of the German master and served as a criticism of the latter who was teaching how to execute men "upright as poles." The principal reason which stimulated Michelangelo to ceaseless investigation (really ad nauseam, as his biographers attest) of studies from the living model and from cadavers is made evident. He wished to inquire into the cause of the sculptured reliefs revealed through the epidermis by the jutting of bones and muscles, stimulated in their continuous variation of accents by the diversity of their expressive movements. Such studies by the artist were certainly developed to their maximum point during the years which immediately precede the painting of the *Judgment*. The extraordinary richness of motifs which the crowd of nudes in the *Judgment* offered constituted the ideal conclusion of his assiduous effort to master the dynamic secrets of the human body.

Such a predominant interest in the nude's expressiveness favored the artist's tendency to separate himself from traditional depictions (in the *Last Judgment*) of a theme which from medieval times had supplied artists with the occasion to flaunt the oddness of their taste (the "demoniacal"). This had been a stimulating motif from which almost every painter had profited. They imagined the devils as strange beings bristling with hair. These beastly creatures were composed from the most absurd elements. Such an attitude had been typical of Gothic taste and its inheritance, cultivated especially in the Nordic countries and perpetuated in the Renaissance. Michelangelo, as a boy, had already done his own version of the demoniacal in his copy of Schongauer's print. Now, he refutes the grotesque idea and invents his demons in a completely human form with muscular bodies and violent gestures, characterized with bestial snouts and monstrous masks. The singular typology of these devils (some of which might have been inspired by Dante's *Inferno*) reveals a decided reticence to accept deformity. He inserts an entirely personal concept into their images. There is an affinity between the damned and the devils (these latter being barely distinct) in the coloring of the flesh and the transformation of the faces which are sometimes animalesque and sometimes characterized by attributes which render their expressions more squalid and revolting than deformed. Sometimes, as in the demons which can barely be distinguished in the shadow of the central grotto, he uses gorilla faces grimacing in a manner which is made horrendous by its realism.

Michelangelo's Humanistic vision in the reality of its figuration excludes the presence of winged Angels from the world of the Blessed and conceives them as distinct from Men only by virtue of their commanding appearance. He also refrains from the insertion of the monstrous and the deformed into the gloomy Infernal atmosphere. He displays figures whose aspect pertains to the family of Man, accentuating their striking strangeness only in the lubricous, repellent masks, as if they were a degeneration of the ideal human form.

Although the limited chromatic variations were introduced in Michelangelo's work at the time of the *Judgment* as dictated by the tragedy of the theme, they were the logical consequence of the pre-eminence of the sculptural element over color. It is this which renders the grandiose scene tragically gloomy. The exceptional power of synthesis manifested by the artist to isolate groups and masses of nudes from the dramatic structure is in accordance with Michelangelo's own idea of giving particular relief to various sculptural motifs in which figures, almost isolated in their autonomy, appear. It is clear that in doing this, he was always aware of the total effect which was certainly studied at length in drawings of the whole which no longer exist.

We may observe in the apparent confusion a careful calculation of the value of these more definite images to which (in the symmetrical section of the fresco) equally monumental figures, almost chiselled in the stone, always correspond.

One of the most interesting of these (opposite the youth who saves the two Reborn with the rosary) is the Damned figure retiring into himself. It is a gigantic human block, held by ugly demons and violently dragged to the Inferno. Plate LXX This nude of a defeated combatant is seen as if wrapped in his own arms which are useless. He is seen from the front, in a gesture of closed desperation, hiding half of his face with his left hand and looking straight ahead with one eye, staring as in a mask of ancient tragedy. This is one of the figures which most impressed Romantic art.

Rodin drew upon it for his *Thinker* for the *Gate of Hell*. This personage, isolated against the background of the cloudy sky and nailed to his demoniacal base which is formed by the devils who cling to him, is worthy of the fertile imagination of Dante and is one of the figures to whom Michelangelo assigned a protagonist's role. The artist did this, not because the figure represented a person recognizable in historic reality or legend, but because it attained a symbolic value of the passions and feelings with which it was invested.

The sculptural power of this figure, as of so many others, separates it from the structure and almost makes it an image in full relief. It also seems more tragic for its suspension in space, and the artist's intention was, indeed, to imprint it with something of deeper expressivity than that which he allowed to the surrounding figures. We have already seen how Michelangelo paints around such powerful figurations (done in a strong sculptured manner). He executes other figures which are quickly sketched and almost absorbed into the mass, barely profiled against the sky or immersed in the crowd of nudes. He thus succeeds in avoiding the monotony which would have resulted from an entirely "finished" execution. This was a defect which we note in the Mannerists and in the sixteenth-century academicians who tried to imitate him.

What does this figure signify? It seems to us to be damaging to an aesthetic comprehension of Michelangelo's work to inquire into the maze of suppositions, seeking answers and meanings which are increasingly subtle. Once again we must follow the artist's expressive values on which he has placed the accent. Such an image of quiet desperation is certainly that of a late repentance which is a measure of the irreparable gravity of the sin. Although the figure is condemned, he displays something of the heroic which Michelangelo had wished to stamp on his dramatic image. The figure does not completely close his eyes to the wreckage of sinful Humanity, nor does he open them petrified with fear. He brings his hand to his face partly covering it in an instinctive gesture. He is driven to watch the entire world which crumbles forever around him and with him, with a single eye dilated with horror. We might say as much for the various sculptured images of the artist. Like a great ancient dramatist who entrusts the interpretation of the deepest and most complex feelings to figures of unforgettable energy, he does not neglect the "choral" function of the overwhelming number of images which wander through the stormy air like nocturnal birds at dusk.

The uncertainty which Michelangelo showed at destroying the lunettes which he had painted above when he did the frescoes on the vault left a trace in the composition of the *Judgment*. There can be no doubt that, if the painting translated the drawing in Casa Buonarroti as it had been conceived (it did not in fact include the two lunettes, but displayed a single tumultuous scene), the composition would have displayed an immediate suggestion of the grandiose synthesis of the masses, as if it were an ideal apsis projected on the plane of the wall. The necessity of filling the lunettes, however, also obliged Michelangelo to shorten the corbel which sustained the "vela" with the *Prophet Jonah* as much as possible. He had to develop the groups of Angels who bear in flight the symbols of the Passion like two open rendings in the clouds through which, almost falling from the sky, descend the figures which extend themselves towards Christ who hovers over the entire scene. It was certainly a solution which hinted at adapting to circumstance in order to avoid the immediate juxtaposition of the *Ancestors of Christ* with the *Judgment*, done in a totally different style. He decided to cover the wall space with an entirely new scene, which would arrive at the limits of the vault and better justify the difference in style between one work and another by means of the different architectural structure. There was also the necessity of inserting the Passion symbols, which were always depicted in the *Last Judgment*, without arranging them in the heart of the composition (which could have been done only by those painters who imagined the scene as a solemn and calm review, where the presence of the symbols of Christ also had their compositional value).

Michelangelo was averse to the effects of supernatural apparitions (as was Caravaggio later, for analogous reasons of the sculptured character of the images) which the Renaissance resolved with harmonious apertures in the sky and splendid lights. Michelangelo's heroic art, based on the human figure in a free play of nudes in space, could not admit such celestial interventions, if not as figures soaring in space and equally strong in construction. Here, in the groups Plates LXXIV
and LXXV which support the instruments of the Passion, he opened the gloomy clouds. He modelled there, as if in a sculptured material, figures in strongly agitated groups. To the left, they bear the Cross, the crown of thorns, and the dice. To the right, they bear the pillar, the sponge, and the ladder.

It is very probable that since these two scenes were the first ones that the artist did, he intentionally sought to harmonize them with the large overhanging "vele" of the *Crucifixion of Amman* and the *Brazen Serpent*. The figures are partly dressed and the nudes, in their complicated and contorted motions, are modelled with great care as to form and color.

Displaying his unequalled knowledge of draftsmanship, the artist seeks out the harshest difficulties of foreshortening and perspective. He overcomes these risky obstacles with the intention of evoking a more decisive depth in space. The figures which bear the Cross in flight seem to be pushed by a stormy wind. One of the nudes, seen from the back, embraces the holy wood, almost in repetition of the Crucifixion gesture. In front of him, other Angels, impetuous Plate LXXIV messengers, cleave the space with swimmers' movements, calling our attention to the Creation scene on the vault.

In the other zone, the cylindrical shaft of the column serves the artist as the pivot around which the nudes circle, almost following the sliding motion of the perfectly polished marble. One of these figures, clinging to the base, seems to want to stop the precipitating motion of the column with his athletic body. We cannot help thinking of the artist's own direct experience in the marble quarries and the difficulties he encountered in the transportation of the columns destined for the facade of San Lorenzo along roads which he himself had designed.

We know well that for Michelangelo, the symbol loses abstract value and becomes a concrete presence, rich in expressive value. It is the very beauty of this column in its proportioned form and smooth marmoreal surface that suggests such an analogy to our minds. Alert and agile Angels move around the perfect column. Their task of showing us their sacred testimony of the Flagellation does not make them forget to avoid direct contact with the relic that they Plate LXXV bear in flight and which they seem to accompany with careful gestures in its magical descent from above.

All this might appear virtuosity (even if it is rather amazing) pushed towards the limits beyond which Mannerism arises. The artist, however, justifies the dangerous pictorial insertion of these two extreme zones of the fresco by the impetus of the figures and their complex movements conceived in relation to the space.

On the other hand, the idea of adding to the sounding trumpets of the *Judgment* the Passion symbols which are almost exalted as Victory trophies is the fruit of the artist's new vision. This upsets tradition and conceives this testimony to the suffering of Christ as a supreme justification of the implacable verdict pronounced by Him who suffered more than any other for Humanity.

The rush of these figures towards the center of the scene is like the unexpected entrance of the brass in a symphony dominated by the serious, mournful sound of the strings. It is an unforeseen and brusque invention in which even the flashing lights around the groups seem to be the reflection of those below, livid as the flash of a steel blade, behind the earth that restores the Dead and the black boat of Charon which unloads the Damned on the threshold of the Inferno.

The significance of the gigantic *Last Judgment* is profound and complex. The admiration suffused with anxious confusion which greeted the work when it was unveiled to the eyes of the artist's contemporaries demonstrates the extent of the unexpectedness of Michelangelo's vision, born from the overturned and fermenting terrain of Christian religiosity in those years.

Unreserved admiration of Michelangelo caused other artists to rush to study the miraculous sculptured effect of its nudes and its compositional novelty. Meditated attention of Churchmen and intellectuals discerned anticipated and revealed spiritual evidence of those problems which were pressing on Catholic thought. More or less clamorous protests finally led to the covering of certain parts of the nude figures by Daniele da Volterra (devoted, however, to the great master). Michelangelo's work could not help but evoke such a series of reactions as well as the ostentation of Aretino's moralistic rhetoric. The artist's inventive freedom must have fatally offended the pietistic aspirations of nascent Mannerism.

In order to indicate, however, that the *Last Judgment* gave form to a new exigence of inwardness, capable of infusing the nude athletes' bodies (the ancient ideal of beauty) with a deeper dramatic life and that the most enlightened spirits of the epoch were aware of this, we refer to a singular testimony. This testimony is derived from the interrogation undergone many years later, in 1573, by Paolo Veronese, at his trial under the Inquisition Tribunal because of his painting of the *Supper in the House of Levi* (now in the Venice Academy).

In his defense, the painter (who then pronounced one of the most beautiful definitions of freedom in art in his phrase "but if in the painting there is more room, I adorn it with figures, according to inspiration") refers to Michelangelo's *Last Judgment* (which he had not seen, however). He says that Michelangelo "in Rome, in the Pontifical Chapel, has there painted Our Lord, Jesus Christ, His Holy Mother, and Saint John, Saint Peter and the Celestial court which are all done as nudes from the Virgin Mary on, in different attitudes and with little reverence."

It is clear that this underhanded reasoning (perhaps suggested to him by his friend Pietro Aretino, with the discredit thrown upon the *Last Judgment*) aimed at creating a model due to "Divine" Michelangelo. The Inquisitor answered, however, "Do you not know that painting the *Last Judgment* in which clothes or such things are not presumed, he did not need to paint clothes, and that in those figures there is nothing that is not of the spirit?"

Although he had been dead for almost ten years, Michelangelo therefore continued to scandalize certain circles because of his presumed license. The Inquisitor's reply shows how the *Judgment* should have been viewed.

The observation that, in the tragic moment of the supreme verdict, clothes were not needed, indicates that the tradition which instead (also because the various hierarchies were recognized there) depicted the *Reborn* with their clothes had been surpassed. The nude had become accepted as a spiritual manifestation which was in accordance with Michelangelo's intention.

This is exactly the opposite of that which Aretino in the midst of the anti-Michelangelo polemic expressed in his venomous letter of November, 1545 (without having seen the original work, but only a copy of same). He gave vent to his wounded pride, profiting by the criticisms leveled by various sources at the *Last Judgment*. "Seeing the complete sketch of all your day of Judgment," he writes, "I have discovered much of the illustrious ability of Raphael in the pleasing beauty of your invention" (as we note, he immediately puts forward the name of Raphael, which he knew was not very pleasing to Michelangelo). He continues, "But I am ashamed of the license, so illicit to the spirit, which you have taken in expressing the concepts." Here is the peroration: ". . . consequently, that admired Michelangelo wanted to show the people no less religious impiousness than perfection in painting."

This is a most cunning argument which creates a contrast between the work's indisputable skill and its presumed irreverence. Finally, his vexation appears and we become aware of his disappointment that Michelangelo did not take into consideration the "imagination" which he had suggested in the letters (which we know so well): "If you had been advised, in composing the Universe and the Abyss and Paradise with the glory and the horror and the fear sketched from the instruction, from the example and from the knowledge contained in my letter that the world knows [here we note his presumptuous pride in having proposed to the artist an instruction to be executed in painting], I dare say that not only Nature, but every benign influence would not regret having given you such a clear intellect."

The greatest perfidy, however, seems to be contained in the concluding statement which appears to be a clear lie, after seeing the letter published in Aretino's correspondence. "Now that I have vented my anger at your cruelty in regard to my devotion . . . destroy this, which I have also done and remember that I am such that even Kings and Emperors answer my letters."

The comparison between Aretino's enraged resentment, which certainly does not show him in his best light, and the statement of Paolo Veronese's Inquisitor indicates the different ways in which Michelangelo's great work was considered when the immediate polemic had been re-absorbed into the historical evaluation. The traces of the disconcerting impression provoked by the *Last Judgment*, an admonishing page which Michelangelo placed before the eyes of Humanity, is, however, still apparent at the time.

The careful and precious study of the genesis and technique of the great fresco, published in 1944 by Redig De Campos and Biagetti, revealed important circumstances which determined with certainty the vicissitudes of Michelangelo's opus. It has also given us the knowledge of the few colors which, chosen among those used for fresco painting, the artist employed in the gigantic painting: lime white, yellow ochre, natural siena, sinopia, burnt yellow ochre, burnt siena, earth green, ultramarine blue, lapis lazuli, natural earth, burnt earth, "life" black.[9]

These are the same colors used, as we have seen, for the painting of the vault, but harmonized among themselves in a much different manner and with a distinct predominance of dark over light tones. With this simple palette, composed entirely of tones which are best incorporated into the plaster without "dry" retouches (which would have been dishonorable for a Florentine painter), Michelangelo gave tempestuous life to his crowd of figures.

None appears to be realized to please the eye, but all speak to us as dramatic images, the expressions of a deep moral and religious content. This is why the chromatic harmonies are in low tones. The powerful shadows bring the modelling of the bodies into relief and the few draperies which vary the nudes tend to monochrome or hint at some iridescent effect (but very moderately, in contrast to the chromatic variety employed in the scenes on the vault, especially in the

Prophets and *Sibyls,* where the color often is of a sustained warm timbre). The sky, which had to appear to be of a compact tonality, of almost marmoreal blue, was first prepared with a reddish color on which a lapis lazuli veining was extended, often allowing the basic color to be seen (especially in the section with the *Reprobates*). This obtained the atmosphere of a kindled dark sunset which also tinges the nudes with dramatic reflections. The disequilibrium which we observe in many sections between the whitish sky and the violence of the dark tones of the figures was, however, not intentional on Michelangelo's part. It is the effect of the transformation of the blue which no longer displays—at many points— its original tone. The studies which have been done on the condition of the immense fresco are reassuring and it is certain that, when it will be possible to undertake a careful restoration of the work, it will be possible to arrive at an effect which is very close to that which was evoked at the original unveiling of the painting.

We can arrive at a certain idea of the original colors by studying the numerous copies which were executed from the original, since the time when the artist was still alive. The best of these copies was done by Marcello Venusti and is Plate LVIII preserved in the Capodimonte Museum in Naples.

This copy was the property of Cardinal Alessandro Farnese, who valued it greatly. It is always on exhibit among the Farnese paintings in the Neapolitan gallery.

It would seem that the first purchaser of the work was, however, Cardinal Ercole Gonzaga, who chose Venusti (at that time, the painter was young and poor) on Nino Sernini's advice. The latter knew that the painter was one of the best of those artists who had so enthusiastically copied Michelangelo's masterpiece. Venusti's copy was done in 1549, before Paul IV had Daniele da Volterra add the draperies to several figures which seemed too naked in 1564. Since the copy is in optimum condition, it also serves as a certain document for the reconstruction of the fresco in its entirety.[10]

Venusti, to whom Michelangelo himself gave the drawings of the composition to translate in painting, was to the extent of his modest ability absolutely faithful in reproducing Michelangelo's work, as can be seen even in the smallest details. He copied it directly from the original, even in regard to the colors which were still intact (at such a brief distance in time from the original unveiling). Venusti's scrupulously accurate copy, however, does not even faintly suggest the vigorous and dramatic accent which the master stamped on the gigantic painting in his inimitable manner, notwithstanding all the care and notable ability shown by the former. We note several qualities in the colors which are much more limpid and firm: the variety of tones that animate the figures, the greater unity of hue in the sky, and the sculptured clarity of the rocks on the ground and the far-off horizon laden with clouds.

In the upper portion, Venusti did not reproduce the corbel of the vault or the beginning of the figure of the Prophet Jonah. He substituted them (perhaps on the buyer's advice) with the image of the Lord from the *Separation of the Land from the Waters* (one of Michelangelo's scenes) and, in an ingenuous, luminous halo, the dove of the Holy Spirit. Except for this variant which is extraneous to Michelangelo's idea, the copy represents a most useful contribution of great precision which reflects Venusti's devotion to the master. Although it transfers Michelangelo's grand conception to a more minute, almost miniature scale, it fundamentally respects the original chromatic values and gives us a genuine idea of the groups of figures which were partially disturbed by Daniele da Volterra's moralistic retouching.

The number of sixteenth-century copies of the *Last Judgment* is some measure of the interest which Michelangelo's gigantic work engendered. There are painted copies, some of which are anterior to the retouching and therefore are more important, and engraved copies, which adhere less to the original. Some of these prints, which were widely diffused in the sixteenth century, represent not faithful copies but rather re-elaborations of the original with variations. They contain arbitrary intrusions which certainly do not lend themselves to a correct study of Michelangelo's masterpiece.

The impressive original, however, which concluded the painting history of the Sistine Chapel with the opening of new and tempestuous artistic horizons, had an enormous influence on the art of those times, through those artists who, arriving in Rome, did not fail to study the work's singular features. One of the greatest painters—whose works pushed sixteenth-century developments to their limits and who, with his hallucinatory vision, was a precursor of Expressionism—to find himself before the *Last Judgment* at a significant moment in his stylistic growth was Domenico Theotokopuli, known as "El Greco." Arriving in Rome in 1570, he came in contact for the first time with the great paintings of the century and, perhaps because of his Venetian studies (as a "young candiotto and disciple of Titian" he had been presented by Giulio Clovio to Cardinal Farnese), he must not have felt too attracted by the "skill" of Michelangelo's design.

The polemic evoked by the nakedness of the figures in the *Last Judgment* was not yet dead, and El Greco inserted himself in that atmosphere in a peremptory manner (as Mancini relates in his biography) in the name of "decency." It seems that the young artist even said that if he were to throw the entire work to the ground and redo it with honesty and decency, as a painting it would not be inferior to the original—a bold plan, perhaps called forth by his intimate mystical feeling of a Byzantine heritage rather than by presumption.

And yet, El Greco not only was interested in Michelangelo's art in Venice (when he copied the model of *The Day* in Tintoretto's possession, in a rare drawing in the collection of prints in Monaco), but he must have taken many notes from the *Judgment* nudes, even if he did not make a painted copy. In his *Dream of Philip II* at the Escorial, several of the Saints came from Michelangelo's opus and, in the wide open mouth of the Inferno to the right, the Damned repeat with hallucinatory clarity the entanglements of Michelangelo's nudes. We find them also deformed in the enigmatic *Opening of the Fifth Seal* of El Greco's final years.

We can consider these references to Michelangelo from a temperament as different from his as that of El Greco (the latter was completely taken by the fascination of the light and color, elements which transfigure the form) as being much more than a transitory episode or simply a stylistic experience. In these references it is even possible to single out what had already partially occurred in Tintoretto's works (which magically evoke Michelangelo's nudes by means of a Titianesque palette). This was the overcoming of the ultimate limits conceded to the sculptured form with its weight and its heroic strength in Michelangelo's tempestuous world with a coloristic evocation nurtured with heightened spirituality. Thus, El Greco developed in painting beyond Michelangelo's *Last Judgment* what Buonarroti realized in sculpture in his final years with the *Rondanini Pietà*: the extreme corrosion of the human form and the interiorization of the heroic effort in the impulse towards Faith.

This is all symptomatic if we think of the *Last Judgment* in relation to the phase of Christian thought in this late Renaissance period, and of the role which El Greco assumed in the Spain of Saint Teresa and Saint Ignatius with his painting filled with yearning for Transcendence.

It is, therefore, natural that, even more than the Sistine vault, the *Last Judgment* lends itself to a variety of interpretations which, starting from the novelty of the composition and the profound thought from which the work sprang, have aimed at a definition of its meanings.

It is legitimate to desire a supposition (as often occurs in the face of a great manifestation of the creative spirit) that, beyond the artistic aspects, which in Michelangelo are essential, might reveal some concept "beyond the veil" which stimulated Michelangelo's imagination and the message he wanted to convey with the tumult of prodigious images.

The inquiry into the *Last Judgment* has thus been extended from aesthetics to philosophy, from theology to ethics through allegory and symbol. (In Dante's work, there is an inexhaustible field for research and study in which, next to severe scientific meditation, the most singular suppositions continually arise. Many of these, after calm examination which does not lose sight of the personality of the "Divine Poet's" art, have been proven unacceptable.) The same phenomenon occurs in relation to Michelangelo's work. It is really amazing that intentions and symbologies have been attributed to it which are so little Michelangelesque. They are even inadmissible in the light of the artist's thought and craft. It is not worthwhile, however, to occupy ourselves with those inevitable attempts (only partly justified by the enormous ideas presented by Michelangelo's personality) which reach the limits of the arbitrary.

This will only disturb a serene consideration of the development of Michelangelo's art which, with every careful investigation, appears to us, in its spontaneous essence, extended towards the vigorous and clear expression of his imaginative world.

The nature of more seriously undertaken research is different. De Tolnay—one of the scholars who has best contributed to the indication of the relationship which links Michelangelo's works to the intellectual history of the time— is the author of the best-informed volumes on the great artist. Speaking of the *Last Judgment* he adds, to the values which compose its admonitory significance, others which attribute vaster horizons to the gigantic composition.

He says that "Michelangelo did not limit himself in his fresco to the representation of human terror at the prospect of annihilation. On the eschatological significance, he superimposes a cosmological significance, revealing the attractions and movements of the figures in the space and the grandiose vision of a heliocentric universe. Christ is the center of a solar system and around Him gravitate, in circular motion, all the constellations. It is not by chance that He is young and beardless with wavy hair and of a perfect body. He is like an Apollo."[11]

In our opinion, however, although the conceptual values behind the world of Michelangelo's sculptured images may be complex and multiple, one cannot follow such an investigation without reservation. We must not forget that Michelangelo is, above all, an artist. As such, his creativity shrinks from superimposing in his work that which would shackle his imaginative inspiration, even if we are convinced that his world is pregnant with profound resonances and unforeseen echoes. The tragic power and the monumental consistency of the *Last Judgment* reach a direct transfiguration of a moving moral and religious idea through stirring but concrete expressive language. Because of this, we experience the dramatic suggestion in such a manner as to prohibit the slackening of its effectiveness with excessive subtlety.

The exceptional vigor of Michelangelo's figurative language, almost arriving at the limits of its possibilities, gives us again (after so much analysis, in the attempt at penetrating his work by investigating its stimuli and most secret motives) the deep, unified impression of a vision dominated completely by imagination. It is supported by the extraordinary vigor of a dominating style which succeeds in determining and molding everything within the absolute of form.

NOTES FOR CHAPTER FOUR

(1) For all historical, critical, and technical references to the *Last Judgment*, one should read: D. REDIG DE CAMPOS—B. BIAGETTI: *Il Giudizio Universale di Michelangelo*, edited by Pontificia Accademia Romana di Archeologia, Rome, 1944, vols. I and II.
(2) D. REDIG DE CAMPOS—B. BIAGETTI: op. cit., vol. II, plate CXXI, number 1.
(3) *Journal du voyage en France du Cavalier Bernin* by CHANTELOU, Paris 1930.
(4) D. REDIG DE CAMPOS—B. BIAGETTI: op. cit., vol. II, plate CXVIII.

(5) F. Steinmann—H. Pogatscher: *Dokumente und Forschungen zu Michelangelo* in "Repertorium für Kunstwissenschaft, XXIX (1906). Also, S. Ortolani: *Pietro Aretino and Michelangelo* in "L'Arte," XXV (1922), pages 15, 26; A. Del Vita: *L'Aretino*, Arezzo 1954.

(6) D. Redig De Campos—B. Biagetti: op. cit., vol. I, page 47.

(7) F. La Cava: *Il volto di Michelangelo nel Giudizio Finale*, Bologna 1925, and for further developments: C. Ricci: *Le scoperte nel Giudizio di Michelangelo: il volto di S. Bartolomeo è quello dell'Aretino* in "Il Giornale d'Italia," June 2, 1925.

(8) G. B. Armenini: *De' veri precetti della pittura*, Ravenna 1586, page 224.

(9) D. Redig De Campos—B. Biagetti: op. cit., page 98.

(10) B. Molajoli: *Il Museo di Capodimonte*, Naples 1961, page 40, figure 10.

(11) Charles De Tolnay: *Michelangelo* in *Enciclopedia Universale dell'Arte*, Rome 1962.

CHAPTER FIVE

THE PAULINE CHAPEL FRESCOES

LAST DRAWINGS

MICHELANGELO hardly had time to reflect on his own gigantic labor on the *Last Judgment* when the Pope gave him a new task—the two vast paintings in the Pauline Chapel which had been designed by the architect Sangallo and was especially loved by Pope Paul III. The first of the two frescoes was executed between 1542 and 1545, and the second between 1546 and 1550. These represent the final paintings of monumental importance which were executed by Michelangelo who, during the later years of his life, dedicated his exceptional activity to the Church of Saint Peter. This was an undertaking which he had accepted as being a profound testimony of faith.

The two Pauline Chapel frescoes have a special significance with regard to the final evolution of Michelangelo's mind and imagination. They are pictorial proofs of an evolution in style which, turning away from the emotional dramatic energy of the *Last Judgment*, seems to accept the narration of sacred facts firstly—in the *Conversion of Saint Paul*—almost as an echo of the trumpets of the *Last Judgment* and the "Dies Irae," then in a severe and concentrated internal resignation in the *Crucifixion of Saint Peter*.

Plates LXXVI and LXXXI

The two frescoes, after undergoing several changes of fortune in the light of criticism, have awakened renewed interest as a result of recent studies. They have been made the example of that "final" painting style of the artist. In the *Crucifixion of Saint Peter*, he shows an elaboration even in his colors in a way which is less sculptural and closer to an intimate research of poetic melancholy. One can determine in this way a considerable difference between the two paintings when comparing them with the *Last Judgment* (especially the *Crucifixion of Saint Peter*). They seem to be a more human vision of religious incidents, thought of in a different way after the outburst of the final tragedy that seemed to have exploited all of Michelangelo's expressive possibilities in painting. He had taken them as far as they could go.

Let us, therefore, consider the Pauline Chapel paintings (after observing the ties that still unite the *Last Judgment* to the *Conversion of Saint Paul*) as the result of a religious meditation in relation also to the artist's overcoming of a spiritual struggle. This meditation is autobiographical in an internal sense, even though translated into the language of painting and addressed as an example to men of faith who look at the monumental work.

The publication in 1934 of the works of art dedicated to the decoration of the Pauline Chapel in *Monumenti vaticani di archeologia e d'arte*[1] was the result of the renewed interest aroused by these latter-day frescoes of Michelangelo. These frescoes were in their turn the stimulus of more profound research into the character of Michelangelo's art as revealed in the two paintings.

In this publication, Fritz Baumgart on the part of historical criticism and Biagio Biagetti regarding the technique and the precious facts ascertained directly on the spot, contribute in a definite way to the estimation of these two last compositions of Michelangelo. There has also been much discussion by De Tolnay, Dvorak and Redig De Campos pertaining to the research carried out on the iconography of the *Conversion of Saint Paul* by H. van Dam von Isselt. The interest in the two paintings centers around the relationship between Michelangelo's painting style as revealed in the *Last Judgment* and its readoption which is seen in the Pauline Chapel paintings. This is shown even more clearly by the accompaniment of the letters, poems, and documents relating to the artist's life which was, at this period, fated by unhappy occurrences, and characterized by a progressive detachment from worldly things.

On the 16th of November 1542, however, a pension was allotted to Urbino the servant so that he might grind colors for the artist, while the latter painted. Michelangelo could then begin the task in the hope that the new agreement made with the Duke Guidobaldo di Urbino for the planning of Julius II's tomb might ease the burden which weighed on his conscience because of the unfinished work.

On the 12th of July 1545, Paul III visited the Chapel where the artist was working. In the following August, he arranged that the wall for which the second fresco was destined be prepared. The *Conversion of Saint Paul* must, therefore, have been finished when, in the same year, a fire broke out in the Chapel, severely damaging the roof, and threatening the painting which was, however, almost entirely saved. The other painting must have been started in March 1546, and was almost finished on the 13th of October 1549 when Paul III, who was then over eighty and only a few weeks from his death, wanted to see Michelangelo's work.

Michelangelo was anxious to settle the big and long-drawn-out question of the undertaking he had made with the heirs of Julius II to work on the latter's tomb before beginning to paint the walls of the Pauline Chapel. This fact is also made clear in the beginning of a long letter which was probably addressed to Monseigneur Marco Vigerio, Bishop of Sinigaglia, which says: "Your Excellency has sent word for me to paint, and not to worry about anything. My answer is that an artist paints with his brain, not his hands. One who cannot work with a clear brain ruins his work. Until this other affair is settled, I shall do nothing good."

In these afflicted words, one can read a paraphrase of what the artist thought about the relationship between the conception of a work of art and the execution of this "concept" expressed so clearly in the famous sonnet "Non ha l'ottimo artista alcun concetto . . ." in which the "ottimo artista" only manages to make the idea concrete when his hand "obeys" his intellect. In the letter, he recalls the stirring thought of a great undertaking which is unfinished and which drags behind in the form of an unfulfilled obligation. This prevented him from giving himself over entirely and with a soul unhampered by worry to the execution of the paintings. Although this is not a direct testimony, it is still significant.

One senses, however, a heavy atmosphere weighing down on the Pauline frescoes which is not caused by any single thing, but by a complexity of external and spiritual facts which tinge these grandiose compositions with a sort of bitterness. The two paintings, for the very reason that they suggest a narrative theme to the painter (even though on the level of a religious evocation), appear to be planned in a greater atmosphere of austere morality. They tend towards an admonitory significance which goes beyond that of the *Judgment* making them two exemplary episodes. One of these, in the lightning-flash of Divine Grace, indicates a new way to Man, who is blind and without faith. The other celebrates the constructive sacrifice of man with the indestructible faith from which the Church is born in its universality.

Michelangelo, therefore, after the terrible vicissitudes of the *Judgment,* turned with an exceptional effort of con-

PAULINE CHAPEL. *View from the principal entrance. Constructed for Paul III by Antonio da Sangallo the Younger. The decoration of the vault with Manneristic stucco had been conceived by Pierino del Vaga, but was almost completely destroyed in a fire and was replaced by another stucco which was very much inferior.*

On the lateral walls are the frescoes, the "Conversion of Saint Paul" (to the left) and the "Crucifixion of Saint Peter" (to the right), Michelangelo's last wall paintings, executed at the wish of Paul III and begun immediately after he had finished work on the "Last Judgment" in the Sistine Chapel.

centrated thought and style to give his characters that fullness of form and that firmly planted position which was vitally necessary to the story, even if it was planned in an atmosphere already detached from the world around it. This is the difficulty in understanding the expressive value of such frescoes in the parable of Michelangelo's painting, without having to consider them either as a final period or a singular return to his former style.

What seems evident, however, is the difference between the two works. The *Conversion of Saint Paul* has many ties with the painting of the *Judgment* while the other is more independent even in its particular coloristic effects which adhere to the severe structure of the masses rendering them more acceptable and rendering the forms more human.

Both scenes have one characteristic in common. They have both been imagined in strict relationship with their environment. They suggest, by means of having the foreground figures cut by the basic limit of the painting, an identification of the observer with the narrated fact. This was something new which was to please the Mannerists very much. Later, it even pleased others who understood the value of intensifying the expression. In the *Conversion of Saint Paul*, it is the two soldiers who come climbing into the field from the bottom, almost exhausted. In the *Crucifixion of Saint Peter*, it is the warriors on the left whose backs are seen, and the weeping women coming forward on the right. In both cases this is done for the same reason. One seems to notice that Michelangelo attaches great importance to his idea which makes the composition more alive and which, above all, does not isolate it in its autonomy in the eyes of the man of faith.

Plates LXXVI to LXXIX The *Conversion of Saint Paul* can be divided into two horizontal zones, from the flashing lights in the background to the line of the ground. As the artist had already done in the *Judgment*, he renders a dynamism of singular energy which can be inferred to have been prompted by his great experience on the *Last Judgment*. This is carried out in an unexpected way. The artist seems to be attracted once again by the rapid and concise narration of the episode as told in the Acts of the Apostles, in which the whole event takes place in a brusque course of events which provokes a sense of excitement in the reader. There is not the least hesitation in the characters of the transformation, unless one counts the amazement of the soldiers who were accompanying Paul to Damascus. When the lightning strikes, they can only hear where the mysterious voice comes from which speaks to their chief as he lies trembling on the ground. "As they were journeying," it says in the Acts of the Apostles, "it transpired that as they were nearing Damascus, all at once a light from Heaven flashed about him and, falling to the ground, he heard a voice which said to him, 'Saul, Saul, why do you persecute me?' and he said, 'Who are you, Lord?' and the Lord said, 'I am Jesus, whom you are persecuting. How hard it is for you to kick back when spurred!' Saul, trembling and amazed said, 'Lord, what do you want me to do?' and the Lord said to him: 'Get up and go into the city where you will be told what you must do!' Even his travelling companions were amazed upon hearing the voice, but not one of them saw anything." That light which "struck him everywhere" is seen by Michelangelo as a sulphurous outburst of lightning which crosses the sky rising up together with the gesture of the Christ from the yellowish halo which surrounds the Saviour clothed in red. It is very clear that the artist wished to give this unheralded phenomenon a natural evidence of its own. The streak of light does not reach the group surrounding the fallen Paul, but disappears, gleaming beyond the horizon like a lightning flash which lacerates a sultry autumn sky. Golden reflections from this light are, however, cast on the figures, to whose clothes (dark red, violet, water-green, warm brown, slate blue) they give a unique chromatic prominence.

In order to hold together such different attitudes provoked by the unexpected miracle, the artist first traced the two great directional lines of the composition which part like an open compass from the Christ's gesture. One connects with the figure of Paul; the other, going through the group of saints and angels around the Christ, reaches the city of Plate LXXVII Damascus. In this way also the circle of angels around the Christ, for which figures Buonarroti in many cases adopted drawings already used in the *Judgment* (as he did also for the fleeing figures on the ground), acquires a logical unity in its movement through space.

The result is an intensification of counterplaced motifs, which have their origin in the central motif of the sudden fall of the principal character who is helped at once by the massed figures of soldiers. They are in costumes derived from the study of Imperial Roman reliefs and the Trajan pillar which the artist could contemplate every day coming out of his house in Macel de' Corvi.

This glance into ancient times, however, reawakens an interpretation of costume which is entirely sculptural, and not at all documentary (an original conception of armor as an element which underlines the heavy masses of the figures in movement). The center of the action which bursts out with the rapidity of lightning is the violent contrast between the prancing of the horse and the crashing fall of the figure of Saint Paul. He is a groping image of sudden blindness, of a hero flung to the ground by a superhuman force.

All these movements depend on this irradiation of forces in a halo-shape, almost symbolized by the prancing horse. It is seen from behind held with difficulty by a servant whose form indicates a line going towards the background of the scene.

At the top, surrounded by figures of wingless angels swimming in the air with the fluidity of young athletes moving freely in water, we see the Christ coming down rending space. He is holding out His right hand towards Saint Paul and indicating to him with His left the city of Damascus on the hill. It appears through the mist like an apparition dreamed up in the desolation of the desert. Every group is ruled by this singular compositional energy. The gestures of the characters seem to obey an ironlike law of opposing movements. We are on the dangerous border line of Mannerism which Buonarroti never oversteps because of his innately rich imagination and because of the solidity of the human figure (an error into which fell numerous imitators of the scene, which is among those most popular among the artists of the sixteenth century).

Among the fleeing and re-grouping figures driven by sudden terror, some stand out in a statuesque manner: the warrior on the left, sheltering himself with his shield and putting his hand on his sword as he looks up; the gigantic image formed by a group of soldiers who have fallen to the ground on the left, instinctively putting their hands over their heads as if to stop the noise of the thunderbolt. In this, besides recalling the *Judgment*, it is possible that Michelangelo also remembered the lightning scene in Luca Signorelli's fresco at Orvieto. Other figures fleeing towards the background point out insistently the sense of depth in a three-dimensional vision which adds fascination to this complex painting.   Plates LXXVIII and LXXX

The artist had already insisted in the *Judgment* on these attitudes which underline spatial depth. In the different groups of resurrected bodies, they seem to penetrate clear through the painted wall. This is also true in the nude figures which are going against the Divine Will, in heavy combat with the angels who are defending Heaven. In this later painting (possibly due to former experience) he was surer of his own particular way of understanding space enhanced by figures. Michelangelo seems to use it as an exceptional element in the composition. He uses it again more coherently in the *Crucifixion of Saint Peter*. Among the terrified soldiers, we can note six or seven figures with their backs turned who seem to be retreating from the foreground. In contrast, there are other figures facing forwards. The same thing is repeated with the figures on the clouds which run forwards or go back in alternating movements.

This "coming and going" of figures indicates a dynamic will which tends to break up the statuesque groupings and to interrelate the various parts of the scene. It almost seems as if the artist is fighting with himself in order to create a composition in which the groups, instead of being isolated by their sculptural quality, have an expressive relationship in a linking together of gestures dominated by the action.

This comes about in a typical conception of the power of the human figure over space. The artist had to indicate the city of Damascus, suggesting a hilly unadorned landscape which serves as a background for the characters, rather than as an environment.

Michelangelo's insensitivity regarding the landscape is evident. From this point of view, the "Humanist" painter's character is rigorous and peremptory. His schematic and summary way of creating the environment in the two Pauline scenes does not represent an exception concerning his own special vision of Nature around us.

When he gave his opinion so decisively a few years earlier on Flemish painting and on the meticulous landscapes of that school (as recorded in the *Dialogues* of F. Hollanda), he spoke in favor of his conception that man should be absolutely dominant. There is no reason to doubt the authenticity of what is referred to in the *Dialogues* (even if the author may have underlined or amplified) in the words of the great master on what best corresponded to his manneristic and Italianized vision which he wanted to develop in Portugal.

Michelangelo's declaration which implicitly states his ideas regarding the human figure is included in a still more profound conception—that of "religiosity." This is a problem which was more present than ever in Buonarroti's art at the time of which we are speaking. When asked by Vittoria Colonna if he thought Flemish art was "more devout" than Italian, Michelangelo replied with a famous criticism of the former school. He underlined the analytical scruple considered in relation to the religious sentiment that Flemish art inspires. These words are sufficiently important to be reconsidered in confirmation of the profound austerity of expression in the later years of his life. "Flemish painting," Michelangelo replied, "will always be generally liked by devout people much more than any Italian painting. Italian painting will draw no tears, while the Flemish will cause many to be shed. This doesn't depend on the vigor or goodness of the painting itself, but on the goodness of the devout person who is looking."

He also gives a singularly ironic definition of Flemish taste: "In Flanders, one can truly say that they paint to trick exterior sight" (a sentence in which the important difference between realist trickery and "interior" and expressive attraction is shaded in); "this painting is composed only with rags, ruined houses, greenery, fields, the shade of trees and bridges over rivers, and what they call landscapes, and the odd figure here and there. All this, although it can seem beautiful to certain eyes, is really done without reason or art, without symmetry or proportion, without discernment or choice, or ease—in a word, with neither substance nor strength."[2]

It is hardly necessary to say how differently Leonardo would have replied, having renewed the relationship between figures and landscape, indicating harmonic developments of sentiments mingling with surrounding nature. In the Pauline frescoes, Michelangelo intensifies the "interior" meaning of form and determines each figure with a very individual dramatic value. In the *Conversion of Saint Paul*, one feels the artist has concentrated his expressive intensity in close dynamic relationship on the images of the prancing horse and the Saint fallen to the ground.

There are several known examples of life drawings which Michelangelo did of the anatomy of a horse and its movements, especially at the time of the *Battle of Cascina* cartoon. This is, however, one of the very rare horses which he painted. It is strange that instead of returning to life studies, he more readily remembered the horses of the *Dioscuri* on the Quirinale. This recalling of ancient art, together with the stimulus derived from classical reliefs and sculptures, underlines the artist's will more than a hypothetic cultural attitude. In the last analysis, it is always movement joined with the strong outstanding effect of the forms which was ever present in Michelangelo's mind. In the case of the fallen figure of Saint Paul, the recollections become more complex.

There is no doubt that this image of a powerfully muscled old man comes from the figure of Heliodorus painted by Raphael in the second Vatican Chamber. If one turns the scheme of drawing around, from right to left, one obtains

Fig. 16—MICHELANGELO *large autograph cartoon (2.63 meters by 1.56 meters). Executed in charcoal and white lead on various joined pages, used by the artist to transfer the compositional design onto the wall prepared for the fresco of the "Crucifixion of Saint Peter" in the Pauline Chapel of the Vatican (1542–1550). It still bears the traces of the holes along the edges of the figures, necessary to the dusting with pounce (Naples, Capodimonte Museum)*

the Saint Paul of this fresco. This recalling of his antagonist's painting is perhaps surprising. Michelangelo is known to have said that everything Raphael knew in painting he owed to him. As the figure of Heliodorus was derived in its turn from the famous fallen warriors in the classical series of the *Dying Gaul*, the relationship can really be understood as an indirect remembrance of ancient art in an idea which was dear to the artist and which can also be seen in the drawings for *Prometheus Bound*. This image of Saint Paul as a bearded prophet (far removed from the traditional figure) is a strange one, however, turned as it is face to face with the viewer. In giving this ostentatious position to the face, the artist must certainly have wished to give it a special significance. It is easy to recognize the connection with the portraits of blind

Plate LXXIX Homer, but also with the face of *Laocoön*. This may not be the end of the allusions. From an autobiographical point of view, we can consider a type of self-portrait which is symbolic of the artist's spiritual situation (Michelangelo had regained his faith after having lived in "blindness" for a long time). One might even see in it a reference to the Pope—considering the abundant beard—who was called Paul. This would justify the unusual type of person which the artist makes of the Saint. Michelangelo was in fact criticized by his contemporaries for not complying with tradition.

We cannot leave this fresco without bringing attention to the outstanding realism of the two soldier-figures who enter in an upward direction from the bottom of the picture. It would seem that Michelangelo wanted to prove above all his painting strength in molding the chiaroscuro and the color and the beautiful image of the young man carrying the shield and helmet on his shoulders. The young man is painted in such a new and modern style, modelled with certainty and originality as is his companion, who is also charged with the weight of the arms which are held up by a short spear.

These two figures, unlike the rest of the *Conversion* scene with its hallucinatory atmosphere, herald the more human pictorial vision of the *Crucifixion of Saint Peter* which the artist was preparing for the opposite wall of the same chapel. Here in the *Crucifixion* (which is the last of Michelangelo's murals) the synthesis of the vast and expressive composition is facilitated by a greater calm and a more acute coherence of composition. In the first fresco, the movements of the groups were centrifugal and tended to disperse the human masses. In this second one, everything concentrates in a centripetal and rotary movement around the gigantic nude figure of Saint Peter. In order to make him stand out more,

Plates LXXXI
and LXXXII he has been nailed to a cross with an extra-long vertical bar which indicates that this will be fixed well down into the hole which is being dug.

The soldiers come upwards on the left. The sad procession of people pass on the right, almost driven by the fatal compulsion of the earthly destiny of a restless, wandering humanity. Both groups acquire extraordinary rhythmical value which is hardly interrupted by the group of figures near the Cross and the soldiers on horseback coming up on the left. The rotary feeling which is given to the whole composition centering round the cross and emphasized by the mimicry of the crucifiers finds its logical justification in the act about to be carried out. Some seem ready to push the great piece of wood with their shoulders in such a way as to make it turn on its own axis and go down vertically into the hole. From this point on, Michelangelo is like a great dramatist. He uses inventions then unknown but also motifs which are dear to his sculptural imagination. The young man who is digging the hole recalls one of the nudes in the *Judgment* who is helping the resurrected. He even reminds us of one of the fighters in the *Battle of Cascina*, who is on the bank of the river Arno. Behind St. Peter's cross in a group which is arguing around a proud young man (who may be taking up the defense of the Apostle) one can recognize figures who are near Christ among the Blessed in the *Judgment*. The manner in which the artist uses his characters is different, however, as is their function in relation to the scene.

There are also figures full of mysterious fascination, such as the group of weeping women in the foreground. They go forward as if driven by the force of events, turning for a moment as they pass to watch the suffering of the Apostle.

Among the soldiers, there are intense faces and eyes standing out in wonder. On the right, a strange hooded figure is seen advancing with arms crossed. He is isolated in his deep sorrow like a barbarian prisoner (certainly painted while calling to mind the great figures of the gigantic marbles which crown the triumphal arches), like the figure impersonated by the artist himself in the group of the *Deposition* in Santa Maria del Fiore. This personage (identified by some with Saint Paul) seems to contain in his proud resignation the secret of the whole fresco, which is composed almost in the Plate LXXXII rhythm of a funeral march.

In order to overcome the sorrowful nightmare which hangs threateningly over the speechless crowd in the center, Michelangelo gave the figure of Saint Peter his maximum care as a painter. It is modelled with a difficult sculptural foreshortening, in an experienced chiaroscuro of sculptural effectiveness. This nude figure of the first Apostle, who was destined to hang head-downwards, is twisted around in an heroic gesture and looks at us with flashing eyes. Anyone who goes into the Pauline Chapel knows this magnetic gaze. Michelangelo knew how to concentrate such an exceptional potency of life. It is like an admonishment and a reproach for our lack of faith. This intense expression which Buonarroti gave Saint Peter fascinated many artists after him.

After the careful restorations of 1934, the colors of the two frescoes have recovered their correlation, revealing at many points a rare vigor and richness of blended tones. This is especially true of the *Crucifixion of Saint Peter* which, in composition as well as chromatic interest, differs greatly from the first fresco. The colors (in the simplicity of their harmonies which correspond to the scrupulous observance of the principles of painting by Buonarroti) seem to be "orchestrated" in a much more vivacious tone. They make one think of the indomitable spirit of renewal which the artist, by then more than 70 years old, still had. It is based on four principal colors: green, red, blue, and yellow. These are enriched in different ways throughout the picture which is lit with golden tones and vibrates in subdued brown and violet. Even if, in this final pictorial labor of Michelangelo, such a vivid care of the colors may be surprising, it is noticeably the design which is exalted in the colors. They are distributed over large areas without being broken up and treated with sensitive blending in the chiaroscuro. They are modelled on the figures and fabrics with careful firmness in a predomination of subtle brush strokes which are short and very sure. They give one the impression of form created by the technique of finely chiselled marble. The fact that Michelangelo also devoted an intense study to the drawing of this fresco is revealed in the fragment of a cartoon drawn to the same scale which is kept in the Capodimonte Museum in Naples. This testimony to the tenacious firmness with which the artist carried out his works is composed of sheets of paper put together and mounted on canvas. It bears the traces of the "dusting powder" with which the artist transferred the design onto the wall before painting the figures. Michelangelo had used such "fogli reali bolognesi" since the *Battle of Cascina* and they show how constant he was in his practices even in the final years of his painting (fig. 16).

Steinmann (1925) had not yet been able to study the frescoes after the restorations. When speaking of this very important graphic document of Buonarroti, he considered the Pauline Chapel paintings almost lost. He concludes: "All the intrinsic qualities of Michelangelo's drawing and color, all that masterly expression of a most intense inner life have disappeared . . . ." For this very reason, he emphasizes the beauty of the great drawing, which, in spite of the damage it has suffered through various changes of home, retains the deep authentic imprint of the great master. We can consider its worth still better by comparing it with the very painting to which it refers. In its simplicity of drafting, in the broad modelling of the forms and the choice of colors, it strictly interprets what the paper contains in the way of expressive vigor and monumental energy.[3]

This unique and precious fragment of the great composition drawn life size allows us to deepen the strong impression which the painting has on us. It consists of three whole figures and the lower part of a fourth at the top. They are the legionaries who are going slowly up the hill where the Crucifixion of the First Apostle takes place. They form the ideal theatrical "wing" for closing the fresco on the left. Michelangelo intensifies mass in human figures, and has used great efforts to create blocked images within closed surrounding limits which render them weighty and gigantic. By this very technique he has given these figures (which are seen from the back) the proportions which were dear to Roman sculptors and which determined the ideal of the "Miles quadratus" in historical reliefs of the imperial epoch or on the Trajan pillars (from which, as we have already indicated, Buonarroti must have derived his inspiration for his soldiers' costumes and armor, which he then transplanted straight away into an ideal world of archaic austerity of his own imagination).

These men going up with alternating movements and counterposed with one another spontaneously suggest the unravelling of the groups. The full-muscled forms can be glimpsed through the folds which emphasize their presence. These constitute the "lines of force" which have always been noteworthy in Michelangelo's works (both in sculpture and in painting) and which become more outstanding in the later-period works such as the *Last Judgment*, the *Palestrina Pietà* and these Pauline Chapel paintings. One of the soldiers has a light-weight "scaled" suit of armor.

The other, a very beautiful figure higher up, is turning to speak to him. In the torsion of his athletic shoulders, the artist is offered the pretext to model an admirable piece of youthful vitality, both in form and color. The handsome face is seen in the painting from under one of those strangely formed helmets which Michelangelo liked so much and of which he emphasized the metal structure. In the drawing, this foreshortened face has an ineffable poetic fascination and seems one of the most intense creations of Michelangelo's imagination.

Finally, it is very useful to compare the treatment of the drawing with that of the painting because we can thus observe their close affinity. On paper, the chiaroscuro is obtained by very sensitive modelling, using little strokes which give the image the sculptural appearance of marble. The same thing is found in the painting, along with more accentuated shadows, because these are favored by the strength of the colors. The continuous modelling of the painting is without brusque relief and almost molded like a sculptural medium.

Certain happenings which could have had a profound influence on the poet's artistic state of mind must not be forgotten in considering the value of the Pauline frescoes, although the latter offer such effective documentation of the extreme development of Michelangelo's painting. They reflect his increasing meditation on problems of religious conscience. Such happenings, in influencing the artist, reveal some significant aspects of his mind in the execution of the composition and his painting research.

The fire which in 1545 had partly destroyed the ceiling of the Chapel and the "stucchi" attributed to Pierino del Vaga cannot have compromised the condition of the painting too much. Michelangelo wrote to his very good friend Luigi del Riccio asking him to have the chapel covered ". . . for preservation if for nothing else, because in the forthcoming season there will be rain, which not only spoils paintings, but even moves walls."

The correspondence with Luigi del Riccio tells us more about Michelangelo at this time and fits in with what is said in Donato Giannotti's *Dialogues*. While speaking of a question regarding Dante, the *Dialogues* tell how Buonarroti was taken up with the idea of death and wished to remain isolated in his house at Macel de' Corvi, or else to be with the few friends who knew how to respect his difficult character and to understand his difficult line of thought. One little piece of Giannotti's writing, among the most vibrant authentic accounts of the artist's life, is enough to make us understand his state of mind during the "Pauline" years.

Michelangelo's friends insist on his coming to dinner with them; he refuses tactfully but firmly, saying that he needs to be alone: "and remember, that wanting to find oneself and enjoy one's own company is not a job which requires

*Fig. 17—*MICHELANGELO *autograph drawing. Red pencil sketch for a "Resurrection" referable to the period of the "Last Judgment" (Paris, Cabinet des Dessins, Louvre)*

excitement or gaiety: but one must think of death! This is the only thought which leads us to recognize ourselves . . . ." Buonarroti then suffers another attack of the illness that had already obliged him to interrupt his work. In 1546 on the 9th of January, Luigi del Riccio wrote to Michelangelo's nephew that, after a serious relapse, "he is already so much better that one can say he is cured. He confessed, took communion and made out his will which I wrote down."

On returning to work, however, the artist received a severe blow when this same Luigi del Riccio died in November of that year. Vittoria Colonna's death on the 25th of February 1547, when Michelangelo was painting the *Crucifixion of Saint Peter,* was another blow.

When Luigi del Riccio died, Buonarroti lost an irreplaceable, patient, and very able friend. He had represented security in the intricate material aspects of Michelangelo's work, and the guarantee of a margin of security in his life in Rome. Michelangelo's sorrow at his friend's death was mentioned in a letter from Monsignor della Croce to Pier Luigi Farnese: "Now that Luigi del Riccio, who looked after all his affairs, is dead, Michelangelo seems to be confused in such a way that the only thing he knows how to do is to despair."

As to the death of Vittoria Colonna with regard to the understanding of Michelangelo's mind during the tortuous passage of his life in which he became more and more illuminated by his faith, we should examine the famous page of Condivi's *Life* in which we seem to hear Michelangelo's very voice. This biography says: "He bore so much love for her that I remember hearing him say that he was sorry for one thing more than any other, and that was that when he went to see her pass away from this life, he did not kiss her forehead or her cheek as one does, but only her hand."

The solitary artist, now more than ever wrapped up in himself, went on with his work in spite of his advanced age. The Pope also seemed to feel responsible for the finishing of this heavy task. He was then 82 years of age and as the ambassador Serristori wrote to Cosimo, "He went up a ladder with 10 or 12 rungs to look at the painting in the chapel which His Holiness was having Michelangelo paint."

The firm unity of Michelangelo's art permits one to speak of painting "manners" only up to a certain point. (These "manners" always go together with his sculpture, often parallel, and sometimes carried out in long intervals with some particular impetus or devotion.) We can, however, recognize that during the painting of the two great Pauline frescoes, a crisis came to a head in Michelangelo's mind and imagination. Although it came to a positive conclusion in his poetry and architecture, it was to leave deep traces in his painting and sculpture.

What is usually called (probably too systematically) Michelangelo's "third manner" is most clearly seen in the *Crucifixion of Saint Peter* in which "the sentiment that pervades it is certainly the one naturally suited to the happening which is represented, but besides this it goes far beyond the amount of pain, struggle, rebellion, and terror that would have come from the crucifixion pure and simple" (Baumgart).

De Campos expresses himself more organically in the conclusion of a synthetic but profound study of the Pauline Chapel. He maintains that in the frescoes of the *Conversion of Saint Paul* and the *Crucifixion of Saint Peter,* the artist tries to go beyond the aesthetic principles of the sixteenth century (they were already vacillating in the *Judgment*) in order to express his new spiritual world. He adds: "It was too late for Michelangelo. He did not create an entirely new language (he could not repudiate himself): he bent the old one to make it say unusual things, according to different rules which he found obscurely by intuition, but always with the same unmistakable accent. Thus came about the third 'manner' in which, when internal dissension comes down to a choice between ethical content and form (as it was then understood), the former always prevails."

When one considers the rightness of viewing the Pauline frescoes as a moral and religious testimony translated into painting, it seems that this demand is expressed in such a deliberately sober and severe style. This style is so different from that of Michelangelo himself in sculpture (in the final *Pietà*) that it causes one to reflect, regarding the painting methods used, on an expressive concentration of the contents. Instead of attempting what would later be possible for a Tintoretto or an El Greco through color and light, it goes back unexpectedly to an almost archaic solution of form.

The fact must not be overlooked that Buonarroti, to obtain the characteristic simplification that he expresses especially in the witnesses in the *Crucifixion of Saint Peter,* looked back with great attention to the fifteenth-century painters who had kept faith (even through their innate narrative spirit) with the simple and solid construction of the bodies, and the vision of a humanity that interprets sentiments with broad and expressive gestures. This leads us to remember that which animates the events of the Antichrist in the first great fresco by Signorelli for the San Brizio Chapel at Orvieto. In this work which depicts the reaction to the preaching of the false Messiah, one can see a protest which is immediately checked, or the excited dialogues among the listeners. They are figures which perhaps Michelangelo recalled when he was imagining the central group for the *Crucifixion* or one of the characters who are coming forward from the background of the scene talking to one another. Such mimicry is the natural result of the absolutely personal development of Michelangelo's thought. In gradually renouncing the ideal of a superhuman tension, this thought comes back into contact with the simple ancient idea that had nourished his early years. It determined these forms which are bound to essential gestures rendered conscious by a certainty that comes from an interior world. It is an archaism which puts Michelangelo the painter once again beside Masaccio, making him meditate on a more intense expressiveness and leading him to a spirit of contemplative narration.

It is only in this way that the artist avoids falling into intellectual subtlety. It is through these same intrinsic qualities that the Pauline images acquire their exemplary, almost moral effect, austerely presented to the eyes of the faithful.

These weighty figures seem to be oppressed by a fate bearing down on their heads. These men react, with gestures that are immediately held back, to the unjust acts which they see being carried out before their eyes.

This way of narrating, taking care to isolate the images in their sculptural structure or putting them together in a subdued commentary on the action, constitutes, if anything does, Michelangelo's novelty in this epoch. It is the final appearance of the solid steadiness of the bodies; not because they triumph in their heroic nakedness, but because they accept their sorrow as man's destiny.

The value of this kind of expression had already been seen in the groups which crowd round Christ the Judge. They comment in different ways on the terrible happening and impose silence on the more courageous ones in this composition. In the Pauline paintings, the same humanity wears the same unadorned clothes, and begins moving in a renewed awareness of life's fragility. It treads the same hard earth that was pressed for the first time by the feet of Adam and Eve.

The monochord rhythm of these figures with their awareness of human destiny concentrated in profound meditation on death (of which the Crucifixion of the First Apostle seems a heroic example) seems to be found again in Michelangelo's lines:

> Burdened with years and full of sinfulness,
> With evil custom grown inveterate,
> Both deaths I dread that close before me wait,
> Yet feed my heart on poisonous thoughts no less.
> No strength I find in mine own feebleness
> To change or life or love or use or fate,
> Unless Thy heavenly guidance come, though late,
> Which only helps and stays our nothingness.

While he was working on the Pauline Chapel, Michelangelo met Titian who came to Rome in 1545. This meeting is significant not only for the interest which we feel in the presence of the great Venetian in Rome (where he had long been invited, but where Cardinal Farnese was the only one to succeed in persuading him to be a guest in the Vatican).

The two artists represented two opposing worlds in art. Michelangelo was the undoubted genius of form, the dominator of marble, but also the creator of the most vast and profound fresco compositions of the Renaissance. He was the artist who had opened the most unknown horizons to painting in a dramatic and heroic conception which was the pointer to a new and powerful vision.

Titian was the evocator of the sixteenth century, the one who had given body and blood to the palpitating and sensual ancient fables, whose living personalities had lived the story of his times through his colors.

Vasari tells us with evident pleasure about the part he had in this meeting which can be considered symbolic of the artistic ideals of his time. It was Cardinal Farnese who gave the biographer the duty of accompanying Titian during his stay, acting as his guide to the ancient and modern marvels of the city. While the Venetian painter was lodging at the Belvedere to execute portraits of the Pope and his nephews, Vasari brought Michelangelo to see him.

It is worth drawing attention to the biographer's words in the "Description of Titian's Works" contained in his *Lives*. They offer us very interesting ideas on the value of the two painters, especially regarding Michelangelo's thoughts on Titian's painting. This extract is so lively and spontaneous that it certainly reflects the immediate impression of the event.

"One day," he writes, "when Vasari and Michelangelo visited Titian at the Belvedere, they saw in a picture which he brought to them a naked woman representing Danaë with Jove in her lap transformed into golden rain. They praised this picture very much (as one does in somebody's presence) but afterwards when they had left him, they began talking about Titian's work. Buonarroti praised him greatly saying how much he liked his coloring and his style; but that it was a shame that they did not learn the principles of good drawing in Venice, and that they had none of those painters who knew best how to teach it. This was so true (he said) that if this man had been helped in art and in drawing as he had been helped by nature, especially in simulating life, no one could do more or better than he, as he has a wonderful spirit and a very sketchy and vivacious style."

This is Michelangelo's opinion on Titian's painting, even if it is in part Vasari's desire to accentuate the importance of drawing as the fundamental thing in art. It is implicitly Michelangelo's opinion of Venetian painting in general, which he knew well through his relationship with Sebastiano del Piombo, if through nothing else. What did Buonarroti admire in Titian's work? Both the coloring and the style. With regard to the coloring, it is noteworthy that Michelangelo had a more lively interest in color not only as understood in its function with sculptured form but also as an element of harmony. In the Pauline *Crucifixion of Saint Peter*, there is reason to interpret it as meaning painting method in the strict sense (a free and broad style based on the brush stroke). According to Michelangelo, Titian lacked art and drawing. By art, he means the amount of faculties which develop with reflection. By drawing, he means how much form and sculptured linear sense he has. This is considered the sovereign language of expression.

He considers the Venetian artist's pictorial faculty to "counterfeit reality" to be a gift of nature. He recognizes in Titian a "wonderful spirit," by which he means his readiness to work, confirming his praises of his sketchy and vivacious "maniera."

His affirmation of the primary importance of drawing does not seem to be anything new for Michelangelo. The priority of drawing as a means of expression was constant up to the final period of his art. Another testimony besides

Fig. 18—MICHELANGELO *autograph drawing. Bistre sketch for a "Resurrection" referable to the period of the "Last Judgment" (London, British Museum)*

137

his painting is in his own words as remembered by Francisco de Hollanda. During a conversation about painting, the great artist confirmed in a peremptory manner: "Anyone who can draw a foot, a hand, or a neck well is capable of painting anything in the world." It should be noted that he does not speak of drawing in the general sense. He refers to the drawing of the human body which he considers the basis of painting. In any case, the recollection of the meeting between Michelangelo and Titian and Buonarroti's opinion seems considerably filtered through Vasari's "Michelangelism."

We do not know to what extent the problems and meditation about color and naturalism were stirred in Michelangelo's mind by his visit to Titian who was in the very act of painting a picture in his own surroundings. It is not likely that a wider acceptance of blended and soft colors or greater attention to the study of human types reflect a significant experience for Michelangelo because the humanity of the *Crucifixion of Saint Peter* differs so greatly from the chromaticism of the *Conversion of Saint Paul.*

Titian, however, had looked long at Buonarroti's work. He shows in several paintings that he valued Michelangelo's grandiose and sculptural vision after that same visit to Rome. He transferred this into his way of understanding anatomy as an energetic urging of the brush stroke which molds his nude figures pictorially into his foreshortenings and his broad gestures. He also adopted a way of placing his figures in space with greater fullness, into his strongly contrasted chiaroscuro, which is still, however, bathed in magic color.

The influence of the Pauline Chapel paintings on sculptural compositions of groups linked together in austere gestures of measured movements was understood in different ways by various painters of the second half of the sixteenth century. They were known even through engravings which were widely diffused, so that the two paintings could be kept under the eyes of painters who never had the opportunity to see the originals. Rome, the Vatican, and the name of Michelangelo were certainly on the lips of all painters, even those who came from far away, so that the two latest compositions by Michelangelo could have their effect even beyond the sixteenth century. Tintoretto was among those who, although being affected by the stimulus of sculptural and compositional solutions, knew how to benefit from them in the enrichment of their own individual experiences. For Tintoretto, Buonarroti's art still represented a dialectic motif compared with Venetian colorism and general luministic effects. If certain allusions in his *Crucifixion* in San Rocco could be traced to the Pauline *Crucifixion of Saint Peter*, it is interesting to note that the absorption of Michelangelesque form and dynamic contrasts in figures is already manifest in a canvas which he painted at the age of twenty, in 1548, *Saint Mark Rescuing a Slave.*

In that year, Michelangelo had not yet finished the second Pauline fresco, but had certainly finished the *Conversion of Saint Paul* three years before. It is with this that the youthful masterpiece of the precocious Tintoretto has symptomatic likenesses. That gesture of the Christ figure and that of Saint Mark at the top, the dynamic effect of the Divine visit on the frightened crowd, might be the result of a parallelism of ideas which would have significance in the artistic development of this period with its many problems. There is no doubt, however, that even without considering the fact that information of Michelangelo reached Tintoretto very rapidly, Buonarroti's influence is evident in this great Venetian's work from his earliest paintings.

The interest in Michelangelo's works is attributed for very different reasons to another painter whom we can now consider the protagonist of the next century and the most definite anticipator of modern art: Caravaggio. His relationship with Buonarroti's work and personality always seems to be that of an active dispute. The special motifs of composition which were deduced from Michelangelo remain the same only in the gestures and the disposition of the whole. Caravaggio goes back to posing a model once again, thus returning to reality; a characteristic which in Michelangelo had reached the typical heroic level.

Caravaggio's position regarding the protagonist of the century which he was about to leave behind him is not without an interesting spirit of revenge. This is perhaps also stimulated by his having Michelangelo as his first name. It seems symptomatic that in his only known signature it is seen alone, traced in the same tint as the blood which flows from Saint John the Baptist's neck onto the floor in the stupendous *Decollation of Malta*.

Buonarroti's example, in either case, helped him to resolve—in his own way, of course—one of his biggest difficulties in painting which was the fruit of his deep stylistic and moral coherence: that of making his Angels, at the top of his paintings of a sacred nature, seem so overbearingly real. This is especially true in the *Seven Works of Mercy* in Naples, in which one Angel who is coming down with the Virgin, blessing the crowd which he uses to carry out the merciful deeds, is derived in the foreshortening and in gesture from Michelangelo's Christ in the *Conversion of Saint Paul*. We cannot exclude the fact that the central part of the *Crucifixion of Saint Peter* in the Pauline Chapel (with the Saint's face turned around to conquer martyrdom and to affirm a truth that goes beyond death) had a still more profound effect on this revolutionary painter. This fact is noted in his own work on the same subject painted for the Cerasi Chapel in Santa Maria del Popolo. Although the problem of composition is very different, and although light comes into it as a new means of constructing form, there is still the fascination of Saint Peter's face which rises vigorously from the inverted Body like a peremptory affirmation of faith. This has an unforgettable antecedent in the same part of Michelangelo's work.

While he was working on the Pauline frescoes, Buonarroti was also drawing other compositions on religious subjects in an intensification of more simplified and unadorned effects. Unfortunately, through an intense desire to reach a new intimacy of style he very often destroyed his sheets (as his contemporaries unhappily recount).

For this reason, the dispersal of such testimonies of this later period was even more important. Besides using them for the paintings he was busy on (such as the one he used for the left-hand part of the *Crucifixion of Saint Peter*) the artist sometimes made drawings in order to have them painted by other artists, or else gave them to friends as souvenirs.

Steinmann has pieced together very carefully the different happenings which show how even preparatory studies or plans for compositions were considered precious relics by his contemporaries. We should not forget that Aretino, as we already said, at the time when Buonarroti was painting the *Judgment* asked repeatedly for some studies as a gift. He implored Michelangelo (a thing he did not usually do) to give him one of the drawings which the artist usually gave to the flames after they had served their purpose.

On the day after his death, Saturday the 19th of February, an inventory was made in his house at Macel de' Corvi. Four cartoons were found together with the big architectural drawings for the workshop of Saint Peter's. One of these was a scene for the *Pietà* with other figures sketched in; another with three big figures and two small boys; a third with only one figure, and the last (which was perhaps the life-size drawing for Christ the Judge and the Virgin in the *Judgment*) with the Savior and the Madonna. Only the second of these precious cartoons is left. This is the one that Buonarroti drew for Ascanio Condivi, the author of the most genuine and simple *Life of Michelangelo*. It was translated by the great artist's young admirer into the mediocre painting preserved in the Buonarroti house, called (mysteriously) *Epiphany* or the *Holy Family*.[4]

This sheet is kept in the British Museum and, notwithstanding the damage which it suffered during the many changes of fortune which finally took it to London, shows the best qualities of Michelangelo's drawing in his later years. This is especially true of the seated figure of the Virgin in the center, in the little Baby Jesus tucked between her knees and in the little Saint John who seems to discover his little playmate in his hiding place with a quick and lively movement. Also noteworthy is the solid figure of Saint Julian, on the left. It is next to the big drawings for the soldiers of the *Crucifixion of Saint Peter*, and documents its contemporaneity with the Pauline frescoes. Its broadness of form and its characteristic forward movement of the figure on the left indicate to the listening Virgin the presence of the faithful. It has the simplicity of plan, the monumental delineation in its images and at the same time that austerity which takes us back to the religious thoughts that sprang from the artist's mind during those years of meditation.

The cartoon of *Venus Kissing Cupid* in the Capodimonte Museum is much more damaged and so much gone over by other hands that it is barely possible to recognize some sign of Michelangelo's original drafting. This also belonged to the Farnese fund to which it was left by the same Fulvio Orsini who gave the precious manuscript containing Michelangelo's poetry to the Vatican.

This cartoon takes us back in time both through its pagan theme and its date, perhaps earlier than 1534 when Buonarroti was still in Florence. The pose of the statuesque nude Venus (which was to have such a wide influence in both contemporary and later painting) already shows us a motif that the artist was to develop in his allegorical drawings and which was to serve for the Saint Paul of the Pauline Chapel. Michelangelo had designed this cartoon for Jacopo da Pontormo. He was one of the most interesting and personal Florentine painters of the first Mannerist school and was esteemed by Buonarroti ever since he saw his first works. It was used by Pontormo for his picture painted on commission for Bartolomeo Bettini. It turned out so beautifully that Duke Alessandro de' Medici took it for himself, having it removed from the artist's own shop.

At the time of the Pauline Chapel, Buonarroti must have recalled his *Venus* as an already far-away dream, precedent to the tempestuous conception of the *Last Judgment*, a yearning for a mythical beauty long ago relegated to "gli amorosi pensieri, già vani e lieti." There were deeper reasons which urged him to carry out sacred themes, and to draw images of the Virgin and Christ with new and trembling care.

Michelangelo's late-period drawings have been rightly gathered together in connection with the Pauline frescoes; those for the *Expulsion of the Merchants from the Temple* and others representing different versions of the theme of the *Crucifixion*. These last ones are the testimony of an intimate spiritual coherence which links the frescoes to sculpture and which end with an impressive catharsis revealed in the *Rondanini Pietà*.

It should be understood that from this time on, Michelangelo's imagination and mind are engaged in an intense meditation on spiritual themes. These include compositions which are almost all inspired by conversations he had with Vittoria Colonna. Some of these were destined for her, such as the *Pietà*. This was conceived in a sententious archaism from which several copies were drawn in low relief and engraving, among which Bonasone's is very well known. This is described by Condivi in the following words: "He made, at this lady's request, a nude Christ taken down from the Cross. It would fall like an abandoned dead body into the arms of His Very Holy Mother if it were not held up by the arms by two small Angels. She stays seated under the Cross, with tearful and sad face and raises both hands to the sky, arms open. On the trunk of the cross is written: "None know how much blood it cost." The biographer adds this significant explanation: "The Cross is like the one that was carried from the Bianchi house in procession during the time of the plague and then placed in the Church of Santa Croce in Florence."

Fig. 19—MICHELANGELO *autograph drawing. Pencil study for a "Crucifixion." Referable to his late period, after the frescoes in the Pauline Chapel of the Vatican (1542–1550; London, British Museum)*

It can be seen from this image of devotion that Buonarroti was concerned with giving a form to the act of prayer rather than carrying out active compositions in his heroic style (at that time alien to his spirit).

These scenes, which are the result of the artist's deeply introspective listening to the motions of the soul, have significance in the documenting of the artist's final spiritual journey. There are others which are executed with an extremely simple technique depending on the vibrant quality of a chiaroscuro which models the forms, while leaving them enclosed in absolutely vigorous schemes. These, with the religious verses and the final *Pietà*, represent the most profound expression that Michelangelo has left in these last years.

The group of ideas for a crucifixion reveal almost in an autobiographical confession the oscillation of the sentiments which were maturing in the master's soul. Everything is concentrated in the dying Christ and the two figures of the Virgin and Saint John at the sides of the Cross. At one moment it is the Christ, hanging heavily on the Cross, almost magnetically drawing the two figures close to him, almost as if they were meeting each other under the big body of the Christ. In another drawing, these two seem to vibrate with the cry of agony of Jesus Crucified.

Like certain characters in the *Crucifixion of Saint Peter* they are drawn into themselves, remaining motionless and turning their heads towards the dying Christ. As in a moving drawing in the British Museum, they seem to palpitate under the arms of the Crucified Christ, almost seeking refuge in the shade of His heroic body (fig. 19).

In these drawings even the form of the Cross changes according to the pose of the Christ. In one, he is abandoned along the diverging arms of the holy wood (as in a study in the Royal Library at Windsor, which is moving in its search for dramatic effect by a refining of the form). There is on the other hand an impressively monumental drawing in the Louvre in which the body of the Christ seems to be contemplated in the immobile symmetry of the pose. It is contrasted by the movements of the lateral figures which are barely indicated and yet driven by an intimate fervour of prayer.

The final testimonies of Michelangelo's figurative art are: these drawings of Crucifixions, the last *Pietà* drawings, especially the *Rondanini* and the one which was found again in Michelangelo's house on the 19th of February 1564, the day after his death (and which was listed as "another statue begun for a Christ and another figure attached to it above, sketched, but not finished").

Michelangelo's solitude, which favored his spiritual meditation, was repeatedly accentuated by the very events of his life. One by one the people who had been near to him in his intense religious meditation, or who represented a more intimate and spontaneous contact with Humanity, departed.

This man, before his contemporaries, had affirmed as few others had done the rights of imagination and the liberty of genius. He had been on familiar terms with Popes and Princes to whom he had presented himself in the full autonomy of an artist who asserted a superior creative necessity. He found himself, however, defenseless and perturbed when, looking around him, he recognized the unbreakable law of time. With its passing, it led him towards death, giving him daily examples of its fatal law. The abandoning by him who had been faithful in the roughness and simplicity of his nature must have been even more touching, as he had helped Michelangelo in everyday life and in his work. The death of Francesco Amadori di Casteldurante, called the "Urbino," who was with him for twenty-six years as his aide and manservant, had an unexpected reflex in his proud and contrary mind. He lived in the great artist's shadow, relieved him of the fatigue of practical matters and took care of all those anonymous jobs for which Buonarroti could not materially find the time. Besides having the job of enlarging the master's drawings as we have already indicated, he sketched the less important parts of the marbles. His presence was so assiduous that the friends who called on Michelangelo were sometimes annoyed by him. This is shown by the words of Benvenuto Cellini, who has left us an unadmiring and almost grotesque portrait of the "Servant Urbino."

The artist, who confessed to feeling more affection towards humble people than towards the great lords of his time, had lavished on his aide and manservant very much of the tenderness which he so rarely managed to express spontaneously and naturally towards others. Between his impassioned soul and the object of his affection there was a confusion of sentiments and thoughts that often prevented him from expressing his mind directly without addressing his ideas in complicated forms borrowed from literature and art.

The death of Urbino came in the master's later years, at the same time that his heroic ideals had given place to a vision of Humanity which seemed to go back to being "primitive" in the fatalistic acceptance of pain, but with an awareness of a more profound and valid life: the life of the Spirit.

We can consider his letter to Vasari in February 1556 to be one of the most spontaneous testimonies of his grief at the death of his faithful servant. It expresses a state of mind beyond the contingent point, and all his internal world comes into it, so that it is a reflection also on his art. This is what Michelangelo writes to "Messer Giorgio Vasari, his dear friend at Florence" : "I can write only with difficulty, but still in answer to your letter, I shall say something. You know how Urbino died: with God's greatest grace for me, but also great loss to me and very great sorrow. The grace is that whereas in life he kept me alive, in dying he has shown me how to die, not unwillingly but with a desire for death. I have kept him with me for twenty-six years and have found him very genuine and faithful. I had made him wealthy and now that I expected him to be the prop and rest of my old age, he has left me . . . ." Michelangelo's sorrow at the death of this man (who had been so assiduously close to him for so long) is almost symbolic of the last period of his life when he lived only for art and his dream of infinite heroic beauty. It almost seems as if the artist, with this death, unexpectedly measures the value of a new reality and turns disconsolately towards everyday life. What had Urbino really represented for him, if not the same human material to mold, to put at the service of his gigantic labor? Urbino had been near his scaffolding during the painting of the *Last Judgment* and during the execution of the Pauline Chapel frescoes. He had probably also served him as a model for the countless studies of attitudes and movements, for that square-built and grave type of human being who expresses the characteristic tone of the figures who populate the *Crucifixion of Saint Peter*. He had, by his simplicity, slowly substituted in Michelangelo's imagination the dynamic and sculptural ideal of the virile nude who animates with his lines, but also with his arrogance, the dramatic heroes who are defeated in the *Judgment*.

Losing him was like realizing in a single moment what a gigantic parabola his creative genius had completed, from the great biblical poem of the Sistine, through the barely suppressed impetus of his statues, to the "terribleness" of the *Judgment* as far as the controlled sorrow of the *Crucifixion of Saint Peter*.

Thus the image of man, interpreter of the mystery of creation and asserter of a superior law of beauty in contest with classical art, struggling with the very limits of his destiny, comes back to live on earth as humanity dominated by a higher law comes forth from the very mystery of his existence.

It will not, therefore, seem strange that in these last years of his life, Michelangelo dedicated himself with renewed ardor almost exclusively to architecture and poetry. These are two forms of expression which had been proper to him even in the most vigorous blooming of his genius in his mature years, but which now seemed more part of his spiritual condition. It was not in homage to the typical attitude of intense Roman religiosity of the sixteenth century that Buonarroti affirmed so often and decisively, having accepted the heavy task of the new Saint Peter's, but only "for love of God." In his dedication to the greatest architectural labor of the century, there is a spontaneous balance of mind and imagination in Michelangelo in the highest testimony of faith which he could give as a conclusion to his life. Architecture fulfilled the need for a catharsis in his drama, which could never have finished in inactivity, but which required expression in the dialectic of forms, without necessarily passing through the refiguration of man. Anyone who wishes to go attentively through the history of Michelangelo's architecture will see that it develops from a concept of the collaboration of the elements of architecture with sculpture. It is nearer the overbearing energy entrusted to architectural means. While conserving the intimate dramatic necessity which was irrepressible in Michelangelo, they act in the contrasts of mass, volume, hollows, and curves in an autonomous way, even if they use measured decorative elements which help them in making their language more supple.

The artist, at this stage of development when faced with the new Saint Peter's, is stylistically and spiritually ready to dedicate himself to it without reservations.

This immense construction which grew slowly but tenaciously in Michelangelo's very hands (in fact he even modelled in clay a sculptured idea of the dome) enthralled the artist into more and more work. As he seemed to hear in the depths of his soul the coming of the final hour, his anxiety grew lest he should not be able to finish the colossal undertaking.

The most important personalities of Florence, his relatives and friends tried to make him go back to his own home. His answer was always the same: the Pope had entrusted Saint Peter's to him, he had to complete the work at all costs and if he left Rome even for a short time, too many "gluttons" would profit by his absence to spoil everything.

His place was in Rome, his world was that of the Vatican "workshop," his daily labor was going into the immense building yard from his house in Foro Traiano to direct imperiously and to oversee the growing architecture. He was ready to speak in violent and peremptory tones against anyone showing sluggishness or, worse, dishonesty in the work. Could Michelangelo's old passion for man cease altogether: the tenacious love for the only language to which he had dedicated his life, and which, by way of the free play of proportion and muscles, had arrived at this wonder of creation which is the human body?

His last thought on a "holy death," of which his faithful servant Urbino had given him such a touching example, was to be one of an absolute and by then peaceful detachment from the longed-for images that had crowded his imagination during an entire life. In defending his plans for Saint Peter's from the criticism of incompetent maligners, however, he let a moving confession escape. It shows us once again the great artist in his entirety and coherence, even if in a style of thought which moves away from artistic practice and enters into theoretical principles.

This confession was in a famous letter which he wrote to Cardinal Rodolfo Pio da Carpi in reply to criticisms which had been aroused in the workshop of Saint Peter's. He was by then only a few years from his death, but it shows how Michelangelo became even greater in his clarity of ideas and in his certainty in an ancient deep-rooted aesthetic conviction. In order to overcome the annoyance of having to speak of art to someone who knew nothing about it, he assumed a tone of lapidary effectiveness. He patiently affirmed that the various parts of an organic work of architecture correspond among each other and follow the same laws as those of the human body. The exceptions were the central elements, "i mezzi," that have no symmetrical correspondence, "just as the nose, which is in the middle of the face, is not obliged to either one eye or the other, whereas one hand is obliged to be like the other and one eye like the other in respect to the sides and the pendants." He concludes with a decisive affirmation: "It is certainly true that the parts of architecture depend on the limbs of man. A man who has not been, and is not a good figure draughtsman, especially of anatomy, cannot understand architecture."

It might seem that this is only a question of a testimony (although born of conviction) of the typically Humanistic ideas on which Renaissance architecture was founded. In this case, however, Michelangelo's words have a very much deeper and more original value.

He starts, it is true, from the concept of symmetry which classical architecture takes from the human body. He makes it physical and dynamic in essence, and in a firm personal conviction, overcomes the principle of the Renaissance canons by that of the human model in its physical energy and living beauty of proportion. It could not be explained why he insisted on the identification of the human limbs with those of architecture. We cannot understand the heat of such a clear-cut affirmation which excludes any understanding of architecture by anyone who is not a good figure draughtsman and a master of anatomy.

Even architecture for Michelangelo was not an art liberated from the language of the human figure, but is developed from the translation of the image of man into expressive elements. It developed even more from that very anatomy which enabled the giving of vitality to forms which the artist had bestowed on his figures of warriors, slaves, and heroes.

We have recognized the validity of this absolute conviction in Michelangelo. One should immediately add, however, that in the transfiguration of the language of human forms into that of architecture, the artist felt that he obtained a contact with a medium which could be better adapted to his intimate desire. This was a desire for severe austerity and great calm, beyond the perturbing presence of man in his particular shape. It is as if in architecture, this tormenting idol freed itself of its carnal clothing, to be reborn as a perennial fountainhead of creative life.

The artist had long ago given voice to his secret spiritual longing in verses of exceptional power and deep inner meaning, beyond that heroic creative force which had for so long served him as the only reason for living. The solution to the drama can be found in his poetry, perhaps even more than in his architecture. It expresses more directly those thoughts and feelings which flee from assuming the material consistency of stone. That is why, as a conclusion to his ideal pictorial parable which is so coherent in its development (and always so bound up with the other manifestations of his spirit), it behooves us to think about these verses which he now wrote only for himself, and which have the mysterious force of a prayer.

Among them all, one famous sonnet, written about ten years before his death, can be taken as the seal of the final sufferings of his art, almost as a spiritual testament. In this, the sentiment unfolds with a singular calm which instills a grave and sure rhythm into the lines. Michelangelo is like a Dantesque castaway, who has finally reached the calm waters leading into the last haven. He seems to turn round to look back at the tempests of the past, and remembers without regret his glorious labors.

He feels himself near a death of which he is certain but not afraid. He trembles for that other eternal death of the soul. All seems vain to him. He realizes that the imagination that had made art appear to him the only idol and sovereign was full of errors. Finally comes the greatest heroic renunciation pronounced by one of the greatest artists of all time. His soul is not content with painting and sculpture because it is turned to another goal, that of Christ.

> Now hath my life across a stormy sea
> Like a frail bark reached that wide port where all
> Are bidden, ere the final reckoning fall
> Of good and evil for eternity.

Now know I well how that fond phantasy
Which made my soul the worshipper and thrall
Of earthly art, is vain; how criminal
Is that which all men seek unwillingly.

Those amorous thoughts which were so lightly dressed,
What are they when the double death is nigh?
The one I know for sure, the other dread.

Painting nor sculpture now can lull to rest
My soul that turns to His great love on high,
Whose arms to clasp us on the cross were spread.

This sublime peace of the soul came to Michelangelo on the evening of the 18th February 1564 when, after the hour of the Rosary, death took him from his house at Foro Traiano, surrounded by drawings and outlined marbles, mute testimonies of the long course of his genius.

NOTES FOR CHAPTER FIVE

(1) L. SABBATINI and F. ZUCCARI: *Gli affreschi di Michelangelo,* in the *Cappella Paolina in Vaticano* with an introduction by F. Baumgart and B. Biagetti, Vatican City 1934.
(2) F. DE HOLLANDA: *Dialoghi* (translated from Portuguese and edited by A. M. BESSONE AURELI), IV ed. Rome 1953.
(3) F. STEINMANN: *Cartoni di Michelangelo* in "Bollettino d'arte del Ministero della P.I." July 1925.
(4) The reproductions of this and other cartoons may be seen in the preceding treatise by STEINMANN: *Cartoni di Michelangelo.*

CHRONOLOGICAL SUMMARY
and BIBLIOGRAPHICAL NOTE

CHRONOLOGICAL SUMMARY

1475—March 6	Michelangelo born in the Castle of Caprese (now Caprese Michelangelo) to Ludovico Buonarroti Simoni and Francesca di Neri di Miniato del Sera.
1488—April 1	His father apprentices him to Domenico and David Ghirlandaio in Florence.
1488—1492	Lorenzo the Magnificent takes him under his protection. He frequents the Medici garden of San Marco.
1492—April 9	Death of Lorenzo the Magnificent.
1494	Michelangelo leaves Florence for Venice and Bologna.
1495	He returns to Florence and works for Lorenzo di Pierfrancesco de' Medici.
1496—June	Makes his first journey to Rome where he remains until 1501 (*Bacchus*; the *Pietà* in Saint Peter's).
1501—1505	Works on sculpture and painting in Florence (the *Bruges Madonna*; *David*; the cartoon of the *Battle of Cascina*; the *Doni Madonna*).
1505—March	Julius II summons him to Rome for the project of the Papal tomb.
1506	Returns abruptly to Florence, because he was not received by the Pope.
1506—November 27	Meets Julius II in Bologna.
1508—1512	Recalled to Rome by Julius II, paints the Sistine Chapel vault.
1513—1517	Divides time between Rome and Florence, working on the architecture and sculpture for San Lorenzo.
1527	The Sack of Rome (Michelangelo is in Florence).
1529—1530	Designs the Florentine fortifications, but leaves the city for Venice. Having returned to Florence in 1530, works on the Medici Tombs.
1534	Receives the commission for the fresco of the *Last Judgment* from Clement VII.
1536—1541	Paints the *Last Judgment* in the Sistine Chapel for Paul III.
1542—1550	Paints the *Conversion of Saint Paul* and the *Crucifixion of Saint Peter* in the Pauline Chapel.
1547—1560	Named architect of the Factory of Saint Peter's, he concerns himself intensely with the Vatican Basilica and other constructions. Writes religious poetry and sculpts the last *Pietà* groups.
1564—February 18	Michelangelo dies at the hour of the Ave Maria in his Roman house at Macel de' Corvi near the Trajan Forum.

NOTE: A complete chronological summary of the life and works of Michelangelo, amply documented and critically written, can be found in the volume of A. Venturi's *History of Italian Art* (*Storia dell' Arte Italiana*) dedicated to *16th Century Painting*, part I, Chapter V, pages 627–716.

BIBLIOGRAPHICAL NOTE

The "classic" bibliography on Michelangelo until 1926 was the *Michelangelo Bibliography* of ERNST STEINMANN and RUDOLF WITT-KOWER, Leipzig, Klinkardt-Biermann, 1927: it is an indispensable tool for studies on Michelangelo, compiled with a clear vision of the various problems, subdivided according to topics and orientated indices. The same STEINMANN, one of the most serious and careful Michelangelo scholars (praiseworthy, among other things, for having assembled over a long period of time, a vast and organic section of books on Michelangelo in the Biblioteca Hertziana in the Palazzo Zuccari in Rome), completed his bibliography in 1930 with the volume *Michelangelo im Spiegel seiner Zeit,* Leipzig, 1930 (pp. 65–95).

Another bibliographical supplement was published by P. CHERUBELLI in the miscellaneous volume *Michelangelo Buonarroti nel quarto centenario dello scoprimento del Giudizio Universale,* Sansoni, Florence, 1942, and includes the studies which appeared between 1928 and 1941. A *Chronological Summary of the Life and Works of Michelangelo* compiled with full, broad citation of documents contemporary to the artist is premised on the treatment of Michelangelo's painted works, in the volume of the *History of Italian Art* of A. VENTURI, dedicated to *16th Century Painting,* part I—U. Hoepli, Milan, 1925, pp. 627–716. It is one of the most reliable, informed references on Michelangelo.

Sources from the artist's contemporaries, of primary importance, are the *Lives* of G. VASARI and A. CONDIVI. Vasari's version, in the two sections of 1550 and 1568, should be consulted in the modern editions; among the many, we recommend C.L. RAGGHIANTI's edition in the "Rizzoli Classics" series, Milan, 1942–1949, and particularly, G. VASARI: *The Life of Michelangelo* (in the compilations of 1550 and 1568), edited and with commentary by PAOLA BAROCCHI, Ricciardi, Milan-Naples, 1962. The five-volume work includes a volume of text, three volumes of critical commentary, and a volume of analytic indices of exceptional thoroughness. It constitutes the best and, by now, indispensable foundation for an in-depth study of Michelangelo.

The *Life* by A. CONDIVI, written from direct information supplied by the artist himself, and which G. VASARI freely drew upon, was published in 1553 by the printer Antonio Blado in Rome, and can be consulted in various modern editions: K. FREY's edition, Berlin, 1887, A. MARAINI's edition, Florence, 1927, or the illustrated edition, with introduction and notes by P. D'ANCONA, L.F. Cogliati, Milan, 1928.

Among contemporary sources for biographical knowledge of the artist, and for a more profound comprehension of his character, one should consult: *Dialoghi Michelangioleschi di Francisco de Hollanda* (translated from the Portuguese), A. BESSONE AURELI, IV edition, Fratelli Palombi, Rome, 1953, and D. REDIG DE CAMPOS' critical edition of *Dialoghi di Donato Giannotti, etc.,* Sansoni, Florence, 1939.

Among the many *Lives* of Michelangelo of literary character intended to re-evoke his personality, see: C. PAPINI, *Vita di Michelangelo nella vita del suo tempo,* Milan, 1949. In order to grasp the artist's spirit, as he directly revealed his most vivid feelings, it is of fundamental importance to study his letters and poetry. For this material, among others, see: G. MILANESE, *Le lettere di Michelangelo coi ricordi ed i contratti artistici,* Florence, 1875; *Lettere di Michelangelo Buonarroti* with preface by G. PAPINI, Carabba, Lanciano, 1913; K. FREY, *Die Dichtungen des M. A. Buonarroti,* Berlin, 1897; F. RIZZI, *Michelangelo poeta;* W. FACON, *Michelangelo poeta,* Bucharest, 1939; V. MARIANI, *Poesia di Michelangelo,* Fratelli Palombi, Rome, 1941, and especially, toe most complete and modern edition of his poetry—*Michelangelo Buonarroti—Rime*, edited by E. Noè GIRARDI, Laterza, Bari, 1960. This exemplary edition includes all of Michelangelo's poems, the genesis of each of which is scrupulously traced. The volume is equipped with a perfect critico-philological apparatus which permits us to study Michelangelo's lyrics in their genuineness. Monographic treatments of orientation on the artist's life and art can be found in the major Encyclopedias; one of the most complete of these is in the *Thieme—Becker Künstler Lexicon* with text by PANOFSKY-TOLNAY, Leipzig, 1930. The *Enciclopedia Italiana*'s article on the artist, written with balance and breadth of information, has also been published separately: P. TOESCA, *Michelangelo*, "Series of the *Enciclopedia Italiana*" II–IV, Rome, 1935. The text of the article "Michelangelo" in the *Enciclopedia Universale dell' Arte*, written by CHARLES DE TOLNAY (1962), is very comprehensive of the various critical opinions and is well documented. The same writer, one of the most important modern scholars of Michelangelo, is also responsible for the more complete, critically executed monograph *Michelangelo*, Princeton University Press, 1943–1960 (Vol. I–V). In all of the aforesaid works (and particularly the last) Michelangelo's painting activity is well treated. Besides these, other information on Michelangelo the painter can be gathered from: A. BERTINI, *Michelangelo fino alla Sistina*, Turin, 1942; F. BAUMGART and B. BIAGETTI, *Gli affreschi di Michelangelo ecc. nella Cappella Paolina*, edited by the Pontificia Accademia Romana di Archeologia, Vatican City, 1934; E. STEINMANN, *Die Sixtinische Kapelle,* Munich, 1922; D. REDIG DE CAMPOS and B. BIAGETTI, *Il Giudizio Universale di Michelangelo*, edited by the Pontificia Academia Romana di Archeologia, A. FACCIOLI, ed., Rome, 1944 (two volumes), with important technical notes on Michelangelo's painting; M. GUERRISI, *"Il Giudizio" di Michelangelo*, Rome, 1947; V. MARIANI, *L'Univers de la Sixtine en Michel-Ange*, Paris, Hachette, 1961—(Chapter V); *Michelangelo (pittore, scultore, architetto)*, edited by L. Goldscheider, Phaidon Press, London, and Sansoni, Florence, 1953; *Tutta la Pittura di Michelangelo*, edited by ENZO CARLI, Rizzoli, Milan, 1964.

For a study of the drawings, it is fundamental to consult K. FREY, *Die Handzeichnungen Michelangelos Buonarroti,* Berlin, 1909, 1911, collection integrated by F. Knapp, *Die Handzeichnungen Michelangelos,* Berlin, 1925; BERNARD BERENSON, *The Drawings of the Florentine Painters,* London, 1903 (two volumes)—new edition, Chicago, 1938 (three volumes); J. WILDE, *Italian Drawings in the Department of Prints and Drawings in the British Museum; Michelangelo and his Studio,* London, 1953; L. DUSSLER, *Die Zeichnungen des Michelangelo*, Berlin, 1959; P. BAROCCHI, *Michelangelo e la sua scuola; I Disegni di Casa Buonarroti e degli Uffizi,* Florence, 1951; *Mostra di disegni di Michelangelo* (Room of Drawings and Prints of the Uffizi), catalog edited by P. BAROCCHI, Florence, Holschki, 1962. For the importance of Michelangelo's anatomical studies, see V. MARIANI, *Anatomia in Michelangelo Buonarroti nel IV Centenario del Giudizio Universale* (1541–1941), Sansoni, Florence, 1942, p. 133.

PLATES

MADONNA AND CHILD
WITH THE INFANT SAINT JOHN
known as the "Manchester Madonna"

Unfinished painting. This charming work can be dated around 1498–1500; much discussed for its authorship which is here confirmed with certainty as Michelangelo's. It is from his youthful period when he still operated within the sphere of Domenico Ghirlandaio and Francesco Granacci, but already shows clear relationships with the *Pietà* in St. Peter's and the *Bruges Madonna*.

DEPOSITION

Partially incomplete painting. This *Deposition* derives from the old Fesch Collection in the Falconieri Palace in Rome. Its origin has been the object of discussion for a long time and some critics still deny its authorship to Michelangelo. It displays, at any rate, the master's autograph. The date is uncertain but would seem to belong to his youthful period: after the *Manchester Madonna* and before the Sistine Chapel frescoes.

THE DONI MADONNA

Executed for the Doni-Strozzi marriage in Florence in 1503, this composition is considered by some to be the only painting on wood which has remained from Michelangelo's work. It follows, chronologically, the *Manchester Madonna* and the *Deposition* of London, and shows characteristics which anticipate the painting of the Sistine Vault.

DRUNKENNESS OF NOAH

One of the sections of the beginning of the great fresco cycle.

DRUNKENNESS OF NOAH
Detail

It is important to note that the small figure of Noah planting the vineyard was left in a sketchy state by the artist. In the pose of the drunken Noah, we see an evident relationship with classic sculptural renderings of the Rivers and an anticipation of the figures of the Medici Tombs in the New Sacristy of San Lorenzo in Florence.

THE FLOOD

This is, perhaps, the first large section executed by the artist at the beginning of the work. It was damaged in the right section where a broad portion of the plaster (on which a tree was painted, to whose trunk was joined the tent, temporary refuge of the castaway) has been lost. In several figures of the left section it is possible to detect (because of a certain crudeness and various details of execution) the presence of collaborators whom the master abruptly dispensed with so that he personally did a large part of the scene, recalling in various episodes the cartoon which he had designed in Florence for the *Battle of Cascina*.

SACRIFICE OF NOAH

Section with the episode of the *Sacrifice of Noah* flanked by two pairs of *Nudes* who support bronze shields decorated with Biblical scenes. This belongs to the first group of scenes painted at the beginning of the fresco cycle. We should observe that in these first episodes painted by the artist, the pairs of *Nudes* still have a decorative character and repeat the same poses in symmetry. Later, however, they assume great freedom of gesture and are clearly individualized in the single figures.

SACRIFICE OF NOAH

In this classically inspired composition, we note the evident references to Greco-Roman sarcophagi and to Imperial reliefs with sacrificial scenes. The drawing and sculptural elements predominate and the composition (also because of its references to ancient sculpture) is executed with studious slowness.

ORIGINAL SIN
and THE EXPULSION FROM EARTHLY PARADISE

This is probably the episode which indicates the artist's first interruption in the painting of the vault (1510–1511). He fills the larger space with two closely linked symmetrical scenes. The relationship is indicated in compositional elements as well as the Guilt-Punishment relationship.

The Demon winds around the Tree of Good and Evil in the aspect of a serpent which ends in a female bust, according to an old medieval tradition. The position of the Angel dressed in red which recalls the Demon's movement, translating it into a primitive gesture, is certainly intentional.

THE CREATION OF EVE

Section with the *Creation of Eve*, flanked by two pairs of *Nudes* which support the bronze shields decorated with ribbons and oak garlands. Various pen and pencil sketches in the British Museum refer to these figures. These sketches clearly show the search for contrasting positions which are executed here with great effect.

THE CREATION OF EVE

Detail

The artist resolves the difficult depiction of Eve's evocation from the body of Adam in an original manner. He places the female figure almost as if it were a link between the creative power of the Lord and the abandoned image of the man immersed in sleep.

THE CREATION OF ADAM

This famous episode offers one of the highest affirmations of Michelangelo's art in the Sistine Chapel. The ample space allows the artist to place the figures with exceptional effect. Adam is among the most beautiful and classic images painted by the artist, who gave his figures the perfect expression of the human body. In relation to it, the Lord, who arrives in flight from the infinite spaces of the Cosmos, appears as a personification of the Creative force, triumphantly accompanied by genii enfolded in the great shadow of a fabulous mantle. The group assumes the aspect of a gigantic cloud.

THE CREATION OF ADAM

Detail

Detail of the figure of Adam in the Creation scene. In this famous image which celebrates the artist's human ideal, the painting style may be linked again to the *Doni Madonna* for the firmness of the drawing and the careful study of chiaroscuro (which is, however, more expanded and full).

THE CREATION OF ADAM
Detail

The meeting of the two hands: the Lord's and Man's. Here the artist, through intensive study, has attained the ultimate mastery of the human form. He expresses, in the diversity of the two hands (Adam's hand inert and lifeless, the Lord's hand palpitating with creative energy), one of the finest conceptions of his genius. He concentrates a world of sculptural values of the most powerful expressiveness into one detail.

THE SEPARATION OF THE LAND
FROM THE WATERS

The Separation of the Land from the Waters, flanked by two pairs of *Nudes* which support decorated bronze shields. The artist increases the dynamism of the gestures and the vigorous counterposition of the nude figures, the fruit of detailed study from a model (even if sometimes inspired from classical art).

THE SEPARATION OF THE LAND
FROM THE WATERS
Detail

The figure of the Lord, who flies over the expanse of the waters, accompanied by genii which bear his garments, is of grandiose effect. He passes over and blesses the new order of the world. The extremely bold foreshortening increases the monumental effect of the apparition.

NUDES

One of the *Nudes* which flank *The Separation of the Land from the Waters*. The dramatic movement of the figure was suggested to the artist's imagination by the idea that the shield which the young man bears has come loose from the supporting ribbons and is about to fall into the chapel below.

THE CREATION OF THE SUN, THE MOON
AND THE PLANTS

Making use of the possibility of repeating the same image in two different actions, Michelangelo imprints a contrasting movement on the duplicate figure of the Creator. In the center, the gold-colored sun seems to illuminate the figure of the Lord with a grazing light as He evokes the two celestial bodies from nothingness with a proud, imperative gesture.

THE CREATION OF THE SUN, THE MOON
AND THE PLANTS

Detail

Detail of the Lord in the *Creation of the Sun, the Moon and the Plants.* We observe the genie to the left, who shades his eyes from the light of the newly created sun. Another genie, to the right in the shade, protects himself from the nocturnal cold.

THE LORD GIVES ORDER TO CHAOS

The Lord gives Order to Chaos flanked by two pairs of *Nudes* with shields of decorated bronze. The constant search for contrasting movements is united here with a deepening of the sculptural effect obtained by a grazing light. Michelangelo left various notes for the nude at the upper left (now in the British Museum).

THE LORD GIVES ORDER TO CHAOS

Detail

Here Michelangelo reached an extreme breadth of painting technique: the drawing form gives way to rapid, ingenious fluidity of the brush-stroke. The coloring passes from one tone to another almost imperceptibly and the manner of sketching the image recalls the characteristic "unfinished" state in which the artist, as sculptor, left many works.

The "divine drunkenness" of the Creation is admirably translated in the pose of the Lord and the whirl of His garments.

NUDES

One of the *Nudes* who bear the decorated bronze shields which are placed over the thrones of the Prophets and Sibyls. This is one of the most accurately painted of the master's figures. The artist has expressed his ideal aesthetic of the nude in a rare equilibrium between reality and imaginative transfiguration.

THE PROPHET ZACHARIAH

The gigantic images of the Prophets and Sibyls which occupy the base of the pseudo-architecture of the vault express the various moments of inspiration, of meditation in the reading of the Holy books, and of the sudden illumination in the revelation of divinatory power. Next to each figure, Michelangelo places two genii who assist or participate in the meditation or inspiration of the Prophets and Sibyls. They often constitute the ideal link between the voice of the Lord and the prophetic function of these protagonists of the great religious poem. At the sides of the marmoreal thrones, Michelangelo has recovered the already elegant balusters with gold. They constitute the only element possessing a purely decorative function.

ZAC RIAS

THE PROPHET JOEL

In this grave, inspired image the artist seems to recall the impulsive but often "cogitative" figure of Bramante (the latter adjective being Vasari's). Contemporaneously, Raphael put the architect into his *Dispute* and the *School of Athens*.

THE DELPHIC SIBYL

In this famous image, which reflects his unexpected inspiration with such efficacy, Michelangelo avails himself of the sculptural appearance of the Sibyl's arm which is crossed over her bosom, to obtain a singularly sculptural relief.

THE DELPHIC SIBYL

Detail

The face with its large open eyes, rich with intense expression, is constructed in rigorous symmetry according to a cross system that was originally traced on the plaster.

THE PROPHET ISAIAH

In the diversity of poses and gestures which the artist assigns to the Prophets, he emphasizes their various personalities. Here, a preceding moment of meditation is followed by the careful listening to the call which reaches Isaiah's ear through the excited words of the genie who alludes to God's voice.

ESAIAS

THE ERITREAN SIBYL

The figure, spread over the space with natural grandiosity, turns over the leaves of the book of the Holy Mysteries while one of the genii lights an ancient oil lamp with his strong hand.

THE PROPHET EZEKIEL

This image, among the most agitated figures in the Sistine Chapel, expresses the reflection of the Divine words transmitted to the Prophet (from the very beautiful child who indicates that Heaven reveals the mysterious truth) with his sudden gesture.

E ZECHIEL

THE PROPHET EZEKIEL

Detail

The singular care which Michelangelo took in painting this Prophet (who proudly extends himself to call the faithful to hear the divine words) reveals the artist's particular affection for this image. The Prophet's face is among the most vigorous conceived by the artist.

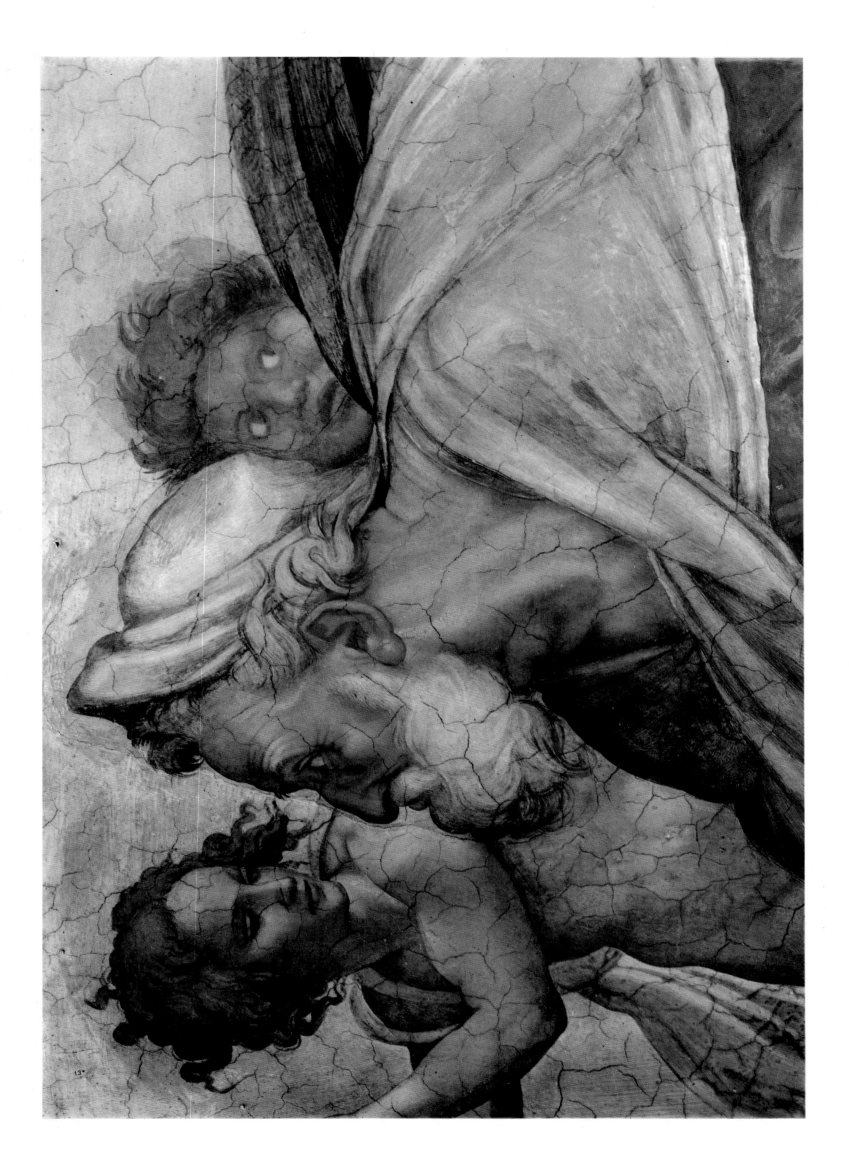

THE CUMEAN SIBYL

The monumental figure of this Sibyl, which seems to be modelled in bronze, reveals typological characteristics which are intentionally southern, in the hawklike profile of the old sun-tanned gypsy.

CVMAEA

THE PROPHET DANIEL

The idea of depicting the Prophet transcribing notes from a large book provoked Michelangelo's grandiose placement of the figure, to which the light gives strong relief. The artist imagines the little genie as a caryatid under the large, sacred book. (This is an exception to the function usually assigned to the genie.)

Rome, Vatican—The Vault of the Sistine Chapel (1508–1512)

THE PERSIAN SIBYL

The exotic accent, which recalls the Orient, is evident here in the amply folded costume and the white turban which is placed on the Sibyl's head.

PERSICHA

THE PERSIAN SIBYL
Detail

From the painting standpoint, this detail reveals the infinite resources in Michelangelo's art. The thin profile of the old Sibyl, who reads the short pages with difficulty, is entirely drawn in shadow and projected on a light background. The colors, motionless in the light, are diluted in delicate harmonies.

THE LIBYAN SIBYL

The figure, done with special care by the artist, assumes extraordinary vitality in its attitude, the result of a lively contrast of gestures. The artist thoroughly studied every element of this figure from life as we see from the drawing in the Berruete Collection in Madrid.

THE PROPHET JEREMIAH

This image, one of the most expressive in the Sistine Chapel, translates the painful spirituality of the Prophet in a new, deep manner, even in the harmonious coloristic agreements.

HIEREMIAS

THE PROPHET JONAH

A masterpiece of invention and style, the surprising image of the *Prophet Jonah* ends (on the main altar) the series of large figures which form the base of the painting decoration.

IONAS

JUDITH AND HOLOFERNES

Angular cloister vault with the scene of *Judith and Holofernes*. This is one of the two squares painted in the first phase of the decoration. Because of this, we note a more evident clarity of the drawing. The almost triptych-like partition of the scene is notable.

DAVID AND GOLIATH

Angular cloister vault with *David and Goliath*. From the first phase of the decoration, this scene depicts the group of protagonists as if it were a sculptured composition. The motif of the youth who overcomes the giant occurs often in Michelangelo's art.

CRUCIFIXION OF AMMAN

Angular cloister vault with the scene of the Crucifixion of Amman. In this scene (one of the last to be painted on the vault), the search for difficult and bold foreshortenings shows the artist's mastery in the freer, more articulate composition.

THE BRAZEN SERPENT

Angular cloister vault with the scene of the Brazen Serpent. The complicated fore-shortening and the excitement of the poses signal the conclusion of Michelangelo's painting of the Sistine Vault. We observe clear relationships with the *Laocoön* group.

MEDALLIONS

Decorated medallions in pseudo bronze on the shields which the Nudes bear, above the marmoreal thrones of the Prophets and Sibyls. In these medallions, Michelangelo depicted episodes from the Old Testament in compositions inspired from medals and coins of classical art. He used an intentionally abbreviated technique which aims for effects of relief and the shine of the metal. The medallion in the center represents the Destruction of the Statue of Baal and the medallion below, the Slaughter of the Sons of Achab.

MEDALLIONS

Medallions in pseudo bronze decorated with Biblical episodes. The medallion in the center depicts the Sacrifice of Isaac and that below, Absalom Ensnared by his Hair in the Tree. The incomplete aspect which the three pseudo reliefs present is due to the particular placement which the artist gave the shields, partly hidden in the shadow of the figures which flank them.

MEDALLIONS

Medallions in pseudo bronze decorated with Biblical scenes. The medallion in the center depicts the Death of Uriah. The different painting treatment is, to a large extent, due to the diverse light conditions in which the artist conceived the medallions (which at a distance had to appear as if they were in relief).

FAMILIES OF THE JEWISH PEOPLE

Cloister vault resulting from the spaces above the windows. Groups of families depicting the Jewish People. In the upper triangle, the group with the mother and sleeping child recalls a motif which was dear to Michelangelo also in sculpture. In the lower triangle, the man's figure is more definite and strongly characterized even in his garments. The mother and child seem to be united in a single destiny of solitude.

FAMILIES OF THE JEWISH PEOPLE

Cloister vault resulting from the spaces above the windows. Groups of families depicting the Jewish People. In the upper triangle, the child seeks the breast of his mother who, almost as if oppressed by a sad presentiment, holds a crude piece of bread in her hand. The scene below depicts the woman who stands out from the others.

Rome, Vatican — The Vault of the Sistine Chapel (1508–1512)   XLVI

FAMILIES OF THE JEWISH PEOPLE

Cloister vault resulting from the spaces above the windows. Groups of families depicting the Jewish People. These are among the most expressive compositions in the series. The pensive group of the mother and child in the upper square is particularly definite. The image below and immersed in sleep is unusual.

FAMILIES OF THE JEWISH PEOPLE

Cloister vault resulting from the spaces above the windows. Groups of families depicting the Jewish People. The artist employs the diminutive triangular form above in order to represent a group in strong relief. Below, the young woman seems to be dominated by a worry which fixes her pose.

THE ANCESTORS OF CHRIST

One of the lunettes above the windows on the walls depicting the Ancestors of Christ: Aminadab. To the left, the figure of the young man in a frontal position seems almost a portrait because of its strong characterization. To the right, the woman combing her hair is among the most vivid images which the artist ever drew from life.

Rome, Vatican—The Vault of the Sistine Chapel (1508–1512)

THE ANCESTORS OF CHRIST

One of the lunettes above the windows on the walls depicting the Ancestors of Christ:
Asa, Jehoshaphat, Joram. The figure to the left in an Oriental costume is almost grotesque.
The new dramatic group to the right, instead, seems to recall the image of charity to life.

THE ANCESTORS OF CHRIST

One of the lunettes above the windows on the walls depicting the Ancestors of Christ: Solomon, Boaz, Obeth. To the left, with singular human penetration, the artist depicts a sleeping mother and child. To the right, he pushes the grotesque almost to caricature in the old pilgrim with the knotty, chiselled stick.

THE ANCESTORS OF CHRIST

One of the lunettes above the windows on the walls depicting the Ancestors of Christ: Roboam, Abias. To the left, Michelangelo, in his free observation from life, possibly intends to create the image of a pregnant woman. To the right, a broken-hearted mother seems to be torn by grief and fatigue. Sketches for this figure are in the collection of the University of Oxford.

THE ANCESTORS OF CHRIST

One of the lunettes above the windows on the walls, depicting the Ancestors of Christ: Naason. The female figure to the left is gazing at herself in a mirror. The young man to the right, who has stopped reading the book on the lectern and seems immersed in profound thought, is more original.

THE ANCESTORS OF CHRIST

One of the lunettes above the windows on the walls, depicting the Ancestors of Christ. In the variety of human motifs in these images, there are several like this old spinner which acquire intense and almost symbolic significance through their austere style.

THE ANCESTORS OF CHRIST
Detail

One of the lunettes above the windows on the walls, depicting the Ancestors of Christ. Broadly sketched in changing colors, this figure of a mother who gazes with ardor at her sleeping child while rocking the cradle gently with her foot is one of Michelangelo's most intimate creations.

THE ANCESTORS OF CHRIST

One of the lunettes above the windows on the walls, depicting the Ancestors of Christ. The depiction of the mother with her two children assumes a monumental character because of the fullness of the painting style and the breadth of the grouping's placement.

THE ANCESTORS OF CHRIST

One of the lunettes above the windows on the walls, depicting the Ancestors of Christ. This figure with the strange, priestly costume indicates as do the others of the same scenes the artist's desire to determine the Biblical character of the images in the Ancestors of Christ lunettes. The child wrapped in a mantle seems ready for a sacrifice.

THE LAST JUDGMENT

A fresco covering the entire wall at the end of the Sistine Chapel. Commissioned by Clement VII, but only begun in 1536 under the papacy of Paul III. Finished in October, 1541, it was unveiled November 1, 1541 and was first shown to the public on Christmas Day of that year. In order to execute the gigantic composition, Michelangelo walled up the two fifteenth-century windows that opened on the walls and destroyed the frescoes from the time of Sixtus IV which were linked to those which are still extant on the lateral walls. Michelangelo also destroyed two lunettes which he himself had done at the time of the painting of the vault, depicting the Ancestors of Christ. In the painting of the *Last Judgment*, these were substituted by the two groups above, containing the Passion symbols.

Copy of the *Last Judgment*, by Marcello Venusti (1512–1579). The accurately painted copy of the great fresco was done by Venusti, a follower of Michelangelo, for Cardinal Alessandro Farnese in 1549. This was executed before Paul III commissioned Daniele da Volterra to cover several of the nudes in Michelangelo's fresco with draperies. The copy is a most useful document for the reconstruction of the integral aspect of Michelangelo's painting (also in regard to the effect of the original colors which have faded somewhat with time). Now in the Capodimonte Museum, Naples.

Rome, Vatican—The Sistine Chapel (1536–1541)   LVIII

THE LAST JUDGMENT
Detail

Central group of Angels with trumpets who call the Reborn to the supreme Judgment and bear the Books of Merits (to the left) and Faults (to the right). In the composition of this central section of the *Last Judgment*, the artist recalls the cartoon for the *Battle of Cascina*. Here, however, the human form has become monumental and idealized into heroic limbs.

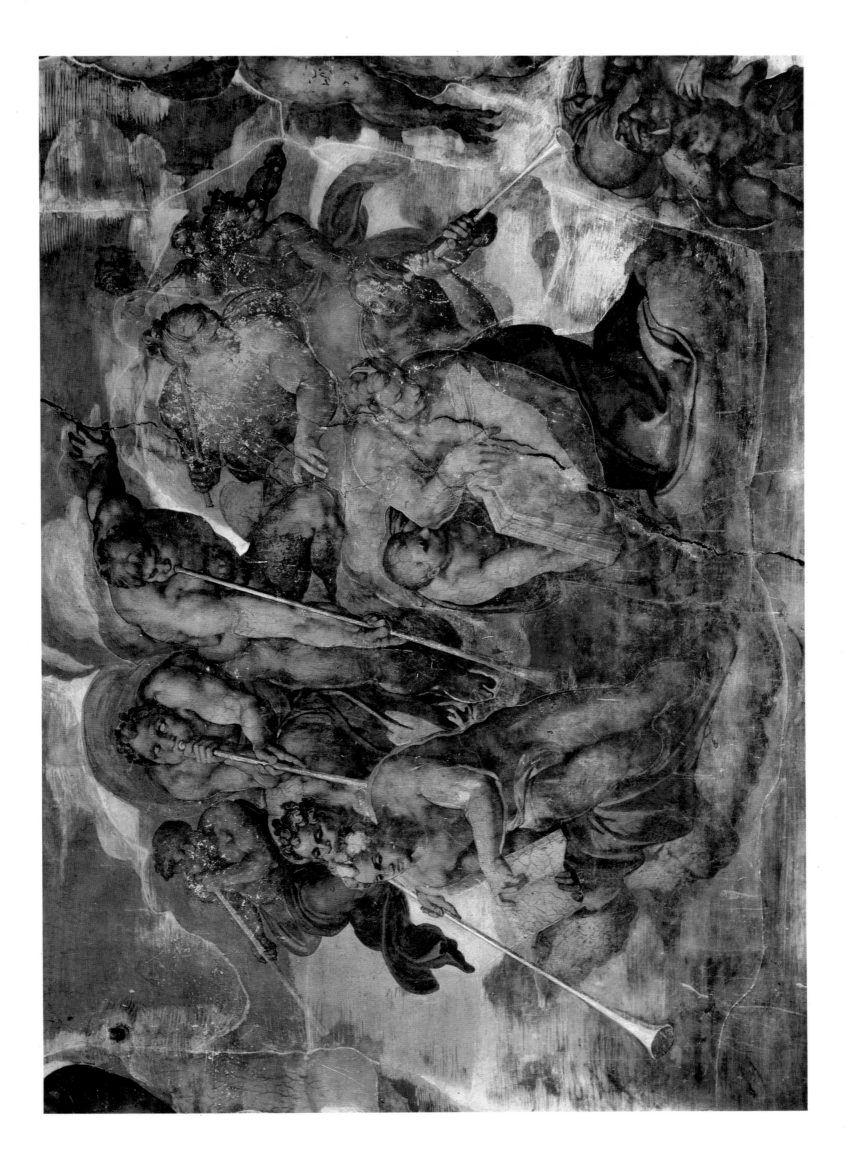

THE LAST JUDGMENT
Detail

Left lower section with groups of Reborn and Angels who deliver the bodies of the newly risen from the Demons. Notwithstanding its darkening by candle smoke, the color was intentionally made gloomy in order to accentuate the dramatic sense of the resurrection of the bodies from the earth. Here and there, the artist has painted skeletons, but seems to have personified Death in the figure wrapped in a mantle in the lower center section, a figure of impressive conception.

Rome, Vatican—The Sistine Chapel (1536–1541)   LX

THE LAST JUDGMENT

Detail

Left section with groups of the Blessed who rise to Heaven, aided by others of the Reborn and by Angels. In these bodies which slowly reacquire life and rise to Heaven, Michelangelo has used the maximum of his drawing knowledge. He has also animated the sculptural forms with intense inner life.

THE LAST JUDGMENT
Detail

Left section with two groups of the Blessed who rise to Heaven, aided by others of the Reborn and by Angels. On the right, two of the Reborn are pulled to safety by means of a Rosary to which they cling.

THE LAST JUDGMENT

Detail

Upper left section. Groups of Saints and Blessed awaiting the sentence of Christ, the Judge. At the center is the harbinger, Saint John the Baptist, dressed in lamb skins. This colossal figure has also been erroneously considered to be a figure of Adam.

THE LAST JUDGMENT

Detail

Central section with Saints and Blessed. On the right among the others is Saint Peter, who comes forward and shows the keys to Christ. Next to Saint Peter is Saint Paul, with the long beard. We note how Michelangelo suggested the idea of space with a diminution of the figures towards the background, and by placing them as an exedra around Christ.

THE LAST JUDGMENT

Detail

Upper central section. Christ the Judge and the Virgin to His right in the shadow of the raised arm that condemns the Reprobate. She meditates under the protection of Her Son. At one time, the artist had thought of placing Her in an imploring position at Christ's feet. In the beardless face below, some scholars claim to recognize the servant Urbino.

THE LAST JUDGMENT

Detail

Saint Bartholomew, who shows Christ the skin and the knife of his martyrdom. The difference between the bearded face of this personage and that of the image depicted in the skin (intentionally colorless, like a bloodless corpse) is clear. The modelled strength is exceptional in the Saint's body.

THE LAST JUDGMENT

Detail

Detail of the skin shown by Saint Bartholomew, in which we recognize the artist's own face. Michelangelo used this to indicate his suffering and bitterness over the criticisms of his work. The impressionistic manner in which the artist sketched this tragic human shadow also reveals a variant in the feet (which had at one time been painted). They are contracted and then corrected with brusque downward brush strokes.

Rome, Vatican—The Sistine Chapel (1536–1541)

THE LAST JUDGMENT

Detail

Right section. Saints and Blessed. Perhaps we can recognize the Cyrenean carrying the Cross. Others maintain that it is, instead, Disma, the "good thief." The admirable harmony of this nude (as of other figures) was ruined by the additions of Daniele da Volterra (who was, because of this, ironically called "il braghettone").

THE LAST JUDGMENT
Detail

Right section with the figure of Saint Sebastian, who shows the arrows of his martyrdom and repeats the act of the archer. Behind him are the pious women. This heroic image, although coming from classical sculpture, restores the ideals of that sculpture in its consciousness of a strength which is not only physical but, above all, spiritual.

Rome, Vatican—The Sistine Chapel (1536–1541)   LXIX

THE LAST JUDGMENT

Detail

Right section. One of the Damned, held by demons and dragged to Inferno. This famous image of desperation rises above the wanton personifications of Inferno as a monument of human sorrow. He seems, in his massive structure, to ignore the precipice into which he is dragged.

THE LAST JUDGMENT

Detail

Right lower section. The Damned who struggle with the Angels and are thrust down to Inferno, grasped by demons. This tempestuous group had already been foreshadowed in a first idea from a drawing in the Casa Buonarroti. Here, the athletically powerful forms are defined with sculptural clarity.

THE LAST JUDGMENT

Detail

Central lower section. Charon, on the boat, strikes the Damned, who have arrived at the threshold of Inferno, with his oar. The artist in drawing this episode from Dante's *Inferno* has (although he also emphasizes Charon's vigorous gesture) freely re-elaborated the scene.

THE LAST JUDGMENT
Detail

Lower section. The Damned, held by the demons and judged by Minos. He is depicted to the right, with the serpentine tail wound around his body and the ears of an ass. This figure, with its caricature-like and grotesque face, alludes to Biagio da Cesena, who had the presumption to criticize Michelangelo's work. The denunciation of the critic's incompetence is evident in the ass's ears.

THE LAST JUDGMENT

Detail

Upper left section. Angels who bear the Cross, symbol of the Passion, in flight. From the carefulness of the execution and the quality of the colors, it is clear that this is one of the first sections executed by the artist. In an early idea, this group and the following one were not foreseen.

THE LAST JUDGMENT

Detail

Upper right section. Angels who bear the Passion symbols in flight. The column of the flagellation, the sponge and the ladder. The perfect conservation of the colors (because of the height of this portion, which protected it from candle smoke) and the extreme care of the design make this group one of the most luminous of all in Michelangelo's painting. This scene and the preceding one are symmetrically composed in accordance with a convergence of light towards the central portion of the *Judgment*.

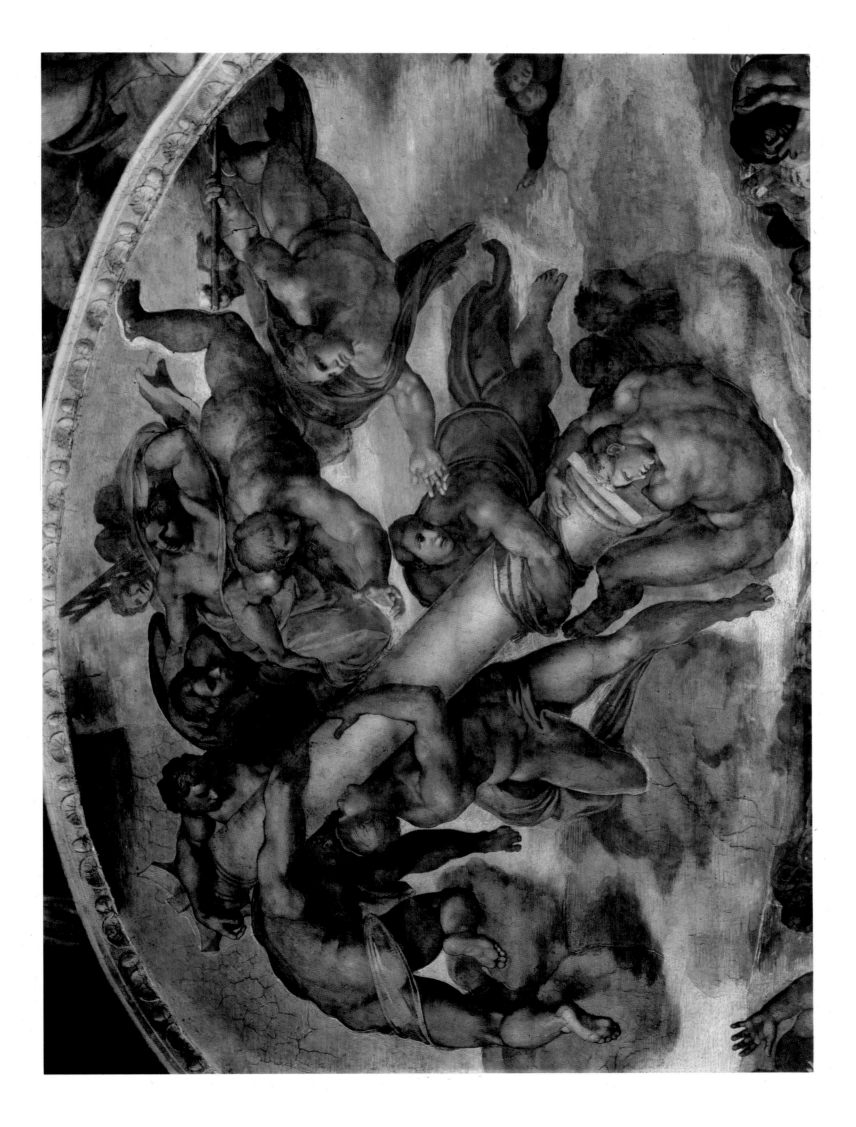

THE CONVERSION OF SAINT PAUL

This is one of the two last wall paintings done by Michelangelo on the walls of Paul III's chapel, consecrated by the Pope at the end of the architectural arrangement in 1540. The frescoes, of extraordinary dramatic intensity, depict the *Conversion of St. Paul* and, on the opposite wall, the *Crucifixion of Saint Peter*. The beginning of the first painting can be set at the end of 1542, at a brief interval from the unveiling of the *Last Judgment*. The master's work proceeded slowly with various interruptions, one of which was caused by the fire which broke out in the chapel, ruining the roof and the stucco of the vault. The completion of the two vast paintings can be set in the year 1550. Paul III, who died November 10, 1549, saw the task almost finished when he visited Michelangelo at work a little before his death.

Rome, Vatican— The Pauline Chapel (1542–1550)   LXXVI

THE CONVERSION OF SAINT PAUL

Detail

Upper section. Apparition of Christ surrounded by Angels and Blessed. As in the central section of the *Judgment*, here too the figures are of different size in order to suggest space. They are placed as an exedra around Christ. The references to the great wall of the Sistine Chapel are clear.

Rome, Vatican—The Pauline Chapel (1542–1550)   LXXVII

THE CONVERSION OF SAINT PAUL

Detail

Detail of the lower section. Saint Paul struck down, helped by soldiers. The composition acquires dynamism from the centrifugal placement of the figures and the rearing of the horse. Bold and new is the young man to the right who climbs with the helmet and the shield on his back.

THE CONVERSION OF SAINT PAUL
Detail

Detail of the lower section. Saint Paul struck down, helped by soldiers. The Saint's pose, in which he is struck down by the thunderbolt, has clearly classical origins. His face, framed with a long beard, is singular and recalls the face of the Pope, Paul III Farnese, who commissioned the painting from the artist.

THE CONVERSION OF SAINT PAUL

Detail

Detail of the lower section, to the right. A group of terrified soldiers. The artist, perhaps remembering the "lightning-struck" figures done by Luca Signorelli in Orvieto, executes the motif with a vigorous contrast of masses modelling the bodies in the colors.

THE CRUCIFIXION OF SAINT PETER

The fresco is opposite the *Conversion of Saint Paul* and was done after the completion of the latter. In the composition of the marching groups and in the colors which pierce the forms, we see the style of Michelangelo's last phase of painting.

THE CRUCIFIXION OF SAINT PETER

Detail

Detail of the central section. Saint Peter crucified. The compositional coherence in this central zone of the painting is admirable. Everything is linked to the movement impressed on the Cross, which is about to be driven into the hole that is being dug out. The artist indicated, in the length of the terminal portion of the wood, the extent to which the cross will be planted in the earth. This emphasizes, even more, the gigantic mass of Saint Peter's body.

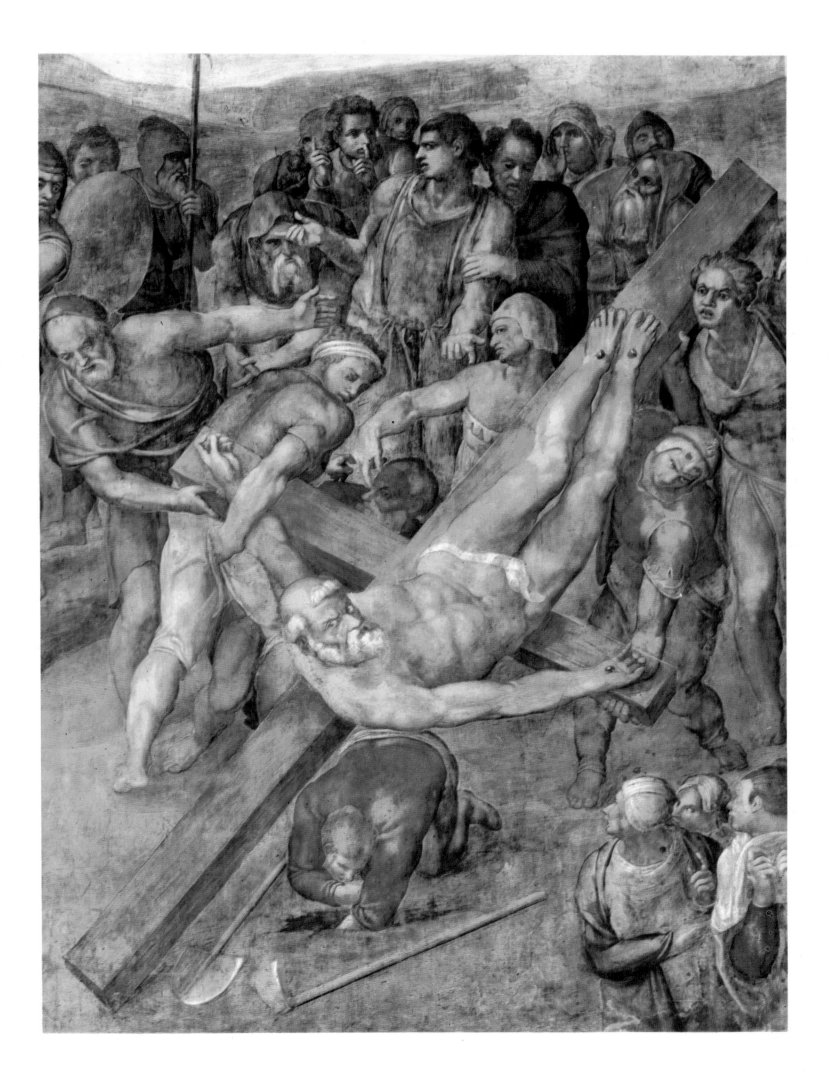

THE CRUCIFIXION OF SAINT PETER

Detail

The face of the First Apostle. In this exceptional painting, the artist seems to have concentrated the highest expressive possibilities. The extremely proud look of Saint Peter assumes extraordinary relief from the constructive firmness of the head, which is turned to us, almost in a peremptory admonition.

THE CRUCIFIXION OF SAINT PETER

Detail

Detail of the left section: legionaries who climb the hill. These figures are referred to in Michelangelo's original cartoon (in the Capodimonte Museum in Naples). We can, however, also note here the value of the artist's new palette which he developed in his last period of painting.

THE CRUCIFIXION OF SAINT PETER

Detail

Detail of the right section. Figures of the mourners who are present at the crucifixion. The severe, hooded figure who comes forward with crossed arms is certainly inspired by the figures of barbarian prisoners in Roman sculpture (several critics identify the figure with Saint Paul).

THE CRUCIFIXION OF SAINT PETER

Detail

Upper right section. Figures who comment on the crucifixion of the First Apostle. Since he also executed the painting in depth, Michelangelo conceived of these witnesses of Saint Peter's crucifixion advancing towards the center of the scene, climbing a hill, and commenting excitedly on the event which is about to occur. The figures seem to be immersed in a sunset which surrounds them with a mysterious atmosphere, heavy with tragedy. The colors, still vivid in the *Conversion of Saint Paul,* are here fused with the chiaroscuro and the drawing loses its incisiveness.